THE HOUSE OF THE NET

The Magical Symbolism of the Hieroglyphs

WENDY BERG

© Wendy Berg 2021

First published in Great Britain in 2021 by Skylight Press,
210 Brooklyn Road, Cheltenham, Glos GL51 8EA

All rights reserved. Except for the quotation of short passages for the purposes of criticism and review, no part of this publication may be reproduced, stored in a retrieval system or transmitted, in any form or by any means, electronic, mechanical, photocopying, recording or otherwise, without the prior consent of the copyright holder and publisher.

Wendy Berg has asserted her right to be identified as the author of this work.

Designed and typeset by Rebsie Fairholm

Hieroglyphs set in NewGardiner, a font by Mark-Jan Nederhof.

www.skylightpress.co.uk

British Library Cataloguing in Publication Data:
A catalogue record for this book is available from the British Library.

ISBN 978-1-908011-91-6

Contents

A brief history of Egyptian magic	7
Becoming Egyptian: The Desert and the Nile	25
Earth, trees and plants	44
Sky, Sun and Moon	68
sabA, the Star	84
The Pyramid	108
The *Ankh* and the House of Life	123
The House of the Net	146
The Eye of Horus	164
Birds, Animals and Insects	177
Hieroglyphs of the Human Body	201
Hieroglyphs of the Subtle Bodies	224
The Temple	246
Afterword: Becoming a scribe	267

Reckless O soul, exploring, I with thee, and thou with me,
For we are bound where mariner has not yet dared to go,
And we will risk the ship, ourselves and all.

O my brave soul!
O farther farther sail!
O daring joy, but safe! are they not all the seas of God?
O farther, farther, farther sail!

Walt Whitman

Hieroglyphs in the tomb of Kagemni at Saqqara,
Chief Vizier to the 6th Dynasty Pharaoh Teti (c. 2321-2290 B.C.)

Photo by the author

A brief history of Egyptian magic

This is a book about Egyptian magic. More specifically, it is a study of the ancient Egyptian hieroglyphs and the magical symbolism contained within them which forms the foundation of Egyptian magic.

Most readers of this book will have some familiarity with the hieroglyphs, especially the well-known examples such as the *ankh* and the Eye of Horus. The hieroglyphs can be used purely as a form of communication whose purpose is to convey information, just as any other written language. But they also function as symbols. They are deliberately designed to contain symbolic references to the inner qualities or causal realities that lie behind the outer world of physical appearances. Symbols can act as a bridge between our perception of the mundane world about us and our understanding of the qualities and energies that inform it; they are gateways that provide entry to worlds of meaning that are beyond our normal comprehension. Their effect is 'magical' because when we look at the hieroglyphs as symbols and ponder their deeper meaning they can bring about changes in our consciousness and enable us to reach a deeper appreciation of the connection between ourselves, our environment and the universal principles that lie behind all creation. It was with good reason that the ancient Egyptians called the hieroglyphs the *medw neter* or Words of the Gods.

The hieroglyphs also teach us a great deal about the magical beliefs and practices of the ancient Egyptians. This study demonstrates how they can be used as a complete approach to Egyptian magic, and one which avoids the obscurity and misconception that has built up over the centuries by returning to the simplicity and clarity of Egyptian magical thought and practice.

Most magical systems utilise symbols because they are one of the best methods of teaching and experiencing the wisdom of the higher realities. They transcend the limitation of words by speaking directly to the imagination and the intuition. The symbolism that supports the wisdom of the Tarot, the Runes, or the Qabalist Tree of Life are all examples of this. Symbols are timeless, and the message conveyed by the hieroglyphs is as revelatory now of the laws and patterns of creation and the deeper causes that lie beyond the visible world as it was 5000 years ago when the hieroglyphs first appeared.

If you have some knowledge or experience of esoteric belief these ideas will be familiar to you, but the symbolic and magical content of the Egyptian hieroglyphs has not been widely recognised. Most contemporary scholarship tends to focus on them solely as 'phonemes' in which each sign represents a distinct unit of sound that can either form a word on its own or be combined with other sounds to form longer words. It is accepted that the hieroglyphs can be used as a type of picture language in which, for example, the hieroglyph of an owl will simply mean 'an owl' but it is not generally acknowledged that there is any deeper meaning to the hieroglyphs, or that they can function as symbols, or that there is any connection between the symbolic content of the hieroglyphs that form a word and the meaning of that word.

This does not represent my own point of view and, as it happens, is also at odds with that of the Frenchman Jean-François Champollion who famously discovered how to translate the hieroglyphs in the early nineteenth century after their meaning had been lost for nearly 2000 years. He described them as "... a complex system, a writing that is figurative, symbolic, and phonetic all within the same text, a single sentence, I would even say a single word."[1] As a description of the remarkable ability of a single hieroglyph to function simultaneously on three levels this can hardly be bettered. A single hieroglyph can indeed be an accurate and recognisable image of the object it represents *and* function as a unit of sound or phoneme *and* symbolise ideas and concepts, all at the same time.

Here is an example of how a single sign can be used simultaneously to represent figurative, symbolic and phonetic meanings: the duck, pronounced *sA*.[2]

sA, the duck

The hieroglyph represents the *Anas acuta* or Northern Pin-tailed duck and could be used in hieroglyphic inscriptions simply to indicate 'a duck.' But the word *sA* also means 'son,' and the same hieroglyph is often seen in the inscriptions carved on temple walls where it is an element in one of the names given to the Pharaoh: *sA re*, which means 'Son of the Sun.' The association of a duck with the sun and the Pharaoh may now seem incongruous, but in the 5th century A.D. the writer Horapollo, one of the last authors to have any real memory of how the hieroglyphs were used before they fell into oblivion, explained in his *Hieroglyphica* how the duck was so protective of its young that the parent birds would offer themselves to the hunter in order to preserve the life of their chicks.[3] The analogy would have been clear to the ancient Egyptians: as well as mediating the life-sustaining powers of the sun to his people the Pharaoh had a duty of protection towards them even to the point of self-sacrifice.

The word 'hieroglyph' is a Greek word meaning 'sacred engraving' but to the Egyptians they were the *medw neter*, the Words of the Gods. These two words are written in the hieroglyphs shown below.[4]

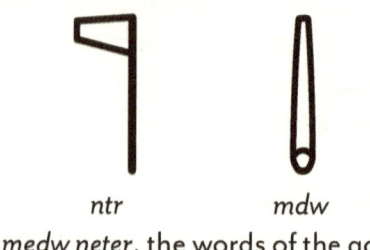

ntr   mdw
= medw neter, the words of the gods

You will notice that the phrase is actually written *neter medw,* but the Egyptian scribes placed the hieroglyph for 'the gods' first in honour of the fact that the gods were more important than words. The next point to note is that although the Egyptian language contained vowel sounds when it was spoken, vowels are not represented in the written signs, so the convention is to insert a vowel, usually an 'e,' where one is needed for ease of pronunciation. Hence *ntr* is usually written as *neter.* You will find frequent examples of this throughout the following chapters.

If you were studying the hieroglyphs with a view to learning how to pronounce them and perhaps teach yourself to read some of the ancient inscriptions, these two words could be committed to memory and their symbolic content would be of little interest. But if we start to think about the possible symbolic meaning of these hieroglyphs it soon becomes evident that the choice of signs to illustrate 'the words of the gods' is neither arbitrary nor coincidental.

There is some scholarly disagreement as to the identity of the object pictured in the first hieroglyph but it is difficult to see it as anything other than a flag blowing in the wind. An analogy might be made with the brightly coloured Tibetan prayer flags that are customarily draped over shrines and sacred places; the prayers and mantras printed on them are believed to be given vitality by the wind, and their words of knowledge and compassion are thus dispersed over the countryside. The flagpoles which were set into the pylon gateways of Egyptian temples probably reached 60 metres in height, and the sight and sound of these flags rippling in the wind would have been an impressive indication of what lay within the temple precincts.

In ancient Egypt the word *'neter,'* as well as describing a god or goddess, also indicated the qualities of regeneration and renewal that the deities brought to humanity. If we assume that the first hieroglyph represents a flag, how might it symbolise these ideas? In early illustrations, the sign consists of coloured strips of blue, yellow and green fabric wound about a pole. The colour of an object was an important expression of its substance or quality and the use of colours in the hieroglyphs were an integral part of their symbolism. Blue represented the heavenly worlds and the concepts of eternity, rebirth and the life beyond the grave. It also represented the fertilising waters of the River Nile, particularly during the period of the inundation when the river flooded out over the land. Yellow symbolised the essential life-giving energy of the sun and the imperishable, incorruptible qualities of pure gold. Green, the natural colour of plant-life, indicated how this positive, creative energy was brought into manifestation in the physical world.⁵ So to the ancient Egyptians these strips of brightly coloured linen tied to a pole and blowing in a stiff breeze would indicate the qualities of eternal life and renewal expressed through the celestial, solar and earthly spheres.

The second hieroglyph, *medw,* illustrates a walking stick. It was used in the word for 'old age' but it was also used in a number of words that refer to speech and learning. A stick can be an aid, a prop, something to lean on, but it can also be used to point to something or to draw attention to an important detail. If we put all this symbolism together we can say that the *medw neter* aid us in our understanding of the gods and of the meaning of sacred words and symbols. We can lean on the hieroglyphs; they support us in our efforts to come closer to the spiritual worlds and they help us by drawing our attention to things that are of significance. Equally – because symbols are gateways that allow passage in both directions – it might be said that the hieroglyphs are 'leant on' by the gods in their attempt to speak to us!

The earliest hieroglyphs discovered so far come from the predynastic period of ancient Egyptian history circa 3,300 B.C. although some recent scholarship suggests that this date should be pushed back by two hundred years or more. Their greatest flowering occurred between 2000 B.C. and 1300 B.C., a period commonly referred to as 'ancient Egyptian' although it is more accurately described as 'Middle Egyptian.' The last known hieroglyphic inscription was carved in A.D. 394 on the walls of the Temple of Isis on the island of Philae.

It is not easy to explain how the hieroglyphs came into being. Egyptian legend describes how the god Thoth or Tehuti brought them as a gift from the gods to humanity, and taught their magical and symbolic meaning to the temple priests and scribes. The rational mind may baulk at this explanation but if, on the other hand, we assume that the hieroglyphs gradually evolved over time in the same way that most other systems of writing have evolved, then we would expect to find evidence of their gradual development over the centuries, and of trial and error as the scribes practiced their craft. So far, little such evidence has come to light. The hieroglyphs not only seem to have emerged in an unusually short period of time but their original shape and form scarcely changed throughout their 3000 years of use, as if it was acknowledged that their original shape and design was significant, perhaps sacred, and that each hieroglyph should always be drawn as it had first appeared.

This book is called *The House of the Net* because in ancient Egypt this was the name given to the school of learning that was dedicated to the study and use of the hieroglyphs. Its function was similar, but more specialised, to the many Houses of Life that played an active part in the work of the temples and were responsible for training the temple priests. The House of the Net or *hwt ibet* was located in the city the Egyptians knew as Khemenu or 'City of the Eight,' its name being a reference to the creation myth of the Ogdoad or eight deities who were venerated there. The city is now generally known by its Greek name of Hermopolis. Both the city and the House of the Net were closely linked with the god Tehuti, whom the Greeks called Thoth. Thoth eventually became subsumed in the later figure known as the Thrice Great Hermes or Hermes Trismegistus – hence the name Hermopolis or 'city of Hermes.'

The confusing substitution of Greek for ancient Egyptian names in the previous paragraph is something we have become accustomed to, but while the habit seems of little importance in itself it is nevertheless symptomatic of a significant obstacle to our proper understanding of Egyptian magic. Many of what we assume to be the original magical beliefs and practices of ancient Egypt have been obscured by the substantial modifications made by the Greek and Roman civilisations who eventually conquered and ruled over Egypt. For example, the Greek name Isis is routinely used in preference to the ancient Egyptian *Aset;* we refer to Osiris rather than *Ausar* and Orion rather than *sAhu*. Instead of *Tehuti* we generally use the uncomfortable Greek word Thoth. But when we refer to the ancient Egyptian gods by their Greek names we obscure the connection between these deities and their spiritual qualities which are revealed to us in the symbolism of the hieroglyphs that spell their names.

Egypt was conquered in 323 B.C. by Alexander the Great who through successful invasion of many lands and nations built one of the largest empires of the ancient world. The city of Alexandria on Egypt's Mediterranean coast became a major centre of Greek culture and trade, and Egypt remained under Greek rule for 300 years until it was conquered by the Romans in 30 B.C. It is not often realised that the famous Cleopatra who ruled Egypt from 51-30 B.C. was Greek, not Egyptian, a member of the Ptolemy family who for the most part remained so strongly allied to Greece that they refused to speak Egyptian. After Cleopatra's death Egypt became a province of the Roman Empire, although vestiges of the Egyptian culture survived until the edicts of the Emperor Justinian in the 6th century A.D. whose enforced closure of the Temple of Isis at Philae in 535 A.D. is generally considered to mark the end of the ancient Egyptian civilisation.

This is not to suggest that the Greek and Roman peoples were antipathetic to what they found in Egypt; far from it. They freely acknowledged their indebtedness to Egyptian wisdom and travelled there in significant numbers to study and learn. The Greek Pharaohs built temples in the Egyptian style at Philae, Denderah, Edfu and Kom Ombo. The philosophers Aristotle, Euclid, Plato, Pythagoras, Herodotus and Strabo were all said to have lived and studied in Egypt and although the relationship between the emergent Greek philosophy and its Egyptian roots has yet to be fully researched, the knowledge that was taught in the Egyptian schools and temples formed the basis of what we now know as Hellenistic thought. It is worth remembering, though, that even by the fourth century B.C. the substance of what was taught in Egypt was probably based as much on oral tradition as reliable fact, because few written records had survived from the height of the Egyptian civilisation some fifteen hundred years earlier. By the time the Greeks and Romans arrived in Egypt the ability to understand and use the ancient sacred language of the hieroglyphs was rapidly diminishing.

The Greeks were particularly drawn to the wisdom of Thoth or Tehuti, recognising him as the god of knowledge, of writing and the realms of the dead. In fact they found so many similarities between Tehuti and their own god Hermes that they amalgamated them into one deity who became identified as an ancient source of wisdom originating from the time of Abraham or Moses: Hermes Trismegistus or the Thrice Great Hermes. The Roman god Mercury also neatly corresponded with the same archetype, and from the stream of wisdom that was attributed to this composite figure emerged the all-encompassing movement of religious, philosophical and esoteric thought known as Hermeticism which soon became the mainstay of the Western Mystery Tradition.

Hermeticism faded in popularity towards the end of the first millennium but was reborn in the mid 15th century when the keen minds of the Renaissance rediscovered the work of the classical authors who had lived and studied in Egypt. The writings known as the *Corpus Hermeticum* which formed the core of Hermetic thought were brought to Italy and translated by Marcilio Ficino. Scholars such as Ficino and Pico della Mirandola believed avidly in the wisdom of Egypt and it was assumed that the revered figure of the Thrice Great Hermes had been responsible in remote antiquity for a vast corpus of esoteric literature of which only the *Corpus Hermeticum* had survived. It wasn't until 1614, when the philologist Isaac Casaubon analysed some of these texts for their style of language, that it was realised that they were largely the product of Hellenist philosophy and probably dated only from the second and third centuries A.D.

However, the impulse behind the Hermetic movement was formidable, and the texts which gradually accumulated under its influence were so numerous and varied that eventually they covered almost every conceivable aspect of the ancient wisdom and the revelation of the Mind of God within the universe. They dealt with vast areas of speculation and philosophy such as the nature of reality, the nature and appearance of the Inner worlds of creation, the nature of the gods and of man's relationship with the gods. They encompassed alchemy, theology, astrology, cosmogony, philosophy, paganism, Christianity and Jewish Qabalah. The Hermetic approach to the Mysteries is eclectic to the point where it is now quite difficult to identify aspects of esoteric thought that cannot be placed under its aegis. However, significant by its absence is any link with the hieroglyphs that formed the foundation of Egyptian magical thought, or with the god who had brought them to Egypt and revealed their potential to humanity. Over the centuries Tehuti became Thoth, and Thoth became Hermes Trismegistus.

Direct knowledge of the magical and religious practices of ancient Egypt had been almost impossible for many centuries before the Renaissance. The ability to understand the hieroglyphs had dwindled during the last few centuries B.C. and the scholars of the Renaissance were almost certainly unable to read or understand a single hieroglyph – even though some of them appear to have had an innate understanding of their symbolic and magical potential. Giordano Bruno, whose cosmological theories were far ahead of his time, recognised how "… the Egyptians used (the hieroglyphs) to capture with marvellous skill the language of the Gods." He contrasted this with the use of the Greek language which he considered mainly to be a platform for intellectual argument and debate between one person and another rather than enabling communication between humanity and the gods. The Greek language, he wrote, "… had brought about a great rift both in memory and in the divine and magical sciences." [6]

His intuitive understanding of the significance of the hieroglyphs was certainly shared by some of his contemporaries.

It has been suggested, perhaps a little uncharitably, that as Bruno and his peers were unable to read the hieroglyphs they had little choice but to proclaim them magical and 'mysterious', but perhaps we should be wary of dismissing some of the greatest minds of the Renaissance. Their view accorded with that of the classical scholars who had studied in Egypt and who, although they had little understanding of the hieroglyphs as a language, seemed to have recognised their symbolic function. Philo Judaeus who lived in Alexandria around the time of Christ acknowledged them to be a system of sacred symbols. In the 3rd century A.D. the Egyptian-born Greek philosopher Plotinus described them as "... signs, a separate sign for each idea, so as to express its whole meaning at once. Each separate sign is in itself a piece of knowledge, a piece of wisdom, a piece of reality, immediately present." [7] His appreciation of the unique qualities of the hieroglyphs is as perceptive as that of Champollion.

Horapollo also believed the hieroglyphs to be a symbolic, ideographic script. His *Hieroglyphica* makes fascinating reading although its blend of fact, fantasy and speculation can probably best be appreciated as an indication of the state of knowledge of the hieroglyphs in Egypt during his lifetime. After his time, the ability to read the hieroglyphs rapidly declined and was soon entirely lost. It was only when Napoleon conquered Egypt in 1798 – and coincidentally provoked a surge of interest in archaeological discoveries – that the famous Rosetta Stone was uncovered in the Nile Delta. It was soon realised that this striking *stele*, a large piece of shining black stone which was probably engraved in 196 B.C., contained three versions of the same text inscribed in Greek, Demotic (a late form of Egyptian written language) and hieroglyphs. The text was written to honour the Pharaoh Ptolemy V, and ironically the very fact of its existence owes much to the Ptolemies' habit of using Greek rather than Egyptian in their communications. Study of the inscription and its partial translation began straight away, but it wasn't until the 1820s that Champollion was able to make the vital breakthrough by realising that the name Ptolemy was inscribed on the stone in three different ways.[8]

Champollion is a fascinating character. He was fluent in many languages including Persian and Chinese yet he said of himself: "I belong to Egypt; it means everything to me." It was said that when he realised he had made the breakthrough into understanding the hieroglyphs he was overcome by emotion for several days. Although he played a vital part in initiating their rediscovery it was nearly 50 years before the first Egyptian texts were fully translated and published. The Victorians became obsessed with all things Egyptian and their enthusiasm for each new discovery and publication played an important role in the rising tide of esoteric movements that occurred during the late nineteenth century.

The numerous sects and mystical societies that emerged during this period culminated in the founding of the Hermetic Order of the Golden Dawn in 1888. In many ways the Golden Dawn defined 20th century magical practice by creating an inclusive and comprehensive occult system that has become one of the prevailing influences on magical work to this day. Members incorporated as many elements of Egyptian magic into their rituals as were known to them at the time, quoting passages from the Egyptian Book of the Dead and making good use of Egyptian god and goddess forms, magical symbols and ritual regalia. The scholarly research of E. A. Wallis Budge, keeper of the rapidly growing collection of Egyptian and Assyrian antiquities in the British Museum, was an invaluable source of material for their magical practice. The myth of Isis, Osiris and Horus was central to the Golden Dawn's more advanced work and the symbolism of the death and resurrection of Osiris was recreated in ceremony and ritual designed to bring about the spiritual regeneration and rebirth of the magical candidate.

Within this comprehensive system, the influence of Egyptian magic, although undoubtedly acting as a powerhouse, was amalgamated with many other esoteric traditions. Alongside elements of Egyptian magic the Golden Dawn rituals included references to Freemasonry, Rosicrucianism, Qabalah, Enochian Magick, Greek magic so far as it was known, material from medieval grimoires and aspects of the Eastern spiritual practices that were rapidly becoming available to the Western world. At the time it could scarcely have been otherwise and although, when compared to our present state of knowledge, there were substantial gaps in what was known of the ancient Egyptian civilisation, the Egyptian rituals of the Golden Dawn were undoubtedly effective in their own right. But, again, the hieroglyphs were significant by their absence, and these sacred signs played almost no part in the Golden Dawn's extensive system of magical training.

The form and content of 'Egyptian magic' established in the early decades of the 20th century tended to rely on formal, elaborate ritual which depended heavily on the invocation of the gods. This emphasis on invoking the god and goddess forms has become established almost to the exclusion of anything else, and it is easy to see why. The vibrantly coloured images and magnificent statues of the Egyptian deities are widely reproduced and provide an entrance into the 'feel' of ancient Egypt that is vivid and exciting in a way that can scarcely be paralleled in any other religion or magical system. But the Greco-Roman interpretation of Egyptian magic disregarded the abundance of deities acknowledged by the ancient Egyptians and focussed primarily on the family group of Isis, Osiris and Horus. The Romans were particularly drawn to Isis and built many temples in her name throughout their empire, laying the foundations of belief in Isis as the goddess above all others and the assumption that 'Isis-magic' is synonymous with 'Egyptian magic.'

An example of this restricted interpretation of Egyptian magical thought is seen in the work of the occultist Aleister Crowley, whose *The Book of Thoth: the Tarot of the Egyptians* was published in 1944 to accompany his Tarot pack of the same name. The cards are filled with rich and complex imagery but you need to look carefully to find many references to Egyptian magical symbolism, even though by this time the hieroglyphs had been thoroughly researched and documented, not only by Wallis Budge but by Alan Gardiner in his comprehensive *Egyptian Grammar* which was first published in 1927.

An equally misleading interpretation of Egyptian magic is conveyed by another prominent figure in 20th century occultism, Dion Fortune. Her novel *Moon Magic* describes how the protagonist, the evocatively named Lilith le Fay, constructs an Egyptian temple in the heart of London which she dedicates to the goddess Isis. She uses the temple to perform a series of magical rituals with her priest which depend to a large extent on the invocation of Isis who is identified with the powers of the moon, hence the title of the novel. The book contains some useful magical teaching but the overall impression given to the reader is that Egyptian magic consists of Isis and little else, and that 'Isis magic' is synonymous with 'moon magic.' The focus on intimate magical working between two people would not have been recognised by the ancient Egyptian priests who, in any case, venerated the moon as a masculine deity.

As will be shown in this study of the hieroglyphs as magical symbols, the essence of Egyptian magic is purity and simplicity. Its intrinsic qualities are clarity and radiance. It is rooted in the natural things of the earth: the sun and the stars, the Nile and the abundance of green and growing life along the riverbanks, the birds and animals, the simple objects of everyday life. Yet it has eternal relevance in its revelation of the relationship between humanity, the natural environment of the land of Egypt and the spiritual realities of the heavenly worlds that shine through earthly things. The intrinsic power of the hieroglyphs is that they capture these qualities and reveal them to us. The hieroglyphs are not mysterious sigils but simple, realistic images of the things of this world, carefully and accurately drawn so that most of them are instantly recognisable. But – and this where their magic lies – they engage with the greater reality that lies behind mundane appearances and are drawn in such a way that when you look at them carefully, and in a meditative state of mind, they open your awareness to that greater reality. They are the alphabet and building blocks of Egyptian magic and a study of their symbolism soon reveals that there is a logical progression of thought within them, which, when followed, quite literally leads us from the earth to the stars.

The hieroglyphs contain a depth and subtlety of meaning that can initially be difficult for us to understand. They represent an entirely different, holistic, syncretic way of looking at the world about us. We are accustomed to a more compartmentalised, 'either/or' way of looking, thinking, and using our spoken and written language. It's said that a picture tells a thousand words but our tendency is to keep images, words and sounds quite separate in our minds. If we look at a simple, realistic sketch of an everyday object we are unlikely to consider that it represents anything beyond its immediate likeness, and if we look at a written word we do not imagine that its individual letters contain symbolic meaning. But to the Egyptian scribes who were responsible for selecting and inscribing the hieroglyphs, each sign was a frame of reference in which appearance, sound and symbolic meaning were intricately related, each element contributing to the whole. As will often be observed in the following chapters, a single hieroglyph can express more complexity and subtlety of meaning than the entire paragraph that is required to explain it in modern English. Hieroglyphs can express the *essence* of something; they reach behind its outward appearance and evoke its unique underlying qualities. They have the ability to synthesise our experience of apparently diverse and separate objects, drawing our attention to parallels and analogies in seemingly unrelated objects and concepts which, on deeper reflection, reveal a common causality.

The Narmer Palette, Cairo Museum

The hieroglyphs are almost certainly the oldest system of writing so far discovered and it is generally agreed that they do not bear any relation to any other language. Some of the earliest examples can be seen on the Narmer Palette, a shield-shaped, ceremonial palette dating from c. 3100 B.C. which shows on one side King Narmer wearing the White Crown of Upper (i.e. southern) Egypt and on the other side wearing the Red Crown of lower (i.e. northern) Egypt.[9] The exceptional standard of the engraving anticipates many of the conventions typical of later Egyptian art. In this early example the hieroglyphs are subsidiary to the illustrated scenes but provide a commentary on them, offering additional information in symbolic form.[10]

A frequent misconception regarding the hieroglyphs is that they were a form of writing comparable to that which we would use to compose a letter to a friend, or a shopping list. It is important to keep in mind that the hieroglyphs were not primarily a means of communication between one person and another but were a means of communication between the gods and humanity. They were used only where they could be preserved for eternity and would have best magical effect, such as on the walls of temples and tombs, on statues and offering tables, wooden coffins, stone sarcophagi, gold artefacts, and on the engraved stones known as *stelae*. They were used for formal scenes, dedications, prayers and invocations, offerings to the gods and sacred and magical texts. The act of inscribing a hieroglyph which was anticipated to last for eternity was therefore undertaken with great solemnity; it was intended to evoke a change of consciousness in the observer and required more than casual attention in the scribe. Only the priests, pharaohs and trained scribes were able to use the hieroglyphs. The scribes who were entrusted with the task of reproducing them were held in great esteem and were accorded a number of privileges in honour of their position. To keep their hands soft and supple they were spared from heavy manual labour, they didn't have to serve in the army and they didn't have to pay taxes.

When the ancient Egyptians wanted to record or communicate mundane affairs they used another form of writing known as Hieratic script which evolved alongside the hieroglyphs. Hieratic is sometimes described as a later development of the hieroglyphs, but this is not strictly true. Hieratic is a cursive script, which means that it is formed with curved, flowing lines that are easily produced by a brush and ink, and it was mainly used on papyrus rather than carved on stone. Although 'hieratic' means 'priestly,' it was the preferred form of writing for legal texts, administrative documents and record keeping as well as lesser sacred work such as copies of funerary literature. The essential difference between hieratic script and the hieroglyphs is that hieratic contains fewer recognisable pictures or images, so it has less potential for symbolism. Towards the end of the ancient Egyptian civilisation, around 600-450 B.C., a third system of writing evolved which was known as Demotic, meaning 'of the people.'

Before we make a detailed study of individual hieroglyphs in the following chapters, there are a few basic rules that are worth keeping in mind. Each hieroglyph can represent either one, two or three sounds and is classified accordingly as a uniliteral, biliteral or triliteral sign. A hieroglyph can represent a word on its own or it can be combined with other signs to produce a word. There are 24 uniliteral hieroglyphic signs and you will often see them reproduced in a chart that links them to their approximate equivalent sound in English, thus forming a recognisable 'alphabet.' It is quite easy to transliterate English words into hieroglyphs by using these signs and it's fun to do this with your own name, although the resulting string of hieroglyphs would not have made much sense to the ancient scribes!

One of the main problems in converting the hieroglyphs into the English alphabet is that they include a number of sounds for which the English alphabet has no equivalent, for example a number of throaty and breathy sounds that we do not normally articulate. There are several systems currently in use for indicating these sounds, each using different combinations of letters from the English alphabet alongside additional glyphs, but there is no overall agreement amongst scholars as to which system is best. To keep things simple, and because the accurate pronunciation of the hieroglyphs is not important to the purpose of this study, in this book only one of these extra sounds is indicated: the 3 or aleph which is pronounced as a glottal stop (as you would say in "uh oh") and which is transliterated as 'A.' You have already seen the A earlier in this chapter, in the words *sA re*, the son of the Sun.

It has been described how the hieroglyphs could function as 'pictograms' but you will find that the terms pictogram, ideogram and logogram are used somewhat indiscriminately by different writers. Strictly speaking a pictogram is an image which clearly resembles what it signifies, an ideogram represents an idea or concept and a logogram is a grapheme or sign which represents a word. Again to keep things simple, the word 'ideogram' is used throughout this book to indicate when a hieroglyph is being used as either a realistic representation of an actual object or person, or as a concept such as joy, or praise, or existence.

In hieroglyphic inscriptions, the signs are usually written from right to left, although they could also sometimes be written from left to right, or from top to bottom, according to how they best fitted the available space. There were strict standards in the accurate depiction of the hieroglyphs but it was also part of the duty of the scribes to create a pleasing aesthetic effect. The clue to working out which way to read a line of hieroglyphs is that the human and animal faces always look towards the beginning of the line, so if the faces are turned towards the right, you read the line from right to left, and vice versa. Although it is necessary to understand these conventions if you are learning to translate and read the hieroglyphs, the focus of this book is their symbolic meaning, so for ease of understanding they have all been drawn in a single line which reads from left to right.

When we look at the hieroglyphs as magical symbols, groups of signs emerge according to the nature of the spiritual qualities that inform their meaning, and which form a natural progression that takes us from the earthly worlds into the heavenly worlds. Although this natural progression has been followed in the succeeding chapters, the commonly accepted method of categorising the hieroglyphs was compiled by the Egyptologist Alan Gardiner in his 'sign list' of some 750 or so hieroglyphs. He divides them into 26 categories, each of which is given a title such as 'Birds,' 'Trees and Plants,' 'Sky, Earth and Water,' and so on. Each category is headed by a letter of the English alphabet and each hieroglyph in that category is numbered.¹¹ Thus his first category, A, deals with 'Man and his Occupations' and the 55 hieroglyphs in this group are labelled A1, A2 and so on. The endnotes to each chapter give the Gardiner reference to the hieroglyphs illustrated in the text.

This book can be read purely as a theoretical guide, but if, as each new sign is introduced, you are able to spend a few moments looking at it in a quietly meditative state of mind you will find that its magical properties begin to unfold. You can do this simply by picturing each hieroglyph in your imagination as it is introduced in the text, holding it in your mind's eye as you read about it, and allowing your own thoughts and realisations to emerge. When the inherent wisdom of the hieroglyphs is combined with the power of human thought and imagination they are transformed into the *medw neter*: the Words of the Gods.

Endnotes
1. Jean-Francois Champollion: *Lettre à M. Dacier*, September 17th 1822
2. *sA*, the duck: Gardiner G39
3. trans. Alexander Turner Cory, 1840, *The Hieroglyphics of Horapollo*, available online at www.sacred-texts.com
4. *medw neter*, the words of the Gods: Gardiner R8, S43
5. Richard H. Wilkinson, *Symbol and Magic in Egyptian Art* (London: Thames and Hudson, 1994)
6. Giordano Bruno, *De Magia, Opera Latina Vol 3*, pages 411-412, quoted from Frances A. Yates, *Giordano Bruno and the Hermetic Tradition Vol III* (Abingdon: Routledge, 1964) page 263
7. Plotinus, *Enneads* V.8.6.1-9
8. Jean-Francois Champollion, *Lettre à M. Dacier relative à l'alphabet des hiéroglyphes phonétiques,* November 24th 1828
9. Image courtesy of Wikimedia Commons
10. see Whitney Davis, *Masking the Blow: the Scene of Representation in Late Prehistoric Egyptian Art* (Berkely: University of California Press, 1992)
11. Alan Gardiner, *Egyptian Grammar: Being an Introduction to the Study of Hieroglyphs* (Oxford, Griffith Institute, 1927)

Becoming Egyptian: The Desert and the Nile

In an often quoted phrase from the *Hermetica,* Hermes Trismegistus tells his pupil Asclepius: "Do you not know, Asclepius, that Egypt is an image of heaven, or, to speak more exactly, in Egypt all the operations of the powers which rule and work in heaven have been transferred to earth below?" [12] The context of this passage within the 'Lament' in which Hermes prophecies the end of the Egyptian civilisation suggests that it can be read as a eulogy, an idealised expression of his feelings for his country. But his statement can also be taken quite literally because Egypt does indeed reveal through the striking contrasts of its landscape the 'heavenly' powers and principles that lie behind the visible world and are given shape in the land. This means that the actual landscape of Egypt can function as an archetype, as a symbol in itself, a universal model of how the principles of creation are brought to earth and made manifest. In particular, we can find in Egypt an expression of the creative, dynamic relationship that exists between polar opposites. The most obvious example of this is the unique juxtaposition of the arid desert and the Nile which is the life-blood of Egypt. The red desert hills form an ever-present contrast to the blue waters of the Nile which reflect the eternally blue skies, the unfailingly glorious sun by day and the brilliance of the stars at night. All of these principles and qualities are revealed in the hieroglyphs.

In Egypt, the wheel of the sun's daily journey around the dome of the sky is constantly visible. Life is ruled and regulated by the sun. It rises from behind the hills on the east bank of the Nile in a fresh and invigorating dawn and rapidly climbs the sky, culminating in the fierce heat of the afternoon. Towards evening, the light mellows as the sun descends to the hills on the west bank of the Nile, creating a brief but pleasant period of dusk before rapidly giving way to darkness. The quality of the sunlight in Egypt is intensely full and bright; it delivers a fuller spectrum of light than is experienced in countries lying further from the equator and the effect can be oddly stimulating if you are unused to such intensity. It is easy to tell the time of day by the sun in Egypt, not only by its height in the sky but by the quality of the light. Above all, the eternally visible daily cycle of the sun instils an appreciation of rhythm and periodicity, of cycles that repeat through eternity. Throughout most of Egypt, almost every day is the same: virtually cloudless blue sky and unbroken sunshine from dawn to dusk. Knowing that the sun will shine tomorrow and the next day exactly as it has done every day since time immemorial inevitably affects your state of mind. Under constant and regular sunshine and clear nights under the stars you become aware of how this regularity of rhythm pulses at the heart of the universe and of how a repeated pattern that is revealed by the passage of time can be found in all natural phenomena, whether a heart beat or millions of years.

With this in mind, when we study the symbolism of the hieroglyphs which make frequent reference to the natural landscape of Egypt, it is useful to have some idea of what that landscape actually looks like. It contains a combination of unique physical characteristics that are not found together anywhere else in the world, the most obvious being the desert and the Nile. The Nile is the world's longest river and, curiously, the only major river in the world which flows consistently from south to north. (Three other major rivers, all in Siberia, flow northwards but only after meandering their way westwards from the Altai mountains before turning northwards to the Arctic Sea and passing through vast expanses of swampy coniferous forest and tundra.) The Nile follows an almost direct northerly line between the Aswan Dam in the south of Egypt to its delta on the Mediterranean Sea.

There is much significance in this concept of 'north-ness' in Egypt. Its importance is demonstrated for example in the orientation of the Great Pyramid at Giza whose north-south axis is aligned to within three-sixtieths of a degree of true north. In Egypt, the continuous flow of energy from south to north created by the immense volume of water moving steadily into the north symbolised, in ancient Egypt, the spiritual progression in human awareness from the things of earth to the realities of the inner worlds which, for the ancient Egyptians, were primarily symbolised by the stars grouped about the northern celestial pole. These are the circumpolar stars, the constellations that are contained within an imaginary circle whose circumference touches the northern horizon. When viewed from the latitude of Egypt these stars do not sink below the horizon and to the ancient Egyptians their constant presence was a constant reassurance of the eternal life beyond the grave. Early writings such as the Pyramid Texts, the Coffin Texts and the Book of the Dead frequently describe the circumpolar stars as the goal of the deceased in the afterlife – although when reading these ancient texts it is important to keep in mind that this same journey into the light of the spirit can be undertaken in aspiration during your life on earth.

Egypt is also one of only three places in the world where a major river flows through desert.[13] This juxtaposition of opposites, and the means by which they can be productively reconciled, is one of the basic principles of Egyptian magic. When we think of Egypt we tend only to think of the Nile, but the desert is of equal symbolic significance because together they perfectly illustrate the polarity which underpins the whole of created life. Creation arises from the coming together of polar opposites: the unmanifest and the manifest, stillness and movement, negative and positive, dark and light, female and male – opposites which, when united, bring the birth of a third, the child of the union. In Egypt you are constantly aware of this polarity; it is written in the landscape wherever you look. You cannot see the Nile without also seeing the desert which borders it on either side.

The desert is rarely mentioned in descriptions of Egyptian magic and tends to be dismissed as the representation of 'chaos' or 'evil.' The word 'desert' conjures the image of a sea of yellow crescent-shaped dunes, but in fact much of the Egyptian desert consists of coarse gravel and stones that support some scanty vegetation and a surprising variety of wildlife. There are of course vast areas of dunes such as the Great Sand Sea in the southwest, but there are also many areas of spectacular scenery. The Black Desert for example is a region of soft orange sand from which emerge hundreds of black, conical hills that are the eroded remains of ancient volcanoes. The White Desert is a fabulous landscape of eroded pillars of white sedimentary rock studded with sea shells and coral that formed millions of years ago on the bed of the Tethys Sea. The Eastern or Arabian Desert which lies between the Nile and the Red Sea is rich with natural resources and was a major source of the precious metals and stones such as carnelian and lapis lazuli that the Egyptians utilised to such effect in their jewellery and funerary artefacts.

Contrary to the traditional conception of the Egyptian desert as an unexplored and trackless waste, from the earliest dynastic period there were significant permanent links between the Nile valley and the centres of population dotted about the desert. Recent exploration has discovered many tracks between these sizeable, organised desert communities and the Nile valley.[14] The Western Desert that stretches into the Sahara contains a number of permanent oases that have been populated since predynastic times. They receive no rainfall but rely on a regular and plentiful supply of water from underground aquifers which support orchards, livestock and a variety of crops. The oasis vineyards supplied the Pharaohs and the more wealthy members of the population with wine, and the oasis towns were served by temples whose gods were the same as those worshipped in the temples along the Nile.

This is not to deny that much of the desert is intensely hot, arid, prone to strong winds and fiercely hostile to life; it is the earth at its most raw, powerful and intense. It represents the ferocious power of solar energy, of light, heat, aridity and apparent lack of movement – but it is not therefore 'evil.' A useful explanation of the equal significance and interdependency of the opposing principles represented by the River Nile and the desert can be found in the 20th century occultist Dion Fortune's treatise on universal energy: *The Cosmic Doctrine*. [15] We can relate the Nile and the desert to the first two principles of creative energy described in this text, which are conceived in highly abstract terms as two vast cosmic 'Rings' that revolve at right angles. The Rings are named 'Ring Cosmos' and 'Ring Chaos.' "Now these two Rings we will call Good and Negative Good; Life and Death; Light and Darkness; Spirit and Matter; Being and Not-Being; God and Devil, because each of these potencies has its root in its respective Ring… Negative Good, when unopposed, resolves itself into the undifferentiated raw material of existence – the first form of manifestation… It is the spin of these two Rings which gives the influences that play upon creation. You are now in a position to know why the mystery of Negative Good is the secret of the Initiates…"

As mentioned earlier, a significant number of the hieroglyphs are images of the natural forms of Egypt's topography, and many of these confront us with the concept of polarity that is expressed within the landscape. Keeping in mind this idea of the desert as 'negative good,' here is the hieroglyph for 'desert.'[16]

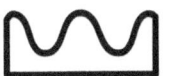

khst = *khaset*, desert

This is an example of a triliteral sign; it contains the three sounds *kh, s* and *t*. Modern convention inserts the vowels *a* and *e* to produce the word *khaset* although we cannot be certain that this is how it was originally pronounced. The hieroglyph was mainly used as an ideogram – in other words it often simply indicated 'a desert.' It could also mean 'hilly country,' 'foreign lands' and 'necropolis,' because in ancient Egypt the cemeteries were located in the dry sand of the desert rather than in the fertile land either side of the Nile. Some of the early illustrations of *khaset* show the hills coloured in red and yellow, with a green line running along the base of the hieroglyph to indicate the river plain, and neatly convey the idea of contrast and opposites within a single sign.

If we look at *khaset* as a symbol it contains several features that merit further attention. First, the hieroglyph doesn't look much like a desert, nor even very much like hills. You will probably find that if you show this sign to someone who is not familiar with the hieroglyphs they will guess it to be an image of undulating waves, or perhaps a crown. A convention of hieroglyphic inscriptions is that one sign indicates 'one of' and three of the same sign grouped together indicates 'many,' so our assumption might be that the hieroglyph for 'desert' or 'hilly country' would be indicated by three hills. Yet this hieroglyph consists of one complete hill and two hills that have been sliced in half. If you try to draw the hieroglyph yourself you will find that it is much easier to draw three complete hills, and cutting two of them in half doesn't seem to make much sense. In fact we might say that the hieroglyph illustrates two valleys rather than three hills.

We can either dismiss this as unimportant and perhaps indicative of a lack of artistic ability on the part of the Egyptian scribes, or we can suppose that it was deliberately drawn like this for a good reason, in which case we need to think a little further. Carelessness was not typical of ancient Egyptian craftsmanship, whether in the hieroglyphs or in the building of their temples and pyramids. Throughout the following chapters our attention will often be drawn to something unexpected in the appearance of a hieroglyph. This is not to suggest that they contain a 'hidden code,' but by looking carefully at these unexpected elements and contemplating the reason behind them we can arrive at a better understanding of their meaning. If we look again at *khaset* we can interpret it as one complete hill which is also depicted in two halves, but we note that each half remains connected to the other through the existence of the complete hill. Were it not for the presence of the complete hill we would not be able to recognise the halves; their identity depends on the presence of the whole.

If we apply this same principle to the fundamental concern of Egyptian magical thought – the apparent division between spirit and matter and the evolving relationship between them – we can say that if spirit and matter were indeed completely separate then the concept of the One Unity would be impossible; there would be no spirit within matter and no possibility of its return. They can only be reunited if the original wholeness and completeness remains available. It has been said that in the beginning, all was One. From the One, in time, the universe came into being, including ourselves and all that we recognise in the world about us. This gradual unfolding of life from the One is sometimes described as the process of involution, and one of the most noticeable effects of involution is that as each spark of light from the One descends from pure spirit into the dense matter of the physical world so it becomes *as if* separate from everything else. Evolution, on the other hand, is the process by which the connectedness between all things is recognised: it is a gradual coming together, a synthesis in which all will eventually again become One. Those who practice the magical arts make a conscious alignment of themselves with the course of evolution by trying to increase their awareness of the spiritual realities which lie behind the forms of the mundane world, discovering and bringing out the hidden light within matter and focussing on the universal principles which unite the outward forms. Bridging the apparent polarity between spirit and matter, or heaven and earth, is human consciousness.

When we consider the desert in relation to the River Nile, initially it will seem that the Nile must symbolise the positive, life-enhancing spirit or 'Good,' while the desert must symbolise the opposite quality of 'Evil' or 'Chaos,' but *khaset* proposes that this explanation is too simple. If we use a magical technique for approaching this hieroglyph we can appreciate how it becomes an expression of metaphysical qualities that we can relate to and interact with. This can be done by entering into a meditative state of mind in which you set aside the physical world and focus your attention on the hieroglyph to the exclusion of everything else. Build the shape in your mind's eye and allow it to take form. Look at the complete hill at the centre and the two halves on either side, and see how they relate to each other.

You may find that when you have built the hieroglyph in

your imagination it begins to transform from a two-dimensional drawing into an energised, three-dimensional image in which the two 'valleys' take on increasing importance. When you focus on the valleys you may find that they draw you into the hieroglyph, as if they have become an entrance to Inner landscapes or other levels of consciousness. Or perhaps the two valleys become channels for the movement of energy both towards and away from you, inviting you into the Inner worlds while allowing energy to emerge from them.

So while the outer or exoteric meaning of this hieroglyph refers to the desert hills, as a magical symbol it refers to the basic concepts of spirit and matter, unity and separation, the appearance of the outer world acting as a gateway to the qualities of the Inner worlds. We might say that the hills represent form and the valleys between them represent energy. Above all, the hieroglyph illustrates the nature of our relationship with both form and energy, and illustrates how it is our *consciousness* which brings them together.

These basic principles that underpin the magical symbolism of the hieroglyphs have been described in some detail because the same principles can be found in many other examples.

Similar ideas are developed for example in the hieroglyph *Akht* or *Akhet*. It represents the sun rising or setting in a valley between two hills and was primarily used as an ideogram which means 'the horizon.' In the Egyptian landscape, the uninterrupted presence of the desert hills along the entire length of the Nile meant that in ancient times the sun could be seen rising and setting from almost any location along the Nile valley, although the view is now often interrupted by modern hotels and high-rise buildings. The symbolic meaning of the 'horizon' was a key element in Egyptian magical thought, and it was perceived as a separate region which had its own special qualities that were over and above the appearance of the physical landscape. In symbolic terms the horizon represents the vastness of the 'inner landscape' that lies between the earthly and spiritual worlds; it is a place of transition between one state of consciousness and another, a state of balance between the polarised energies symbolised by the Nile and the desert. The Great Pyramid at Giza, for example, was originally called 'The Horizon of Khufu' suggesting that within the pyramid the spiritual presence of the deceased Pharaoh remained as a mediator of these qualities to the land and people in a permanent condition of spiritual potency.

Akht = *Akhet*, the horizon; spiritually potent

The word *Akh* can also be translated as 'to shine' or 'to be spiritually effective or potent.' [17] The hieroglyph not only illustrates the physical event of the rising or setting sun but invites us to relate to the qualities symbolised by the sun and to embody them within our own selves. Here, the sun represents each individual who undertakes the evolutionary journey that alternates between life and death, or night and day, and in doing so acquires the ability to mediate between them. *Akhet* develops the idea expressed in *khaset* that the valley holds as much meaning and potential as the hills. We have greater 'spiritual effectiveness' when our Inner light shines like the sun, or when we are able to embody the energy of the valley in equal measure with the form of the surrounding physical environment. The sun god *Ra* or *Re* was one of the most important gods of the Egyptian pantheon and the symbolic 'taking on' of the sun's powers, of shining like the sun with the radiance of spiritual light, represented an advanced stage of spiritual achievement.

The hieroglyph therefore functions as a symbol of all those who, having grasped and experienced these opposing states of spirit and matter in themselves and in the universe about them, are able to maintain a creative equilibrium between them. The sun may be rising into day or setting into night but in either case it is a time when the realisations of one state of existence can be merged with another.

The second major feature of the Egyptian landscape is, of course, the River Nile. The name 'Nile' comes from the Greek word *Neilos* which means 'river valley' but the ancient Egyptians knew it as *iterw* which simply means 'river.' It is written in hieroglyphs as follows: [18]

= *iterw*, the river

The first four of the five hieroglyphs that comprise the word *iterw* are among the most commonly used uniliteral hieroglyphs and represent, reading from left to right, the flowering reed, the small loaf of offering, a mouth and a quail chick. Although these signs contain symbolic meaning – and this will be looked at in later chapters – their primary use here is as sounds or phonemes. The significant hieroglyph in *iterw* is the final sign, which is not pronounced. A sign such as this is often used at the end of a group of hieroglyphs and is known as a 'determinative' because it defines or determines the meaning of the previous hieroglyphs. One consequence of the rich symbolic potential of the hieroglyphs is that when they are combined in a word the precise meaning is not always obvious, hence the need for the determinative which limits and defines the context. In *iterw*, the determinative is the hieroglyph *mu*, which represents 'water.'

Given the importance of the River Nile as almost the only source of fresh water in Egypt, to say nothing of its powerful symbolic presence, it can perhaps come as a surprise that it is not represented by a single distinctive hieroglyph. It seems that for the ancient Egyptians the name of the river was of little importance; what mattered was the symbolic properties of the water itself.

Here is the hieroglyph *mu* again: [19]

mu = water

Mu is always shown as above, with three 'zigzag' lines placed one on top of the other. The most frequent number of zigzags in each line is seven, although the number varies between four and ten. There is no apparent significance in this variation which is probably just a reflection of individual style or a response to the available space in which the hieroglyph could be drawn with pleasing symmetry. In many examples, the ends of each line are slightly extended downwards.

If you didn't know that *mu* represents water you might find yourself puzzling over what it does illustrate. It's not an obvious choice of symbol for water. Water does not describe the sharp angles of *mu* but flows in soft curves. In the magical traditions of the West, water and earth are often considered to be feminine elements in contrast to the masculine elements of fire and air, but the lively, angular appearance of the hieroglyph does not evoke the receptive, reflective qualities we usually associate with water. *Mu* can also refer to bodily fluids such as semen, urine and spittle.

It is good to have a picture in your mind of the physical appearance of the Nile. It is wide, sparkling under blue skies, its surface often rippled by a stiff breeze. Its low banks are thickly covered with flowering reeds, and in many places the flow of the river is interrupted by small, reed-covered islands. We do not know whether the ancient Egyptians had knowledge of the actual source of the Nile, although their expeditions to the fabled land of Punt may have taken them into the heart of Africa. The Nile has two main tributaries: the White Nile whose source is in Lake Victoria, and the Blue Nile whose source is in the fertile tablelands of Ethiopia. The Blue Nile was responsible for the yearly inundation that brought the vital black silt, rich with nutrients and minerals, that was deposited along the flooded river plain. Although we tend to think of rivers as 'feminine,' this flooding of the waters and the resultant fertilisation of the land is perhaps more accurately understood as symbolic of masculine power, and certainly the river was thought of as male by the ancient Egyptians. Unfortunately the inundation which played such a vital part of Egyptian life is now a thing of the past; since the building of the High Dam at Aswan Dam in the 1960s the Nile's flow has become restricted to a more or less constant rate throughout the year and this effect is likely to be even more pronounced when the Grand Ethiopian Renaissance Dam on the Blue Nile is completed.

A third major tributary of the Nile, the Atbara, joins the river some two hundred miles north of Khartoum, and from here the river sweeps fiercely between sandstone hills until its passage is impeded by a series of five cataracts, intrusions of hard black igneous rock polished smooth by the action of sun, wind and water over millions of years. At the furthest north of the five cataracts is the island of Abu, now known as Elephantine Island. In ancient Egypt, Abu was regarded as the source of the Nile whose waters, it was said, flooded out from between two boulders in a cavern deep beneath the island. It was of course as evident five thousand years ago as it is today that the Nile does not flow out from beneath the island but there can be no doubt of the unambiguous masculine symbolism! Abu is also the location of two of the 'Nileometers,' a series of engraved lines cut in a narrow channel in the rock where the height of the Nile's floodwaters on a certain day of the year was measured as an accurate assessment of the anticipated volume of that year's inundation.

Returning to the hieroglyph *mu*, we see that the sign gives no indication of the source or destination of the flowing water. It is not flowing from something into something else and has no apparent beginning or end, although the hint of an extension at the ends of the lines in some examples suggests that it derives from something which is beyond our sight or comprehension. Nor are there any restrictions to the water's flow; it is not contained. *Mu* offers us a glimpse of something infinite and eternal, having no obvious connection with the physical world and no apparent limitations. Rather than illustrating the physical element of water it seems to represent something as nebulous as moving energy – of which water is a physical example.

There can scarcely be a more difficult subject to comprehend than 'energy' but this makes *mu* a particularly important hieroglyph in terms of magical symbolism. One of the problems in discussing energy is that we tend to define it according to our background of thought and belief. Those more esoterically inclined often qualify the word with adjectives such as 'balanced,' 'blocked' or 'healing.' Those of a more scientific frame of mind speak of light, heat or sound; they distinguish between chemical, magnetic and atomic energy and refer to potential (stored) energy and kinetic (moving) energy.

We can only perceive energy indirectly by observing its effect, so it would be more accurate to say that if we describe the energy of something we are really describing its condition, quality or state. In esoteric terms, as pure spiritual energy becomes more complex and dense it can be said that its light decreases. Conversely, as dense matter becomes infused by spirit it can be said that its capacity for revealing its light is increased, a process that is sometimes described as the regeneration of matter. In esoteric belief it is assumed that there is a correlation between the quality of energy being experienced and the consciousness of the individual. The phrase 'tuning in' to energy is often used, suggesting that its qualities can best be experienced when there is a close correlation between the 'wavelength' of the consciousness of the observer and the frequency or quality of the energy being measured.

By looking at the hieroglyphs we can observe how this same focus on the quality of energy was a preoccupation in Egyptian magical thought. We are not certain how the following word was pronounced – it could be either *nw, nnw* or *nwnw* – but it means 'primordial waters.' [20]

nw = *nnw*, the primordial waters

The use of the hieroglyphs in this word is highly abstract. The spherical pots or water jars indicate the primordial ocean of space, *nwn*, which rather than being completely without form – and therefore incommunicable through words or images – is envisaged as an enclosing sphere. The 'content' of the spherical jars is without substance. It can perhaps best be likened to the Unmanifest. "The Unmanifest is pure existence. We cannot say of it that it is *not*. Although it is not manifest, it *is*. IT is the source from which all arises. IT is the only 'Reality.' IT alone is substance. IT alone is stable; all else is an appearance and a becoming." [21] This is the primordial substance that becomes the source material of every created form. Interestingly, there are three jars where we might have expected only one – but this leads us into deep waters!

The second hieroglyph, *mu,* is not pronounced and therefore acts as a determinative, telling us that the content of the 'water jars' of space is in some way analogous to the element of water rather than, for example, the element of air. The final hieroglyph is another unpronounced determinative: the hieroglyph *pet* which means 'the sky.' It confirms that the symbolic meaning of the previous two hieroglyphs belongs to the sky or heavens rather than to the physical earth. [22]

The hieroglyph *mu* derives from another hieroglyph, or at least is closely related to it: a single zigzag line which is pronounced '*n*.' [23]

〰〰

n = n, to, for, belonging to

This sign means 'belonging to.' It was also used as the prepositions 'to' and 'for,' and conveys the sense of 'moving towards.' While *mu* can refer to liquids generally and to the waters of the Nile in particular, '*n*' refers to the quality behind the physical appearance, the moving or flowing energy which lies behind the mundane manifestation of all things. Its basic meaning of 'belonging to' represents the sense in which one thing or person is connected to another at a metaphysical level; it suggests identification, integration and union. The notion of 'belonging' not only refers to the movement or exchange of energy as it flows between two things and forms a connection between them but also to our awareness that this energetic connection is taking place. The appearance of this hieroglyph in a word prompts us to consider the nature of the underlying relationship between one thing and another even if – especially if – it is not immediately apparent. The hieroglyph symbolises the universal principle of synthesis, the omnipresent existence of connecting energy, and our ability to observe that connection.

Here are some examples of how the hieroglyph '*n*' was used. The following word means 'prayer' or 'to pray for.' [24]

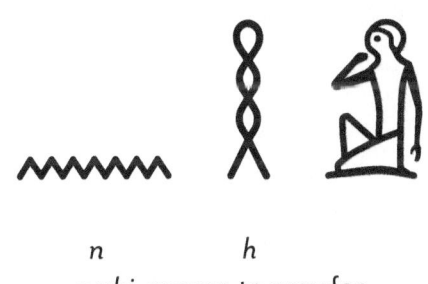

n *h*
= *nhi*, prayer, to pray for

The word begins with '*n*,' and the idea of moving and connecting energy. The second hieroglyph depicts the lamp wick made from twisted linen or flax that was essential for maintaining the perpetual flame of the oil lamps used in the temples. The lighting and dousing of the lamp wicks played a significant role in the daily life of the temple, and the kindling of a flame is perhaps one of the most consequential symbolic actions we can make, a deliberate bringing down of the supernal light into manifestation through our own conscious effort. The determinative in this word is a seated figure raising a hand to their mouth. (Many words are determined by a hieroglyph of the human figure in a variety of different postures.) The three signs represent the progression of spiritual energy into increasingly dense levels of manifestation: first there is pure energy or movement, then light, and finally sound: energy manifesting through three different levels of vibration. The combined symbolism is a remarkably perceptive illustration of the true nature of prayer: not a naive request for what we think we need, but a means by which we can attune ourselves to spiritual energy and then give voice to it.

A similar use of '*n*' can be seen in the word below which is an alternative spelling of the word *neter* (singular) or *neterw* (plural), 'the gods.' [25] (Many words could be spelt with a variety of different hieroglyphs.)

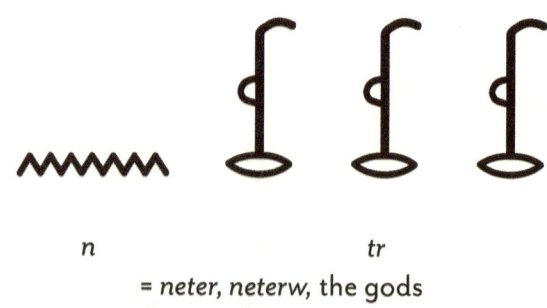

n   tr

= neter, neterw, the gods

The symbolism in this word helps us to understand what the ancient Egyptians meant by 'the gods.' The second hieroglyph is often described as a palm branch which has been stripped of its leaves, with notches made in the stem to keep a count or tally. The hieroglyph was associated with the concept of time and the measurement of the passing of time by the marking of each year or season. The shape on the side of the branch does however look more like a budding growth than a notch, and this accords with the meaning of the hieroglyph: 'fresh,' 'vigorous,' 'renewed' and 'young.' Horapollo describes how "... they (i.e. the Egyptians) represent the year by a date-palm, because this tree alone at each new moon sends forth a new branch, so that it produces twelve new branches a year."[26]

The symbolic meaning of *neterw* in this combination of hieroglyphs tells us that regeneration is brought about through natural, cyclical patterns and, as was mentioned in the previous chapter, it suggests that the usual rendering of *neterw* as 'the gods' might more accurately be translated as 'regeneration' or 'the embodiment of universal, cyclic principles of growth and renewal.'

The use of the hieroglyph '*n*' at the beginning of this word reminds us that the gods do not exist in isolation but that their fundamental quality is that of universal, regenerative energy. Again, here is the idea of movement, transference and exchange of energy which promotes a sense of universal connectedness.

The following word '*nehet*' means 'shelter' or 'refuge.' [27]

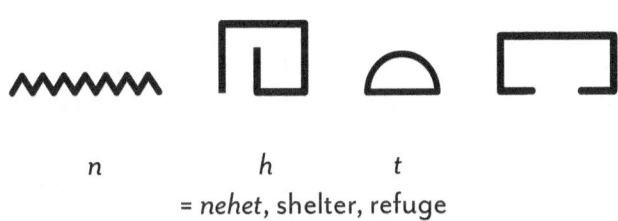

n   h   t
= *nehet*, shelter, refuge

The hieroglyph *n* is followed by a sign which represents one of the simple reed shelters that can still be seen alongside the Nile to provide shade for the field-workers and their animals. The third hieroglyph represents a small loaf of offering, '*t*' which indicates that the word is feminine. The word is determined by the final sign *pr* or *per*, which means 'house.' [28] The clue to interpreting this group of hieroglyphs is established by the initial sign which suggests that the meaning has less to do with the physical appearance or properties of the building but with the type of experience or quality of energy that it provides: protection, shelter, and refuge.

The same idea is developed in the next word which is also transliterated as *nehet* but means 'magical protection.' [29]

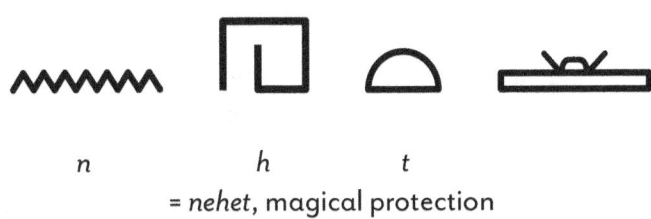

n   h   t
= *nehet*, magical protection

Here, the final sign is the hieroglyph depicting a roll of papyrus that has been tied and sealed. It is pronounced *medjAt*, but it functions here as an unvoiced determinative. This is one of the most frequently used determinatives and will often be encountered in the following chapters. Its appearance indicates that the preceding hieroglyphs represent an abstract idea or concept rather than an actual object. *MedjAt* refers to the ability to 'know' in the sense of having an intuitional grasp of the universal qualities behind all things rather than perceiving them as separate. It suggests that our habit of believing things to be disconnected and separate, and of thinking of ourselves as disconnected and separate, makes us vulnerable and in need of magical protection. Magic, according to the hieroglyphs of *nehet,* is the ability to see the connection between all things and to realise our own connectedness with all that is.

As a final example of '*n*' the following word, *hnn* or *henen*, begins with the delightful hieroglyph of a pair of arms rowing. The determinative is of a man striking or pointing with a stick, which means 'force' or 'effort.' The whole word means 'to inflame or irritate,' 'to disturb or interfere' and corresponds remarkably well with modern phrases such as 'stirring it' and 'muddying the waters!'[30]

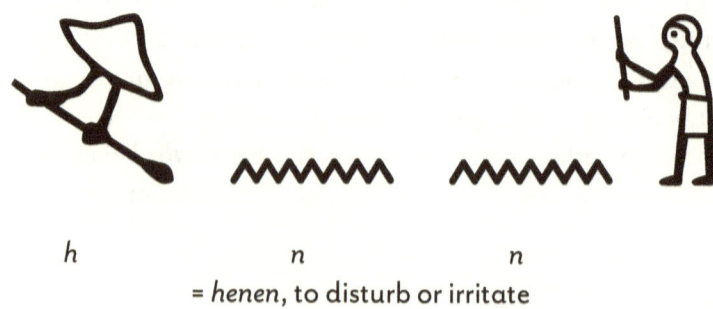

h   n   n
= *henen*, to disturb or irritate

In this chapter we have explored some of the basic principles on which the symbolism of the hieroglyphs is built, and these same principles will be seen at work throughout the succeeding chapters. Contemplation of the hieroglyphs as magical symbols leads us to a greater understanding of how Egyptian magic was originally taught and practiced. They reveal how the physical appearance of the things about us reveals the qualities and energies behind all creation. In particular, the unique landscape of Egypt symbolises universal concepts such stasis and movement, dryness and moisture, sterility and fertility, chaos and control, states of being and consciousness, and above all the relationship between energy and form. In Egypt, the productivity of the land depends upon human mediation to channel the life-giving waters of the Nile into the otherwise arid soil just as the evolving relationship between spirit and matter depends on the mediation of human consciousness to bridge the apparent gulf between them. When we contemplate the magical symbolism of the hieroglyphs we too, through our minds and imagination, bring heaven to earth.

Endnotes

12 ed and trans Walter Scott, *Hermetica: the writings attributed to Hermes Trismegistus* (Bath, Solus Press, 1992) page 136
13 The other two examples are parts of the Yellow River in China, and the Colorado River in the southwest of the USA.
14 see for example J. C. Darnell, with the assistance of D. Darnell and contributions by D. Darnell, R. Friedman, and S. Hendrickx, *Theban Desert Road Survey in the Egyptian Western Desert, Volume 1: Gebel Tjauti Rock Inscriptions 1-45 and Wadi el-Hôl Rock Inscriptions 1-45* (University of Chicago, Oriental Institute Publications 2002)
15 Dion Fortune, *The Cosmic Doctrine* (York Beach ME, Red Wheel/Weiser 2000) pages 23, 25
16 *khaset*, the desert: Gardiner N25
17 *Akhet*, the horizon: Gardiner N27
18 *iterw*, the river: Gardiner M17, X1, D21, G43, N35a
19 *mu*, water, Gardiner N35a
20 *nwn*, primeval waters: Gardiner W24, W24, W24, N35a, N1
21 Dion Fortune, *The Cosmic Doctrine*, page 19
22 the hieroglyph *pet* is discussed in more detail in Chapter Four
23 *n*, we, us, belonging to: Gardiner N35
24 *nhi*, prayer, to pray for: Gardiner N35, V28, A2
25 *neterw*, the gods: Gardiner N35, M6, M6, M6
26 Horapollo, *Hieroglyphica: Book I*, Section 3
27 *nehet*, shelter, refuge: Gardiner N35, O4, X1, O1
28 A detailed discussion of *pr* or *per*, the hieroglyph for the house, is found in Chapter Thirteen
29 *nehet*, magical protection: Gardiner N35, O4, X1, Y1
30 *henen*, to disturb or irritate: Gardiner D33, N35, N35, A24

Earth, trees and plants

Where the desert and the river come together, fertile land is created. This chapter looks at the symbolism of the hieroglyphs that represent the features of the land along the Nile valley, and the plants and trees that grow there.

First, the hieroglyph *tA*, which means 'the land.' [31]

tA = the land

This sign combines two separate hieroglyphs: a long, narrow strip with rounded ends, and underneath it three small circles in a horizontal line. The sign is so abstract that its meaning is almost impossible to guess from its appearance, so our first question must be why it has been designed in this way. Or, alternatively, to consider why the gods conveyed this particular design to humanity. It is quite difficult to design an unambiguous symbol for 'the land.' Does 'land' mean a country, a continent, a farm or a vegetable plot? Does it refer to the whole Earth or to a handful of earth? *tA* contains no indication of size or context and there is no hint of vegetation growing on it, which deprives us of what might have been a clue to its size or identity. Nor is it clear whether we are looking down on this symbol as if it was an island, or holding it before us in our mind's eye as if it was suspended in mid air.

The rounded ends are also puzzling. A square or a rectangle would be a more obvious symbol for a plot of land or a field. In the language of symbolism the square is often an indication of physical manifestation – there are no right-angles in space – in contrast to the circle or sphere that symbolises the wholeness of the heavenly worlds. In fact there is a circle or sphere in *tA*, but it has been divided into two halves, and these are kept apart by the parallel lines.

But if we think about this hieroglyph as a magical symbol rather than as an unsatisfactory illustration of 'land' there is plenty to interest us, not least in what it tells us about the ancient Egyptians' view of earth and heaven and the relationship between them. If we contemplate the significance of the divided circles or spheres in the upper part of the hieroglyph we might see one half of the sphere representing the physical earth and the other half as an indication of space. The parallel lines between them convey the idea that their separation is only apparent; whatever the distance between them, they remain connected. The parallel lines are an indication of space or time, and they suggest the existence of a creative tension or polarity between the two extremes. A single line might have sufficed, but parallel lines suggest that this is a two-way relationship.

A final point of interest is the orientation of this part of the hieroglyph. If it was depicted vertically, with one half-sphere above the other, we would be likely to identify the upper half-sphere as 'heaven' and the lower as 'earth.' The horizontal arrangement suggests that what we assume to be earth is ultimately no different to spirit – and vice versa – and that this apparent separation may just be a projection of our own beliefs and understanding of reality. This interpretation is reinforced by the second element of *tA*, the three small circles. They are always placed beneath the first element of the hieroglyph and therefore draw our attention to what is *within* the land rather than growing on its surface. These three circles can indicate seeds but they also symbolise the presence of spiritual energy and the unity and entirety of the heavenly worlds that are present within land. They tell us that the land is not inert matter, but 'dense spirit.'

Putting all this together, we find that the symbolism of *tA* confronts us with fundamental questions regarding how we perceive 'spirit' and 'matter.' It invites us to consider how the seeds of spirit within the earth can be brought out into the light and encouraged to flower.

When these three circles are used as a separate hieroglyph, *nbw*, (shown below) they represent grains of sand or minerals.[32] The word 'grain' was used as we use it now, to refer to any small particle of something that is commonly found in large quantities. The hieroglyph indicated for example the finely ground lead sulphide that was used for kohl eye-paint, and to represent gold, and copper.

○○○

nbw = nebw, grains of sand, gold, incense, kohl

Nebw also represents the grains of incense used in temple ritual. The Egyptians referred to incense as 'the fragrance of the gods' and the correct mixture of ingredients was regarded as a vital part of the ceremony. Plutarch notes that the incense *kapet* (now better known by its Greek name *kyphi*) had sixteen ingredients, and he describes how they were blended "... not at random, but while the sacred writings are being read to the perfumers as they mix the ingredients." He adds: "... the air at night is a composite mixture made up of many lights and forces, even as though seeds from every star were showered down into one place. Very appropriately, therefore, they burn resin and myrrh in the daytime, for these are simple substances and have their origin from the sun; but the *kyphi*, since it is compounded of ingredients of all sorts of qualities, they offer at nightfall."[33] In other words, the spiritual qualities of the grains of incense were recognised, brought out and released through human mediation in a series of ritual actions that invoked a beneficial and elevating effect on the human psyche. The fragrant smoke of the burning incense became a vehicle through which the wisdom of the gods could be brought down into human perception – thus the whole exercise of mining the grains of incense, blending them and burning them became a bridge between the earthly and heavenly worlds.

In the above extract, Plutarch makes an interesting point regarding the Egyptians' reverence for the inherent properties of a substance – in this instance the blended incense – and the ways in which these properties might be identified and used appropriately. The substance of a material object is important because it is through our awareness of its qualities and attributes that its origin in the spiritual world can be discerned. It was the responsibility of those who worked within the temples to seek out these spiritual treasures and offer them up to the gods.

This concept of the inherent sacredness of the earth is suggested in the symbolism of *tA*, as in all the hieroglyphs. The three circles represent the spirit that lies dormant within the land until its potential is brought out through human mediation. The hieroglyph draws our attention to what is hidden, and to those aspects of earthly substance that humankind is able to discover and bring out into the light.

The Egyptians used a variety of colourful semi-precious stones in their jewellery and in the sacred artefacts of their temples and funerary goods, together with a great deal of gold. The beauty of the famous gold and lapis funerary masks of the Pharaoh Tutankhamun is but one example of the extraordinary skill of the Egyptian craftsmen and of the apparently limitless resources at their disposal. Much gold was obtained from the Eastern desert, where it was easily recoverable from alluvial deposits and in the sandy detritus that filled the desert valleys by swirling it around in the nearest supply of water.

Although different minerals were indicated by the 'three grains' hieroglyph, gold was held in such high esteem for its actual and symbolic properties that it was represented by a separate hieroglyph. The hieroglyph for gold, also pronounced *nebw*, is shown below.[34]

nbw = *nebw*, gold

This sign is usually said to indicate a gold necklace, with beads or droplets of gold suspended from a semi-circular plate and with the heavy ties of the necklace hanging downwards. But as we found in *tA*, there are a couple of 'not quite right' elements in the design of this hieroglyph which draw our attention to its symbolism. If the ties curved upwards it would be more easily recognisable as a necklace, an arrangement which is used to good effect in the hieroglyph for 'necklace' which is shown below. This is a realistic depiction of the distinctive Egyptian collar necklace, the *wsh* or *wesekh* that typically was made from dozens of tiny beads threaded into rows of contrasting colours.[35] The contrasting ends of the collar where the rows of beads are fastened together and the two short ties are clearly shown.

wskh = *wesekh*, the pectoral or collar necklace

A brief survey of illustrations of ancient Egyptian necklaces and pectorals reveals that the design used in the hieroglyph *nebw* is not typical of them, and indeed it is difficult to find any illustrations of necklaces which resemble the hieroglyph. The *nebw* hieroglyph has a flat top and the sturdy, vertical necklace 'ties' look more like table legs than ties of thread or fine gold. This effect appears to be quite deliberate as there are a number of examples in which the hieroglyph supports the kneeling or standing figure of a goddess.

Earth, trees and plants

The red granite sarcophagus of Rameses III shows the goddess Nephthys kneeling above a *nebw* on which the descending 'droplets' are particularly emphasised.

The red granite sarcophagus of Rameses III, now in the Louvre, Paris, showing the goddess Nephthys kneeling on the hieroglyph *nebw*, 'gold.'

Photo by Frank Kovalchek

Gold is the ultimate demonstration of the ancient Egyptians' belief in the sacredness of physical material. They regarded it as a living substance rather than an inert metal; they believed it to be the essence of the sun's radiance contained within the earth. Its nature was shown forth in the golden bodies of the gods and goddesses who were untarnished by the shadows of the material world. One of the epithets of Osiris was 'Eternal Gold,' Hathor was known as 'the Golden One' and the sun god Re was also known as 'the Mountain of Gold.'

There is a fascinating image of dancers carrying out what is described as the 'gold movement' in one of the wall paintings in the tomb of Watetkhethor, a priestess of Hathor and daughter of the Sixth Dynasty Pharaoh Teti (2350-2338 B.C.) who was buried alongside her husband Mereruka at the funerary complex of Saqqara. A similar image is displayed on the tomb of Iymery, a high priest during the reign of the Fifth Dynasty Pharaoh Khufu, in which two men perform 'the dance of seizing the Golden One.'³⁶ In these illustrations, two dancers are miming an action in which they appear to be holding up a large piece of cloth between their outstretched hands just as we might hold and shake out a bedsheet. Dance played an important part in the Egyptian funeral, with separate dances depicting each of the five stages of the journey of the deceased into the afterlife. The first stage, in which the 'gold dance' took place, described how the deceased entered the boat of the sun god Re in order to travel across the heavens before entering the Innerworld or *dwAt*.

The illustrations of the 'gold movement' suggest that it mimicked the process of winnowing for gold. This was done either by placing the sand and gold mixture into a fine woollen sheet and shaking it up and down so that the gold particles became electrically charged and attached to the blanket while the sand particles blew away, or by heaping the gold and sand into a bag with long hanging ends which were held out between two people, and water passed through it. The 'droplets' beneath the hieroglyph *nebw* might illustrate water filtering through the cloth, revealing the pure, washed gold safely contained within the bag.³⁷

If we put these elements of symbolic meaning together, in addition to being a simple ideogram for gold, *nebw* also appears to refer to an important stage in ancient Egyptian magical and spiritual practice, that of 'becoming gold.' This represents a stage of spiritual awareness that is achieved when the impurities and shadows of earthly existence have been filtered away, leaving the essential gold of the Self to shine through. We might make a parallel with the ability to fully identify with the light of the Soul or Higher Self so that it permeates and shines out through our everyday personality or Lower Self. Or, in Qabalistic terms, bringing down the qualities of the Sephirah Tiphareth into Malkuth.

When the hieroglyph *nebw* is used as a symbolic funerary table or altar, the presence of the goddess above the altar indicates how we too might be transfigured, becoming like the 'gods' or spiritually evolved beings whose bodies shone as gold. The hieroglyph symbolises the journey of the deceased through the after-life and, equally, the evolutionary journey of humanity in which our inner light is gradually revealed. The seeking out and extraction of gold was part of the Pharaoh's sacred and magical duty to his people, and his ability to discover the 'treasures' hidden in his land and to refine them into glorious offerings to the gods was a demonstration of his ability to mediate between heaven and earth on behalf of his land and people.

Keeping all this in mind, we can return to the hieroglyph *tA* and appreciate how its many levels of symbolism are used to enrich the meaning of other words and phrases. For example, here is the word *sstA* or *seshetA* which means 'secret,' 'hidden.' [38]

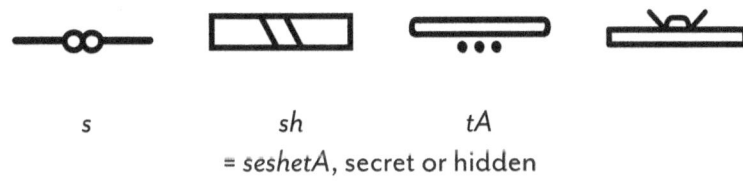

s   sh   tA

= *seshetA*, secret or hidden

The first hieroglyph of *seshetA* represents the door-bolt that was used to fasten the great double-doors that enclosed the innermost sanctuary of the temple. The second depicts a lake, pool or enclosed stretch of water, either natural or artificial, such as the sacred lakes of the temples. The third hieroglyph is *tA*, the land. The final hieroglyph is a determinative: the sealed roll of papyrus which tells us that the previous signs should be interpreted as an idea or concept rather than at their face value.

The overall symbolism of this word therefore describes a hidden, guarded place, which is neither water nor land although it possesses the qualities of both. The illusory nature of the 'landscape of the consciousness' was encountered in the region known to the Egyptians as the *dwAt*, an area of the Inner world in which the symbolism of lakes and marshy areas predominated. Some parts of this region were benign, other less so, and it is comparable to the many astral landscapes of modern Western magic which offer a similar admixture of reliable information and illusory glamour. Equally we might say that *seshetA* refers to the mystery of the physical landscape which, when unlocked, reveals the secrets of the universe.

tA is also found in the expression *tA neter*, written below. It is formed of signs we have already looked at and illustrates how with only a small vocabulary of hieroglyphs it is surprisingly easy to construct words and phrases that contain a depth of symbolism. *tA neter*, 'god's land,' was the name given to the fabled land of Punt.[39]

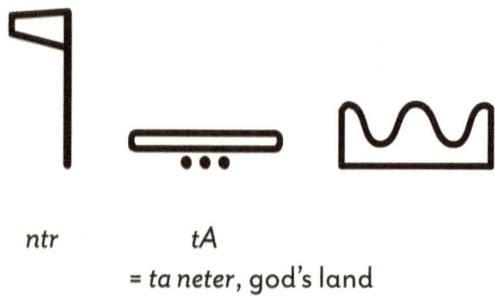

ntr   tA
= ta neter, god's land

The determinative is this instance is *khaset*, the desert, which tells us that the country or area in question is mountainous, a desert, but probably not a part of Egypt. Modern opinion is that Punt likely consisted of an area around the Red Sea which included what is now Eastern Ethiopia and parts of Somalia and Eritrea, but to the Egyptians it was 'god's land' because it was a rich source of gold and therefore the source of all that was immortal, incorruptible and untarnished by earthly shadows.

tA is also used in the following word, *djet*, which means 'eternity.'[40]

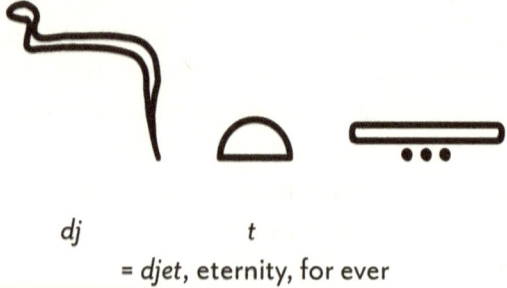

dj   t
= djet, eternity, for ever

The first hieroglyph in this word is the cobra, the frequently used biliteral sound *dj*. This sign is used in a number of words that describe the divine power and authority held by the Pharaoh. It is followed here by the feminine '*t*' of the small loaf of offering. Without the determinative of *tA* we might read the word simply as 'royal power' but the use of *tA* in this group of signs tells us that all the qualities symbolised by this hieroglyph are relevant to the concept of 'eternity.' The phrase 'eternal Egypt' has become something of a cliché but it represents a fundamental principle in Egyptian magical thought: the land of Egypt does indeed embody sacred truths and universal principles – such as those symbolised by the hieroglyph *tA* – which are relevant for all times and places.

The relationship between heaven and earth is symbolised in another hieroglyph: *mr* or *mer* which means 'the hoe'.[41]

mr = *mer*, the hoe

This hieroglyph is an accurate depiction of the Egyptian hoe, which consisted of a straight wooden handle containing a cavity into which a broad blade was fitted and tightened with a wooden peg or strap. A rope of woven palm-fibres was wound around a notch in the handle and fastened through a couple of holes in the blade; this maintained the distance between the two pieces. Scenes illustrating the various stages of temple construction show the Pharaoh using the hoe, if only symbolically, to dig the building's foundation trench and to demonstrate the symbolic importance of his spiritual role at the basis of the temple's work. In the language of symbolism we note that the hoe comprises a curved line connected to a straight line, suggesting the curve of space or spiritual worlds joined to the straight edge symbolic of the material world. The ideal, perfect nature of the relationship between them can be seen in the word below, *mr* or *meri*, meaning 'to love, want or desire.'[42]

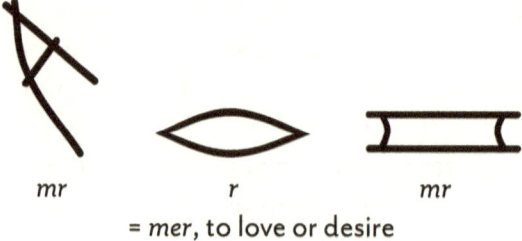

mr   *r*   *mr*

= mer, to love or desire

The hoe, *mer*, is followed by the hieroglyph of the mouth, '*r*' which contributes the idea of expressing or giving voice to something. The final sign, which is also pronounced *mer*, represents a canal. These last two signs are both examples of what is known as a 'sound complement,' a hieroglyph which has the same sound as a preceding hieroglyph but is not pronounced. Sound complements were often used to provide an additional element of symbolism, or even to enhance the aesthetic appearance of a group of signs. In this instance the hieroglyph of the canal adds to the symbolic meaning of the word. It represents one of the navigable, man-made waterways that were excavated through the Nile's floodplain to ensure a regular flow of water from the river into the surrounding fields, and contributes the analogy of the fertilising relationship between the river and the land.

The design of this final hieroglyph is quite abstract. A canal might more realistically be illustrated by two parallel lines open at either end but, like *tA*, these parallel lines are connected by two semi-circles. The obvious difference is that while in *tA* the semi-circles are convex to suggest that they are two halves of a single whole, in *mer* the semi-circles are concave; they appear to be segments of two different circles. The hieroglyph therefore symbolises the concept of two separate bodies being brought and held together, rather than a single whole being divided into two. This of course is precisely the purpose of the Egyptian canals: they are channels made by human effort through which the life-giving waters of the Nile are brought to the dry land, thus initiating a creative relationship between the polarised 'opposites' of arid desert and fertile waters through human mediation.

With this in mind the additional meanings of this final hieroglyph *mer* as 'supporters,' 'devotees,' 'servants' and 'weavers' makes perfect sense. The canals are the servants of the land and its people; they are vital to the fertility of the land although they depend upon the Nile for their existence. This in turn becomes a metaphor for those who consciously involve themselves in the evolutionary processes of regeneration and renewal: they are devotees of the Great Work, the weavers of synthesis, the servants of the Mysteries who mediate between heaven and earth. Again we can only wonder at the depth of symbolic meaning contained in these three hieroglyphs.

Similar ideas are found in the word *uAt,* which represents a road.[43]

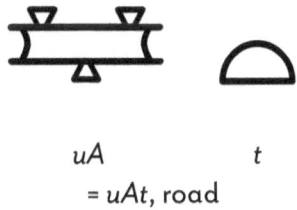

uA　　　　　t
= uAt, road

Here is a further example of two parallel lines linking segments of two separate circles, in this instance to represent the obvious fact that a road joins one place with another. But the hieroglyph *uA* also means 'far,' 'long ago,' 'from a long time past,' 'to begin a journey, or to prepare a way for' and 'to take someone's example.' The symbolic meaning of the sign therefore refers to the connection that can be made between the present and the past rather than between one physical location and another. This accords with what we know of the extreme conservatism of the ancient Egyptians, who recognised a specific period in their remote past as the time of perfect balance between heaven and earth, and which they believed should be perpetuated through eternity. They referred to this time as *zep tepi,* the First Time, a period distinguished by the remarkably precise mirroring between significant constellations and the Egyptian landscape.[44] The symbolic meaning of *uAt* therefore refers to the idea of an imagined or spiritual journey that returns to and relives this moment of perfection, with the aim of retaining the spirit of that time within the present reality.

The three identical objects at the sides of the road are usually described as shrubs, although it is difficult to identify them with any certainty. They are customarily drawn as shown, with two 'shrubs' on the upper surface of the road and one on the lower, but their depiction varies considerably between examples, and in some illustrations a long stem extends across the road and out the other side. They might perhaps represent stone boulders which have been used to support the road or to raise it from the surrounding fields. Keeping in mind the meaning of the hieroglyph, it could also be conjectured that these shapes represent stages or markers on the spiritual journey – but readers must draw their own conclusions.

The hieroglyph uAt, 'road'. From the tomb of Princess Idut (also known as Seshseshet) at Saqqara, c. 2360 B.C.

Photo by the author

The final example of a hieroglyph associated with the landscape is *sepat*. Here, there are no curved lines; all reference to the symbolism of circles has disappeared, and while this makes the sign less interesting it does serve to confirm the symbolism of the previous examples. This hieroglyph is the ideogram for land that has been divided by man-made boundaries, such as the provinces or 'nomes' which were the local administrative districts that existed in Egypt throughout most of the Pharaonic period. The word nome comes from the Greek '*nomos*' meaning the body or spirit of the law; the Egyptian term was *sepat*. The number of divisions in the sign varies from one example to another and probably has no significance.⁴⁵

sepat = district, province or nome

For most of the dynastic period of ancient Egypt there were forty-two nomes, twenty in Upper (i.e. southern) Egypt and twenty-two in Lower Egypt (i.e. the area from the south of the modern city of Cairo to the delta including the Mediterranean coast). Each nome had its own capital city and ruler, and each was distinguished by its own title and emblem. For example, the hare was the emblem of the fifteenth nome of Upper Egypt whose capital city Khemenu or Hermopolis was closely linked with Tehuti and his wisdom.

The following word combines five of the hieroglyphs we have looked at so far, with one new addition. It means *tA meri*, the beloved land, Egypt.⁴⁶

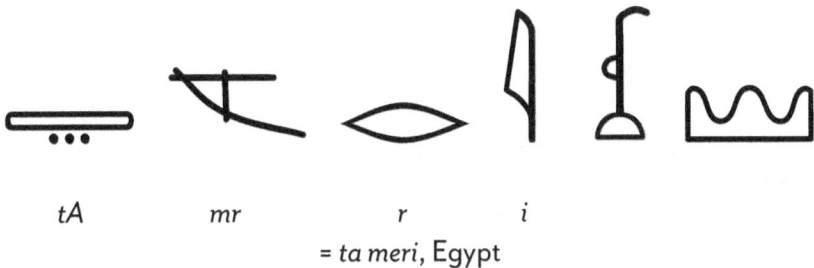

| tA | mr | r | i |

= *ta meri*, Egypt

The symbolism of the first three signs will be familiar from previous examples. These three hieroglyphs are sufficient to spell 'the beloved land,' but the three hieroglyphs that complete the word provide additional layers of symbolism. The fourth sign represents the flowering reed that grows in profusion along the borders of the Nile and illustrates the loose, branching clusters of flowers at the top of the reed. The sign is pronounced '*i*' and was generally used as a phoneme, but also means 'me' or 'my,' and 'to come' or 'return.' It is associated with the *sekhet iaru* or 'Field of Reeds' described throughout the funerary texts. Often also referred to as the 'Field of Peace,' the Field of Reeds was an Inner location encountered by the deceased soon after death, or by the magical initiate undertaking the same spiritual journey. It was a place of repose, a space which provided opportunity for reflection on the life that had recently been left behind; it allowed time for the necessary purification and renewal to take place before the journey through the Inner worlds continued. The idyllic nature of the *sekhet iaru* has been likened to the Christian Paradise or to the Elysian Fields of Greek mythology, a blissful place undisturbed by the challenges of the human condition. The purpose of this hieroglyph within the word *tA meri* is to indicate the significance of this region within the magical landscape of Egypt. The physical geography of Egypt not only displays the polarised opposites of the desert and the Nile but, equally importantly, expresses what lies in between and the qualities represented by this state of being.

The fifth hieroglyph is the budding palm branch which was discussed in Chapter Two. It is not pronounced, so it functions as a determinative which adds to our understanding of the previous hieroglyphs. It refers to the passage of time, it means 'to be young' or 'vigorous' or 'to be renewed' and is connected with the notion of the gods as a realised manifestation of the cyclic patterns of renewal. Its presence in this word reminds us – should we need such reminding – that the Egypt is a sacred landscape, and that the presence of the gods as expressions of the power of spiritual renewal is manifested in the land itself.

The final sign is *khaset,* the hieroglyph for the desert, which was also discussed in Chapter Two. Its inclusion in this word as a second determinative serves to remind us of the significance of the desert within the overall symbolic representation of Egypt.

tA meri includes two of the many hieroglyphs that illustrate some of the plants and trees that grow alongside the Nile and in the fertile river plain. Another example is the hieroglyph *imA* which represents the sycamore tree, although the same sign was widely used to represent trees, shrubs and bushes in general.[47]

imA = the sycamore tree

Although usually referred to as a sycamore, this tree is actually a variety of fig, the evergreen *Ficus sycomorus* which is a different species to the sycamores of northern Europe. It grows to a height of 20 meters and was the tallest tree in ancient Egypt, with a dense crown of spreading branches and large leaves that provided welcome shade. As there are few native trees in Egypt it was valued for its many uses: coffins and funeral furniture were made from its wood while its fruits, bark and latex were used in medicine for their anti-inflammatory properties. There are now very few of these trees remaining. In ancient times the Sycamore Fig was pollinated by a particular type of wasp which is now extinct in Egypt, and as the tree does not create viable seeds it does not easily reproduce, so its propagation depends on farmers taking cuttings or planting leafy branches straight into the ground.

The tree might be thought of as the Egyptian Tree of Life. Legend tells how Tehuti inscribed the names of the blessed dead on the leaves of the sycamore. It was associated with the goddesses Isis, Hathor and Nut who in many illustrations are seen reaching out of the tree to offer food and drink to the deceased. The feminine connection with the tree is indicated in its symbolic meaning: 'kind,' 'gentle,' 'pleasing' and 'gracious,' and the tree later became associated with the Virgin Mary who was said to have rested with Joseph and the infant Jesus under a Sycamore Fig during the flight of the Holy Family to Egypt. A tree that is claimed to be a descendent of this original sycamore can be seen in Matariya, a suburb of Cairo, where it stands beside a well reputed to have been created by Jesus.

The hieroglyph also means 'brilliance,' 'radiance' and 'splendour,' especially when determined with the hieroglyph of the rayed sun, as shown below. [48]

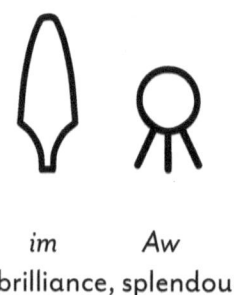

im   Aw
= brilliance, splendour

This aspect of the sycamore's symbolism is briefly alluded to in Chapter 109 of The Book of the Dead which describes how the sun god Re passes between two 'sycamores of turquoise' before striding towards the gate of the East, through which he then ascends as the dawn. The wording suggests that the two sycamores are located just before the sun reaches the final gate of the horizon, a part of the unseen world of pre-dawn and pre-manifestation. The notion of two pillars forming a gateway between the outer and Inner worlds has persisted from early history as the crucial period in which the soul momentarily pauses between the worlds before taking the final descent into physical manifestation. In Egypt, the two sycamores were symbolised by pairs of tall, slender obelisks that were erected in front of the pylon gateway of the temples. The possibility that this symbolism of two trees or pillars at the threshold between the worlds was adopted in the Hebrew tradition of the two pillars Jachin and Boaz seems quite possible, although there is not a great deal of historical evidence to support the idea.

The attractive hieroglyph shown below is the lotus, and illustrates the plant's stem, distinctive heart-shaped leaf, and its rhizome or roots.[49] The sign is pronounced *khA* and means 'a thousand.'

Earth, trees and plants

khA = the lotus plant, one thousand

The habit of the lotus is well known: the rhizome is anchored in the mud at the bottom of a lake or river until it is ready to germinate, at which point a long stem emerges and reaches up through the water towards the sunlight. The leaves float on the surface of the water but the flower is held several centimetres above it. There is an obvious parallel with human evolution, each plant representing the individual soul that reaches towards the light of the spirit, passing through muddy emotional waters and levels of astral illusion to the clear light of day. Perhaps less well known is the lotus's unusual ability to exist in apparent stasis for many hundreds of years until such time as its seed miraculously revives and stirs into life. This long period of dormancy can be paralleled with humankind's ability to remain in the discarnate realms for long periods before returning to incarnation on earth, and with this in mind the hieroglyph's other meanings of 'to remember' and 'to hold in mind' become clear. Human consciousness has been defined as 'awareness plus memory' and our ability to remember what has occurred in the past – whether this is a few minutes ago, our childhood, or what we have learnt and assimilated in previous lifetimes – is one of our principle tools for evolutionary growth. It enables us to achieve a better understanding of the present by comparing it to the past, and to realise new plans for the future.

The following word, *khA khA ib,* means 'to delight the heart,' the final hieroglyph of the heart being the determinative.[50]

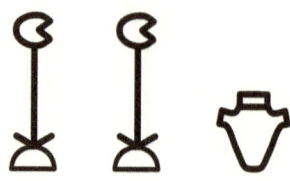

khAkhA   ib
= khAib, to delight the heart

To the ancient Egyptians, the heart represented the seat of the intelligence: not the intelligence of the rational, reductionist, concrete mind that we now tend to value more highly but the intuitively based intelligence that makes connections between apparently disparate objects and events and is able to perceive them as part of a greater whole. 'To delight the heart' beautifully describes the joy that is experienced in those brief moments when everything seems to come together and we intuit the underlying connectedness of all things.

Another frequently seen hieroglyph is the lotus flower shown below, pronounced *ssn* or *seshen*.[51] It appears in many finely worked illustrations of natural scenes.

ssn   = seshen, the lotus flower

The blue lotus was one of the most revered symbols of ancient Egypt. An aquatic plant with beautiful colour and perfume, its flower opens in the morning and closes towards dusk in a rhythm that was seen as a representation of the pattern of life, death and renewal and of the universal cyclic background of creation. Another remarkable feature of the Egyptian landscape is that if viewed from above, the Nile itself describes the image of a lotus. The river from the First Cataract at Elephantine Island northwards forms the stem, while the division of the river into the distributaries of the delta represents the flower. In ancient times the river divided into seven branches in the delta region, although nowadays only two remain.

The remarkable shape of the Nile 'lotus' can best be appreciated from space, but the ancient Egyptians seem somehow to have known what it looked like from above. The funerary texts contain evocative descriptions of how the perfume of the lotus reached the nostrils of the sun god, as if the Nile itself was a fragrant flower on a cosmic scale.

Another well-known plant is the papyrus, which is depicted in the hieroglyph below. Fibres taken from the stem of the plant were used to make the thin sheets of material that could be written on with pen and ink. The hieroglyph is pronounced *wadj* and means 'green,' 'fresh,' 'hale,' 'sturdy and vigorous,' 'fortunate and happy.' [52]

wdj = wadj, green, vigorous, happy

The shape of the papyrus stem was widely imitated in the temples, where papyri-form columns, brightly painted in blues and greens and shaped like a single papyrus stem or bundle of stems, represent both the marshy areas along the borders of the Nile and the mythical marshlands that were believed to surround the first island of creation.

The colour green represents renewal, of 'making green,' and the qualities of 'green-ness' are a central concept in Egyptian magical thought. Green-ness indicates the spiritual renewal, happiness and prosperity that can be experienced through contact with the deities. The underlying idea is of regeneration, of discovering and upholding the qualities of youth, vitality and the 'green feelings' of contentment, strength and good fortune. Green-ness was particularly associated with Osiris, and with the goddess Wadjet, the deity of Lower Egypt. Her symbol was the *wadjet* cobra or the 'cobra at rest' whose ability to shed a layer of skin and reveal the new skin lying beneath is symbolic of renewal and rebirth. The *wadjet* cobra is the second hieroglyph in the word below, the third being the sealed roll of papyrus which indicates that the previous two signs are to be read for their symbolic rather than literal meaning.[53]

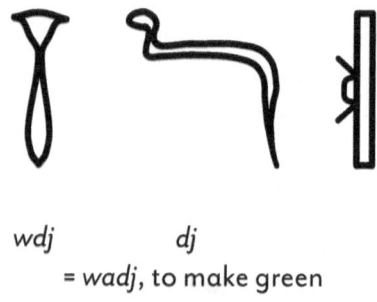

wdj   dj
= wadj, to make green

One of the primary myths in Egyptian magic tells of the life, death and rebirth in the stars of the god Osiris, and the miraculous conception of his son Horus. The original Green Man, Osiris was often portrayed with green skin to demonstrate his connection with the cycles of renewal in nature and the prospect of eternal life in the stars. The well-known symbol of the Eye of Horus (discussed fully in Chapter Nine) is also known as the *Wadjet* Eye.

Finally, here are two hieroglyphs which look similar but have quite different meanings. Each depicts a variety of the flowering reed or sedge found along the edge of the Nile, although botanists are not certain of their precise identity. The first of these, pronounced '*n*', is often used in groups of hieroglyphs such as that shown below which describe the 'weariness' or 'inertness' of the 'dead' – or in other words the living individual who has not yet achieved a state of enlightenment and spiritual rebirth. [54]

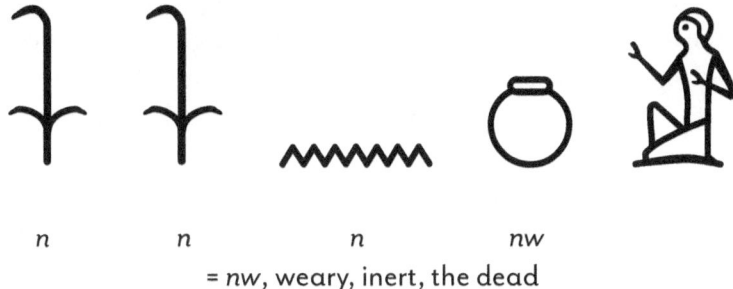

n   n   n   nw
= *nw*, weary, inert, the dead

In this word, the flowering sedge is followed by the sound complement '*n*' which we explored in the previous chapter; it indicates the idea of belonging, or of energy moving between two objects. It is followed by the water jar, *nw*, also discussed previously, which represents the concept of the Unmanifest or the primeval sea of space from which all substance derives. The final determinative is of a seated man or woman, which tells us that the previous hieroglyphs are to be understood as qualities or states of mind experienced by human beings.

The words 'weary,' 'inert' and 'helpless' are often used in the funerary texts to describe the condition of Osiris who, having been ritually slain by Set, remains in a deathlike state until he is discovered by his sister-wife Isis, who by magical means revives him to life and potency. When we consider the symbolic meaning of this story our customary understanding of the states of 'death' and 'life' are shown to be less exact than we might have supposed. Osiris's state of death to the physical world is as much symbolic as actual, a period of inertia or a passive state of existence before his rebirth as a shining spirit. The hieroglyphs in the word above describe the ability to return at will to a deeply meditative state that taps into the reservoir of the Unmanifest and it is this, together with the initiatory magic of Isis, which provides the regenerative energy that brings Osiris to life. On a much smaller scale, we experience the same renewal after deep meditation or restful sleep.

A similar sign to the hieroglyph '*n*,' but displaying two rows of leaves at the base of the stem instead of one, is the *swt* or *sut* plant which from earliest times was used as an emblem of the kingship of

Upper Egypt.⁵⁵ The sign is shown below. The inclusion of a second row of leaves seems to have been sufficient to represent the essential difference between symbolic 'death' and living kingship, perhaps suggesting that the Pharaoh as the embodiment of Osiris was able to maintain both states of being within himself in a perpetual state of renewal. Next to it is the hieroglyph of the honey bee, *bt* or *bit* which was the emblem of Lower Egypt.⁵⁶ The hieroglyphs were often combined in hieroglyphic inscriptions to indicate that the Pharaoh was sovereign of the Two Lands of Upper and Lower Egypt and had that he united within himself the qualities they represented. The bee was said to have been created from the tears of the sun god as they fell to earth, so this lovely example of symbolism links the plants of Egypt with the insect that pollinates them and with the Pharaoh who mediates their qualities to his people.

swt   *bt*
= *nesw-bit*, King of the Sedge and the Bee

Endnotes
31 *tA*, the land: Gardiner N16
32 *nebw*, grain: Gardiner N33 and N33a
33 Plutarch, *Isis and Osiris* (Loeb Classical Library Volume V, 1936)
34 *nebw*, gold: Gardiner S12
35 *wesekh*, the pectoral necklace: Gardiner S11
36 see Kent R. Weeks, ed Peter der Manuelian and William Kelly Simpson, *Giza Mastabas Volume 5*, Boston, Department of Ancient Egyptian, Nubian, and Near Eastern Art Museum of Fine Arts, 1994 Also: http://encyclopedia.jrank.org/articles/pages/51/Funeral-Dances.html
37 This suggestion was made by Ippolito Rosellini, the Egyptologist who, with Champollion, led a French/Tuscan expedition to Egypt.
38 *sesheta*, secret, hidden: Gardiner O34, N37, N16, Y1
39 *tA neter*, god's land, Punt: Gardiner R8, N16, N25
40 *djet*, eternity: Gardiner I10, X1, N16
41 *mer*, the hoe: Gardiner U6
42 *meri*, to love or desire: Gardiner U6, D21, N36
43 *uAt*, road: Gardiner N31
44 The hieroglyphs for *zep tepi* are discussed in further detail in Chapter Eleven
45 *sepat*, nome or administrative district: Gardiner N24
46 *tA meri*, the beloved land, Egypt: Gardiner N16, U7, D21, M17, M5, N25
47 *imA*, the sycamore tree: Gardiner M1
48 *imAw*, brilliance, splendour: Gardiner M1, N8
49 *khA*, the lotus plant, one thousand: Gardiner M12
50 *khAkhA ib*, to delight the heart: Gardiner M12, M12, F34
51 *seshen*, the lotus flower; Gardiner M9
52 *wadj*, green, vigorous, happy: Gardiner M13
53 *wadj*, to make green: Gardiner M13, I10, Y1
54 *nw*, weary, inert: Gardiner M22, M22, N35, W24, A1
55 *swt*, kingship: Gardiner M23
56 *bit*, honey bee: Gardiner L2

Sky, Sun and Moon

This chapter explores some of the hieroglyphs that illustrate the sky, the sun and the moon. The first of these is *pt* or *pet,* which means 'the sky.'⁵⁷

pt = *pet*, the sky

Pet is rarely used phonetically; it usually functions either as an ideogram meaning 'sky' or as a determinative. It is another abstract sign, consisting simply of an elongated rectangle whose two lower corners are slightly extended downwards and taper into a point. *Pet* often forms the upper border of illustrated scenes where it acts as a counterpart to the hieroglyph *tA,* the land, which delineates the lower border. The proportions of these hieroglyphs were adjusted according to the dimensions of the scene and where necessary were elongated to such an extent that they appear to consist only of two long parallel lines.

As with all the more abstractly drawn hieroglyphs, *pet* challenges us to consider why it was drawn in this way, and the reasons behind its design are by no means obvious. The sky has no visible form, so its presence can only be suggested by the illustration of what it contains, such as the sun, moon or clouds. If you didn't know that *pet* represented the sky it is unlikely that you would guess correctly. There is something apparently naive about the hieroglyph; it looks rather like a child's drawing in which the sky is a narrow band of blue across the top of the paper just wide enough to hold a bright yellow sun. It is interesting that although *pet* is often depicted covered in stars, it is never shown in combination with the sun or moon.

What is particularly puzzling about *pet* is that it contains two right angled corners and two corners of 45 degrees, which the sky does not! As we have observed previously, curved lines readily symbolise the things of heaven while straight lines and angles indicate human-made, earthly things, and the hieroglyphs generally conform to these principles. Straight lines and corners suggest limitation, definition and artificial boundaries, so a more obvious choice of design for *pet* might have been a semi-circle to indicate the dome of the celestial sphere.

The shape of *pet* is echoed in illustrations of the enfolding form often adopted by Nut, the deity of the night sky. Many images of this goddess depict her as the all-embracing arch of the starry sky where her arms and legs reach down to the ground and her star-covered body stretches across the heavens. A visual reference to Nut can certainly be seen in the hieroglyph but it is by no means just a 'shorthand' version of the image of the goddess. It is a symbol in itself; it represents spiritual realities in an abstract form. The ancient Egyptians did not believe that the sky was a flat blue lid somewhere up in the air and were perfectly aware that the celestial bodies were not pasted onto a two-dimensional surface. Their extensive knowledge of astronomy included an awareness of the relative movement of the stars and planets. The shape of the hieroglyph does however seem to depict the sky as a *layer* of something that separates the familiar, recognisable, physical world below from the 'something else' that lies above it, and the use of *pet* to indicate the sky when there is no obvious need to do so – after all, we all know that it's there – suggests that the Egyptians may have had something like this in mind.

The hieroglyph can also be translated as 'heaven' or 'the heavens,' 'the distant one,' 'gateway' and 'portal' – words which all suggest a religious or metaphysical interpretation. Heaven is more than 'the sky,' it is a specific Innerworld region, the realm of the afterlife and the land of the gods, and the hieroglyph symbolises the gateway to their world. *Pet* represents the level of the Inner worlds that contains the bodies of the stars. The presence of *pet* in an illustrated scene draws our attention to their presence and to the energies and principles they represent, encouraging us to think about the effect they might have on us. In the temples, *pet* was often engraved on the lintel over doorways which led into a sequence of rooms progressing towards the inner sanctuary, so that when you walked beneath the hieroglyph you were reminded that your aspiration was to move from one level of consciousness into another. The use of the *pet* in an illustration tells us that we are not just looking at a mundane scene; it reminds us that what manifests in the earthly world is always linked with the powers and beings of the Inner planes of creation.

There is a surprising relationship between *pet* and *tA*. Intuition tells us that *tA*, the land, should be formed of straight lines and *pet*, the sky, formed of curved lines rather than the other way round. Hieroglyphic wisdom, it seems, doesn't tell us what we think we know but dares us to think differently. These two hieroglyphs invite us to consider the earth as an expression of spiritual principles and the heavens as the origin of earthly forms.

This link between the mundane and heavenly worlds is emphasised by the downward movement at the lower corners of the hieroglyph. The sharp angles at the lower edges make an emphatic statement of focussed, dynamic, downward-flowing energy. They ask us to consider how this energy descends, or how it can be invoked from the heavens into the earth. The use of angles rather than curves suggests that the nature of this descending energy is a directed, specific force rather than free-flowing or random.

The ancient texts describe the sky as resting on four 'pillars' although illustrations often show staves or wands rather than pillars. Scenes that were framed above and below by *pet* and *tA* were sometimes completed on either side by the hieroglyph of the *wAs*

Sky, Sun and Moon

or *uas* wand, shown below: sky above and earth below connected by a magical staff.[58] Here is a forerunner of the Tarot card of the Magician who raises one arm to the sky while his other points down to the magical tools on the table in front of him. Just as *pet* could be extended to cover the upper edge of an entire scene so the *uas* wand could be expanded vertically to such a height that it is easy to overlook its zoomorphic features at either end.

wAs = the *wAs* or *uas* wand, 'to have dominion'

Many different types of wands and staves were used in ancient Egypt and the subtle distinctions in their meaning is not always easy to determine. There can be little doubt however that they represent the ability to mediate or channel aspects of spiritual energy. The *uas* is the most frequently illustrated example of the Egyptian wands, and one of the earliest examples can be found on an ivory comb belonging to Pharaoh Djet, the fourth Pharaoh of the First Dynasty who reigned c 2980 B.C. The comb, now in the Egyptian Museum in Cairo, was discovered in the Pharaoh's tomb at Abydos and shows two wands framing the picture and supporting the sky.

In later examples this wand acquired more distinctly animal-like characteristics, developing the long ears, slanting eyes

The ivory comb of Djet, c 2950 B.C. (Cairo Museum)

and downward-sloping muzzle of the so-called 'Set animal,' an unidentified creature linked with the god Set. The fork at the base of the wand might be a stylised representation of the animal's legs although it has also been likened, perhaps with increasing improbability, to a device for catching snakes, a herdsman's crook and a dried bull's penis. As Set was particularly associated with the desert we can suppose that the wand was also associated with the raw, fierce, solar energy of the desert, so that those who wielded this wand were thus demonstrating their ability to invoke and control that energy.

The wand is the archetypal tool of the magician, the symbol of the Adept, an indication of the magician's ability to understand, embody and utilise certain aspects of universal energy. It symbolises the magician's ability to align his or her personal will with divine will in order to assist in bringing regeneration and renewal. The *uas* wand is usually said to represent 'dominion,' a word which conjures up the popular image of a wizard brandishing their wand to project a blast of energy to control mighty powers – but we can assume that the *uas* wand was not used in this manner. In illustrated scenes it is usually held by deities such as Ptah, Osiris, Hathor and Set but, interestingly, is almost always held in the *left* hand. This is an important point, because the left hand is generally recognised as representative of the receptive, Yin or feminine aspect of the psyche while the right hand expresses the positive, Yang, outward-going energy that we would tend to associate with the magical wand. In fact the *ankh* is usually held in the right hand, and often extended in an active ritual gesture towards another person just as we might assume the *uas* wand to be used.

A number of illustrations show the *uas* wand in an everyday setting. In the Theban Acropolis on the West bank of the Nile (opposite the modern city of Luxor) the tomb of an official named Menna is beautifully painted with scenes of daily life. Menna's title was 'Scribe of the Fields of the Lord of the Two Lands' and one of the paintings shows a procession of surveyors in a cornfield. They are holding a rope which has been knotted at regular intervals and was presumably used for measuring distances; some of the workers carry writing materials, and a woman is bringing them food and drink. One of the men is holding a *uas* wand in his left hand. He does not appear to be in a position of authority over the others but, like them, is dressed in a loincloth and appears to be part of the group. The impression given by this painting is that the wand is one of the tools of the land surveyor rather than a ceremonial or ritual instrument.

The scene is discussed by Martin Isler in *Sticks, Stones, and Shadows: Building the Egyptian Pyramids*.[59] Isler suggests that the *uas* wand was originally a staff used as a gnomon, a means of measuring the passage of time, and for ascertaining geographical direction. The word 'gnomon' comes from a Greek word meaning 'one who knows, discerns or interprets,' so one who holds a gnomon is therefore 'a knower of time.' The gnomon projects a shadow that varies in length according to the height of the sun: the shortest shadow is cast at midday when the sun is on the meridian and longest when it rises and sets. The forked base of the wand would make it easier to keep it steady and ensure that it was exactly perpendicular to the ground rather than accidentally tilted to one side. The angled head would function in the same way: if the staff was tilted, the angled head would reveal a 'bump' in the shadow.

If this theory is correct, and the evidence of these illustrations must surely be taken into account, it would explain why the wand is usually held in the left hand. Rather than being a symbol of projected force it becomes symbolic of the wielder's ability to understand and interpret the natural rhythms and laws of the universe. Keeping track of time is of vital importance for the smooth functioning of an organised society, and before the mechanical clock was invented the ability to know the hour of the day, to record the passing of time by measuring the shadow of the sun or moon and to understand the complex cycles of periodicity that these shadows revealed, were indicative of a profound knowledge and authority. The tracking and comparison of the various cycles of time including the vast and slow-moving changes associated with the precession of the equinoxes and the relative movements of the stars was the particular province of the god Tehuti. In this case 'dominion' suggests an ability to know, understand and transcend the limitations of time as they are usually understood.

Another use of the *uas* wand is found in the hieroglyph below which shows the wand suspended beneath the hieroglyph *pet,* the sky. *khAwy* means 'night,' 'darkness' and 'obscurity.' The distinctive forked base of the wand is present but the staff is broken and the head has gone. [60]

khAwy = night, darkness

A more obvious symbol for 'night' might be the hieroglyph of the sky covered in stars that is so often seen in Egyptian illustrations, so it is interesting that the above sign makes no reference to the celestial bodies but depends for its meaning on the absence of the wand's 'head.' This does tend to confirm that there is a symbolic link between the head of the wand and the sun or the sun's light. When this symbolic connection is severed, darkness occurs, whether actual darkness or possibly the implied loss of the magician's abilities.

Another variation of the *uas* wand is shown below. This is the *djAm* wand which displays the same long curved head and forked base but has a wavy or corkscrewed stem. [61]

djAm = electrum

Not many of these wands have survived but a beautiful example can be seen in the bas reliefs from the Theban tomb of Nespekashuti which are housed in the Metropolitan Museum in New York.[62] The wand is held by one of the men taking part in the procession of funeral offerings and it is interesting to note that he is holding it in his right hand. His left hand improbably balances what looks like a piece of furniture. The wand-bearer does not appear to be in a position of authority over the others in the procession but is dressed similarly to them, a part of the crowd.

Electrum, symbolised by the *djAm* wand, is a naturally occurring alloy of silver and gold which the ancient Egyptians used as a coating on the surface of the pyramidions that capped the pyramids and obelisks. As the *uas* wand appears to represent the authority of those who have command over the qualities of solar energy and of time, we can conjecture that the electrum of the *djAm* wand extends this meaning to include a knowledge of, or dominion over, all that is symbolised by the bodies of the moon and stars in addition to that of the sun.

Re = the god of the sun, or *herw* = daytime

The daily passage of the sun overhead during the day and beneath the earth during the night forms an imagined enclosing ring about the River Nile's linear flow from south to north. These two features are essential components in the basic structure of Egyptian magical thought and it is useful to keep them in mind, because this 'ground plan' is not the same as the circle and equal-armed cross or quartered circle which is customarily adopted in Western magical systems. The quartered circle with its catalogue of corresponding elements, angels and archangels, god and goddess forms, psychological attributes and symbols that are apportioned to each cardinal direction in Western magic was not a feature of the Egyptian temple. Very few of the gods or goddesses were specifically connected with a particular direction although it is tempting to try to make them so, and there are few symbols or attributions that can be allocated to the cardinal directions in any meaningful way. Nor can the deities be usefully equated with the Sephiroth of the Qabalist Tree of Life or, indeed, with any other magical system.

There is, though, an important distinction in Egyptian magic between North and South, and between the East and West banks of the Nile. The Nile's flow of movement from South to North means that the South represents the past while the North is the direction of the future. The East bank was thought of as the land of the living because the sun is 'born' in the East, and the West bank was the land of the dead because this is where the sun descends into the Inner worlds. As a rule, the tombs and funerary temples were built on the West bank while the living temples to the gods were built on the East bank – although nowadays of course both banks are equally populated by the living.

To return to *re,* the sun, there are variations in the depiction of this hieroglyph. Often it was drawn as two concentric circles as shown above, but it could also be depicted as a single circle. There is also some variation in the relative size of the two circles; sometimes the inner circle is almost as large as the outer, sometimes it shrinks to a central point. The circle with a point at the centre is now widely accepted as both the alchemical symbol for gold and the astrological symbol for the sun, and its origin is probably correctly attributed to the ancient Egyptians. The variations in the comparative sizes of the two circles is a significant element of the symbolic meaning of this hieroglyph. A single circle represents the totality of the celestial sphere, completeness, the One, but two concentric circles represent the relationship of one thing to another, or between an individual and the totality. A 'dot' in the centre of a circle might indicate the initiatory spark of the spirit within the vast ocean of cosmic space, or the masculine principle enclosed by the feminine, or the sun as a point of light within the universe. It can represent ourselves as individuals within the totality of our perceived world or environment.

If, on the other hand, the inner circle is expanded so that it nearly matches the circumference of the outer circle the symbol becomes a wheel, and this gives rise to a range of symbolism associated with the passage of time. We use expressions such as 'the wheel of the year' and 'the turning of the seasons' to describe the journey through time as we experience it on earth and measure in periods of a day, a year, or an astrological Age, as if we were propelled by the power of the sun. In many mythologies the sun is depicted as a wheeled chariot driven by the sun god, although the Egyptians preferred the symbol of the sun boat.

The following phrase, *re neb,* means 'every day.' The second hieroglyph is an illustration of a shallow basket and symbolises 'all things' and 'everything.' It also indicates 'Master' and 'Lord' – or with the addition of the feminine *'t'* it means 'Queen,' 'Mistress.' [63]

re   neb
= every day

The hieroglyph *re* could also be combined with the sign for a butcher's block. Pronounced *khr* or *kher,* it indicates 'that which is under,' 'segmented,' 'owned or possessed.' The sense is not so much of something being underneath something else in a physical sense, but that it comes under the aegis or jurisdiction of a greater authority. [64]

khr = kher, that which is under

The butcher uses his knife to cut and separate, or to end life, and the hieroglyph suggests that just as the butcher will use his knife to dissect a carcass, so do we attempt to divide the flow of time into manageable portions which we can grasp and remember. Our comprehension of time is generally the product of our ability to measure it by mechanical means or, when these are not available, by forming subjectively based notions derived from our memories of past events such as when we last changed jobs, or moved house, or took a holiday. The symbolism of the hieroglyph might be compared with the symbolism of Saturn and its indication of the principle of limitation.

There are also a number of hieroglyphs referring to light, and to the different qualities of light. Here for example are the hieroglyphs that spell *hedj tA*, the dawn: [65]

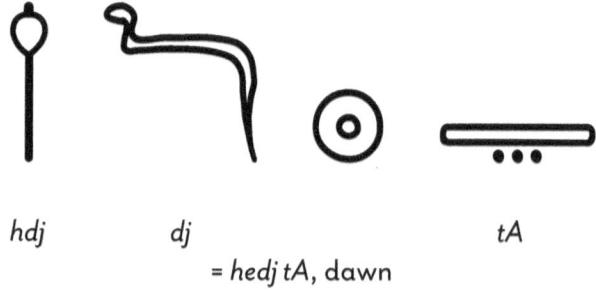

hdj   dj   tA

= *hedj tA*, dawn

The first of these hieroglyphs is the mace, perhaps originally a weapon of war but later adopted as a ceremonial staff or ritual wand. The word *hedj* means 'bright' or 'white.' As we have seen previously, the hieroglyph of the cobra at rest, *dj*, is associated with ideas relating to royalty, royal authority and renewal. The hieroglyph of the sun acts as the determinative which tells us that the word refers to the passage of time, while the final hieroglyph is the familiar *tA*, the land. The symbolism is clear: the clear, pale light of dawn brings regeneration and renewal to the land, and this energy of the rising sun is especially connected with the Pharaoh who transmits these properties to his land and people. In every description of the Pharaoh's duties we can also consider how the same qualities can be applied to our own lives and aspirations.

The depiction of rays of light extending from the sun's surface is a familiar addition to the sign, and was well known to the ancient Egyptians. It was especially popular during the reign of the 18th Dynasty Pharaoh Akhenaten who introduced the monotheistic solar cult of the Aten and was frequently illustrated beneath an exuberantly rayed sun. The rayed sun, the hieroglyph *Ahw*, is shown below.[66]

Sky, Sun and Moon

Ahw = sunlight, radiance

Ahw means 'light,' 'splendour,' and 'radiance.' It could also mean 'to dry' and 'to wound,' perhaps in recognition of the less beneficent aspects of the sun. The hieroglyph was also used as the determinative in words referring to the *hnmmt,* the Sun Folk or People of the Sun, the name given to what may have been a group of priests located in the ancient city of Heliopolis or *Iwnw,* the City of the Sun – although the word was sometimes used by the ancient Egyptians to describe themselves. [67] In the after-life, the *hnmmt* were encountered after a successful crossing of the Milky Way, the 'Winding Waterway' of the funeral texts. The word *hnmmt* (so many additional vowels are needed to make sense of this string of consonants that it is usually left as it is!) probably derives from the root *nmi* which means 'to travel or traverse by water,' or perhaps from *nmt* which means 'to traverse or stride over' with its suggestion of the striding figure of Orion. [68]

Iwnw was the centre of the worship of Re and Atum and its main temple was reputed to be the most splendid in Egypt, containing a floor that was so perfectly polished that you could see the night sky reflected in it. The city is now almost entirely lost beneath the streets of Cairo but was one of the principle centres of learning in ancient Egypt and the chosen destination of visiting Greek philosophers such as Pythagoras, Solon and Plato. Comparatively little is known of the work of the priesthood of *Iwnw* but it was the birthplace of the Ennead, the nine gods or creative principles whose influence dominated Egyptian magical thought for many centuries.

A third aspect of the sun's energy is seen in the combination of the hieroglyph for the sun with the enraged or 'striking' cobra, often described as the uraeus serpent. The combined sign was known as the 'Eye of Re.' [69]

re = The Eye of Re

The cobra is the emblem of the serpent goddess *Wadjet* or *Uadjet* who presided over Lower Egypt while her counterpart, the White Vulture *Nekheb*, was the titular goddess of Upper Egypt. 'The Two Ladies' became the exclusive symbol of the Pharaoh who enjoyed the combined benefits of their protection. When Re emerged as the foremost representation of the sun, the fierce, poison-spitting aspect of the cobra-goddess became identified with the Eye of Re which symbolised the more aggressive aspect of the sun's energy.

After the relatively straightforward symbolism of the hieroglyph for the sun it can be surprising to find that there is no single hieroglyph for the moon. It is included in all four signs shown below although none of them comprises a definitive ideogram for 'moon'. The crescent moon is depicted horizontally because this is how it appears in Egypt.[70]

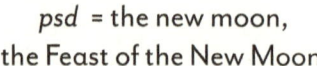

psd = the new moon, the Feast of the New Moon

Abd = one month

There was little overall consistency in the use of these signs and although our natural assumption is that they refer to the new, full, waxing and waning moons they seem to have been used fairly arbitrarily. The first hieroglyph was sometimes used to represent the new moon and the Festival of the New Moon. The third and fourth signs could both be used as an ideogram for 'the moon,' especially when ascribed the phonetic value *iah*, which name was also given to *Iah*, one of the gods of the moon. Perhaps the most important point to keep in mind when considering the symbolism of the moon is its dissimilarity with current Western esoteric practice in which the moon is regarded as an aspect of feminine energy. The ancient Egyptians saw the moon as masculine, not feminine. As mentioned earlier, the significance of the cycles of the moon as an exact measure of time were part of the wisdom conveyed by the god Tehuti: "He who Reckons the Heavens, the Counter of the Stars and the Measurer of the Earth."

Another use of the hieroglyph of the moon can be found in the word *psdt* or 'Ennead' shown below.[71]

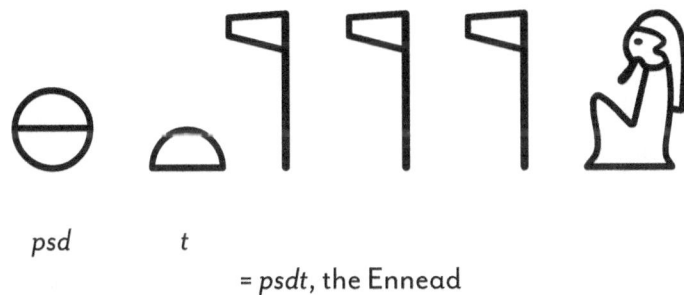

psd   *t*

= *psdt*, the Ennead

The word is spelt phonetically: the hieroglyph for the new moon *psd* is followed by the feminine sign of the small offering loaf, which means that the remaining signs are all determinatives. Here again we see the flags that symbolise the *neterw*, 'the gods,' and the final sign is a frequently used determinative for divinity. The use of the hieroglyph for the moon in a word that refers to the Ennead or nine gods of the solar centre of Heliopolis is puzzling until we remember that the sign doesn't necessarily refer to the moon itself but often indicated the division of time as it was measured by the moon. Periods of nine days or years are especially relevant in the systems of measuring time used by the ancient Egyptians where the solar and lunar cycles are combined – and they may also refer to the nine month human gestation cycle or, on a higher scale, the gestation of the Ennead of the gods.

A further example of the hieroglyphs' wide frame of reference is found in the following word which illustrates the plant known as the *wAh* or *Cyperus esculentus*, the Tiger nut or Earth almond.[72] The second sign depicts seeds or grains. The Tiger nut was one of the oldest cultivated plants in ancient Egypt, having been grown from at least the fourth millennium B.C. and is a remarkable superfood. Its tubers have a high nutritional value and were ground to make milk, or roasted and mixed with honey, used medicinally, and burnt as fumigants for houses or clothing. The offering loaves in the temples were made from ground and sweetened tiger nuts, perhaps an early example of the 'moon cake.'

wAh   = earth-almond

Finally, the sign below, *smA* or *semA,* is usually translated as 'the priest who clothes the god' or 'priest of the clothing.' [73] Little is known about this sign which combines the hieroglyph of the moon with a more direct 'wand-like' energy. Readers are invited to form their own conclusions as to its symbolism.

smA   = semA, the priest who clothes the god

Endnotes

57 *pet*, the sky: Gardiner N1
58 *wAs* or *uas* wand, to have dominion: Gardiner S40
59 Martin Isler, *Sticks, Stones and Shadows: Building the Egyptian Pyramids*, Norman, University of Oklahoma Press, 2001, p 136
60 *khAwy*, night, darkness: Gardiner N2
61 *djAm*, electrum: Gardiner S41
62 The image can be seen on the Metropolitan Museum website: www.metmuseum.org
63 *re neb*, every day: Gardiner N5, V30
64 *kher*, that which is under: Gardiner N7. The hieroglyph of the butcher's block as a separate sign is Gardiner T28
65 *hedj tA*, the dawn: Gardiner T3, N5, I10, N16
66 *Ahw*, sunlight, radiance: Gardiner N8
67 *Iwnw* was located in what are now the suburbs of north-east Cairo
68 see Jose M. Serrano, *Origin and Basic Meaning of the Word Hnmmt (The So-Called "Sun-Folk"), Studien Zur Altägyptischen Kultur 27*, 1999, page 353-68. http://www.jstor.org/stable/25152809.
69 *re*, the Eye of Re: Gardiner N6
70 *psd*, the new moon: Gardiner N9, N10. *Abd*, one month: Gardiner N11, N12
71 *psdt*, the Ennead: Gardiner N9, X1, R8, R8, R8, A40
72 *wAh*, Earth almond: Gardiner N11, N33
73 *semA*, the priest who clothes the god: Gardiner Aa25

sabA, the Star

It was mentioned in Chapter Four that *pet,* the hieroglyph for the sky, is never shown in combination with the sun or moon but is frequently covered in stars, a convention which demonstrates the profound significance of the stars in the ancient Egyptians' perception of the universe. The light pollution which dims our night skies together with the fading of the stars in our consciousness makes it difficult for us to comprehend the potency with which they were experienced by the ancient Egyptians, for whom the celestial bodies must have seemed so very much brighter and closer to the earth than they appear to us now. The stars were their spiritual home, and their aspiration was to return to them. They perceived each star as the spiritual embodiment of a human being who had spent time on earth but in spirit was transformed as Osiris, whose immortal, stellar body strides out across the sky as the constellation of *sAhu* or Orion.

Although the ancient Egyptians had a comprehensive knowledge of the night skies, the focus of their sacred and magical beliefs was the area of stars we know as the circumpolar stars and which they called the *ikhemu sek* or Imperishable Stars, the constellations that wheel about the northern celestial pole. The stars in this area of the sky do not sink below the horizon when viewed from northern latitudes, and to the ancient Egyptians their constant presence represented the eternal, undying light of the spirit, the essential spark of Divinity within each human being which remains untouched by the symbolic darkness of earthly life.

The hieroglyph shown below is *sbA* or *sabA*, the star.[74]

sbA = sabA, the star

The 'arms' of the star were typically drawn as shown, slender isosceles triangles. The centre of the star is often marked with a small circle, or occasionally as two concentric circles. In some later examples the arms are more like elongated ovals, and these are sometimes crossed by a pair of parallel lines.

The most obvious aspect of the hieroglyph's symbolism is that there are always five arms, never six, seven or any other number. The likely reason for this is that a five-pointed star creates an immediate correspondence with the basic configuration of the human body: the head, two arms and two legs which were later memorably illustrated in da Vinci's drawing of the Vitruvian Man. In some illustrations of *sabA* the 'head' of the star is drawn shorter than the 'arms and legs' to emphasise this association.

A less obvious but nonetheless important consideration is whether the hieroglyph represents stars in general or a single star – and if so, which star? As we have said, the convention of hieroglyphic drawing is that one sign represents one of something and three signs represents many, but although a single star is used in most hieroglyphic inscriptions it doesn't appear to refer to any one particular celestial body. The star Sirius held especial significance for the ancient Egyptians but it had its own name and hieroglyph, which we will look at later in this chapter. *SabA*, it seems, represents the *concept* of a star or the quality of 'starriness' rather than any specific celestial body, a notion which can now seem quite strange to us.

This quality of 'starriness' is confirmed by the sometimes frustrating lack of precise astronomical reference in ancient writings such as the Pyramid and Coffin texts, where although the stars are frequently referred to it is not easy to connect what is described to what can actually be seen in the night sky. These texts, we must remember, are not intended to provide a factual description of the celestial bodies but are a guide to the various stages of transformation of consciousness. The journey to the stars is an internal one: it represents the expansion of the mind into a heightened state of awareness that can be likened to 'stellar consciousness,' a condition in which the quality of 'starriness' is fully assumed and the entire being is permeated with the white light of the spirit which is visibly manifest in the stars.

In most modern, solar-oriented civilisations this internal assumption of 'starriness' is difficult to understand. We know that the sun represents the centre and focus of our universe as our source of life, light and strength, and we associate the moon with romance and illusion, discerning its influence in the ebb and flow of Inner tides and rhythms. But we are not accustomed to thinking about stellar energy in the same way, and the relevance of the stars to our everyday life on earth is not easy to recognise. For a start, there are so many of them. We have some familiarity with the qualities associated with the twelve constellations of the solar zodiac but if we now use the word 'star' at all, it tends either to be a synonym for 'celebrity' or in the expression 'you're a star,' meaning 'thanks, you've done me a favour.'

There is still considerable debate over many of the Egyptian constellations as they are depicted on the walls of tombs and on coffin lids and it is not easy to correlate the familiar 48 'classical' constellations listed by Ptolemy with the very different configurations that were evidently perceived by the ancient Egyptians.[75] For example, we know that their constellation *sAh* or *sAhu* is the group of stars we identify as Orion but we cannot be sure how many of the stars in our modern constellation correspond with the constellation recognised by the Egyptians. It has been suggested that *sAhu* lies mostly to the south of the modern constellation, his head consisting of the three stars that we now identify as the belt and his right foot reaching down to touch the figure of Eridanus.[76] It has also been suggested (and we will look at this suggestion in more detail later in the chapter) that *sAhu* consisted only of the single star *Rigel*.[77]

Another area of confusion is that the Pyramid and Coffin texts frequently refer to the god Horus as the 'Morning Star,' a term we now use for the planet Venus. The correlation of Horus with Venus is an attractive idea but there is little evidence to suggest that the ancient Egyptians made this connection, and in fact the planets in general were not of particular significance to them. We know that the Egyptian term *ikhemu sek* or Imperishable Stars refers to the circumpolar stars but so far as we know they identified only two constellations in this group: the asterism of seven stars we call the Plough or Big Dipper but which they saw as the thigh or foreleg of a bull, and our modern constellation of Draco which they saw as a hippopotamus tethered to a mooring post.

However, rather than becoming distracted by these difficulties, we can learn a great deal about the Egyptians' understanding of the stars simply by looking at the symbolism of the hieroglyph *sabA* and the way in which it was combined with other hieroglyphs.

As a first example, the following word is also pronounced *sabA*, but means 'door.'[78]

sabA   A
= sabA, door

The second hieroglyph in this group is a vulture, also pronounced 'A,' and a sound complement that is so frequently combined with the hieroglyph *sabA* that it seems to have been regarded as intrinsic to its meaning. The bird is the White Scavenger vulture or *Neophron percnopterus*, one of the oldest species of vulture and often seen in

Egyptian illustrations as a sign of 'spiritual sovereignty,' the symbol of an advanced stage of spiritual development. The birds and animals depicted in the hieroglyphs are never chosen arbitrarily, and the symbolic potential of their physical appearance and behaviour is always fully utilised. The White Scavenger vulture is a surprisingly attractive bird, very different in appearance to the hunched form and ugly features of the more familiar Bald-headed vulture. It has pure white plumage, a golden yellow face and a distinctive white 'ruff' around its head and neck which may have been imitated in the *nemes* headdress worn by the Pharaohs. Its wings are tipped with black feathers that are dramatically revealed when the bird is in flight. In addition to its impressive appearance the White vulture displays advanced skills amongst its kind, being one of the few birds able to use tools: it breaks open large eggs by dropping pebbles on them, and uses a twig to gather and roll up tufts of wool to make a soft lining for its nest.

The third hieroglyph in this word is *per,* meaning a house, building, temple or doorway. It functions here as the determinative, and the potential ambiguity in its meaning enhances rather than obscures the overall sense of the word. When we have attained the qualities symbolised by the previous two hieroglyphs, have we reached the temple of the stars which is our final spiritual home or have we simply opened a 'door' in our consciousness that will lead to further enlightenment? Either way, the combined symbolism of these three hieroglyphs suggests that 'starriness' is a transformative energy which is active in all parts of our spiritual journey whether it signifies our final destination or remains a stage upon the way. The difference is probably not one that we can usefully contemplate.

The ancient Egyptians understood 'stellar consciousness' as something that represented our highest spiritual self and was an active and specific source of wisdom. This is expressed in the following word: *sabAyt.*[79]

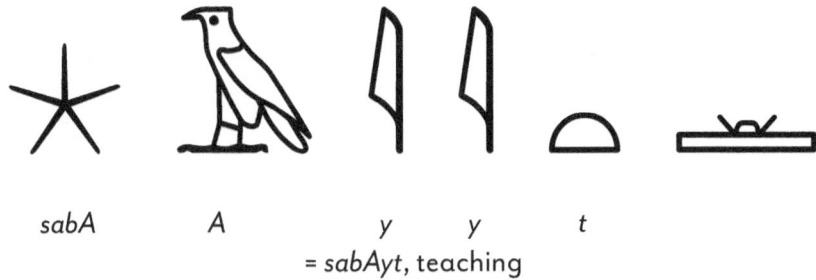

sabA   A   y   y   t
= sabAyt, teaching

The word *sabAyt* means 'written teaching or instructions.' Here again is the combination of the star and White vulture. The word concludes with the feminine '*t*' and the determinative of the tied and sealed roll of papyrus which tells us that the overall meaning is an abstract idea. The phrase also includes two hieroglyphs of the flowering reed which, as we saw in Chapter Three, is linked to the symbolism of the *sekhet Iaru* or 'Field of Reeds,' the Innerworld equivalent of the marshy areas that border the Nile and a place of respite and contentment. S*abAyt*, 'teaching,' suggests that the ultimate source of our wisdom and knowledge, both of ourselves and of the world about us, is the stars.

The same idea is found again in the following word which also means 'to teach,' or 'teaching.' Here, the determinative is the hieroglyph of a man holding a stick in order to draw attention to a significant point.[80]

sabA   A
= sabA, 'teaching'

The combination of the star and White vulture also appears in the following group of hieroglyphs which form the word *Akh Akh* which is an alternative spelling of 'stars.'[81]

A   kh   A   kh
= AkhAkh, stars

The determinative of *AkhAkh* is the group of three stars that provide the frame of reference for the preceding signs. The identity of the second hieroglyph is still is open to debate although it is generally agreed to represent either a sieve, a placenta or a ball of twine, and each of these possibilities offers a wealth of symbolism. A ball of twine can be likened to the unravelling of our path of destiny: the knowledge of our spiritual goal is with us from birth but only gradually becomes visible as we follow it from the 'darkness' of the mundane world into the bright world of the spirit. We use the metaphor of the thread to describe how we become the weavers of our lives, discovering that what we initially perceived as disconnected events and experiences are part of a unified whole that we create through our imagination. The thread can represent time, and the chain of cause and effect which binds us or becomes a tool in our hands. It becomes the thread of the sequence of our lives through the cycle of birth, death and rebirth in which an understanding of how our present life is part of a greater series of lives enables us to move forward.

If on the other hand we interpret the hieroglyph as a sieve or placenta, the symbolic meaning becomes linked with the idea of filtering, refining and purifying. We know that the ancient Egyptians used sieves; there are illustrations of them making beer with sieves of reeds and palm leaves to strain the wheat and malt mixture, and the hieroglyph is used in the word for 'brewers.' But the process of refining refers here to the refining of our being which is achieved through the conscious clearing of the unwanted 'shadows' that accumulate in the emotional and mental bodies. A word composed of three such hieroglyphs means 'unique' and 'the exception,' suggesting the removal or refinement of all unwanted parts so that only the pure essence of the substance remains.

The hieroglyphs of the White vulture and sieve which form part of the word *AkhAkh* were also used on their own to spell *Akh* or 'spirit,' confirming the relationship between 'spirit' and 'stars.' [82]

A   kh
= *Akh*, spirit

The following word gives us an alternative spelling of *AkhAkh*.' [83]

A   kh   A   kh
= *AkhAkh*, to grow green like the plants

The determinative in this word is a sprig of leaves or herbs which defines the meaning as 'to grow green like the plants.' The meaning suggests that to become an *Akh* or shining spirit is an entirely natural process of growth and renewal.

If we put together the abundance of symbolism contained in the above words and hieroglyphs we can form a useful interpretation of the quality of 'starriness' as it was understood by the ancient Egyptians. The star represents a distinct type or quality of energy which is expressed as the pure white light of spirit, yet it is possible to access this state of being or consciousness during our lifetime. It is a state in which the divine spirit of the individual becomes the ruling element of their whole being. The hieroglyph of the star represents an image of spirit, but it is more than that. The star – in the sense of our own, individual star – functions as a source of wisdom and knowledge; it represents an interior place or state of mind and, at the same time, is a doorway to that place in which spiritual wisdom can be accessed and manifested. It is both the means and the end. The evidence of the hieroglyphs suggests that the ancient Egyptians considered each star in the sky to be an actual manifestation of the spiritual essence of each individual human being. If this seems a little fanciful it is worth keeping in mind the extent to which our present way of thinking about ourselves and our universe is almost completely solar centred. The sun is indeed the Earth's primary source of life-energy but we tend to forget that the sun is also a star; we think of it as somehow unique, as if in a category all of its own. It can be a useful exercise to imagine transferring our relationship with the sun to another star.

The hieroglyph of the star can also be pronounced *dwA*, in which case it gives rise to a different group of words. *DwA* is shown below, followed by the hieroglyph of the kneeling man whose hands are raised in adoration to form the determinative that defines the word as 'to praise or worship.' [84]

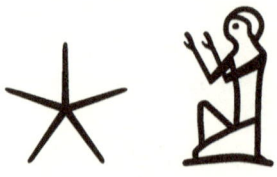

dwA = praise, worship

As this word indicates, there is a difference of emphasis between *sabA* and *dwA*. *SabA* is associated with the higher levels of consciousness and the spiritual enlightenment that characterises this level. *DwA*, on the other hand, suggests an attitude of awe and respect rather than gnosis or spiritual wisdom. For the ancient Egyptians, praise and worship of the stars was not mere lip-service but a genuine acknowledgement of what they represented, together with a realistic appreciation of what was needed in order to reach them. The approach to the stars represented by *dwA* precedes that of *sabA*; to reach the stellar wisdom of *sabA* you must pass through the stages of *dwA*, gaining an understanding of what the stars signify and of what must be achieved before attaining the condition of 'starriness.'

Confirmation of this is found in the word *dwAt* or *duAt*, the name given by the ancient Egyptians to an area of the Inner worlds through which the questing soul passed before reaching the later stages of spiritual enlightenment. *DwAt* is usually written as below and is composed of four hieroglyphs that we have already explored.[85]

dwA   *A*   *t*
= *dwAt*, the Inner world

The word *dwAt* is often translated as the Underworld or Netherworld, suggesting a dark and punishing subterranean region rather like Hades or Purgatory. The analogy is misleading; the *dwAt* is not a place of spiritual darkness but represents an Inner environment that corresponds to a level of consciousness. It is neither the sunlit world of everyday life nor the starlit world of spirit but an in-between stage, an interior land that is visited in dreams and reverie or entered into by use of the creative imagination. Such regions can be places of inhibition and fear as well as guidance and understanding. The recently deceased or the magical initiate travels through this region and confronts its challenges, so that gradually the interior light of the spirit dawns and becomes the guiding light. We can see the same concept in the word shown below: *dwAyt*, which means 'dawn' or 'morning.'[86]

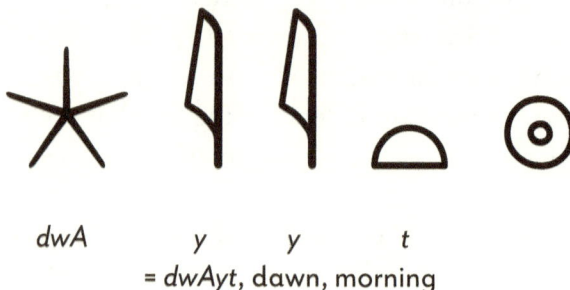

dwA   y   y   t

= *dwAyt*, dawn, morning

This group of hieroglyphs flows beautifully in whichever direction you read it. It depicts that brief but special quality of early dawn in which the incipient light of the sun blends with the still visible brightest stars, and it refers also to the corresponding stage of consciousness in which the strength of the outerworld personality, which is represented by the sun, gives way to the light of the spirit. The inclusion of the flowering reeds forms a link with the *sekhet iaru* or 'Field of Reeds' which was a substantial area in the landscape of the *dwAt*.

The word *dwAt* could also be written with a single hieroglyph:[87]

dwAt

This combination of star and circle symbolises the union of sunlight and starlight which is the ultimate aim of those who travel through the *dwAt*. It reminds us that the achievement of 'starriness' brings us to wholeness, to the One. Here, each aspect of the individual is now fully integrated, so that the many different lights of existence are shining as one: the light of the sun, of the stars, divine spirit with human spirit; terrestrial fire joined with celestial fire.

Finally, the star hieroglyph could also be pronounced '*wnwty*' and when pronounced thus it means 'astronomer,' 'hour-watcher' or 'star-watcher'. From the same root derives the term *wnwt*, the priesthood.⁸⁸ Here, the stars and the sun are again conjoined, providing us with a definition of the priest as one who has achieved knowledge of their powers and integrated those powers within themselves.

wnwty = astronomer   **wnwt** = priesthood

There are many references in the funerary texts to the Milky Way or 'Winding Waterway' which was regarded as the celestial equivalent of the River Nile. For example in Utterance 437 of the Pyramid Texts the king is exhorted to raise himself as Osiris and to take the roads to the sky where Horus is waiting: "For you have travelled across the Winding Waterway in the northern sky as a star crossing the sea beneath the sky." In Utterance 359 the king invokes the aid of the god of the sun to help him summon the ferryman who will take him across the waters. "Oh Re, commend me to *mAhAef* the ferryman of the Winding Waterway, so that he will come to me in his boat and ferry me across to the other side, to the eastern side of the sky ..." We can add to our understanding of the Winding Waterway in Egyptian magical thought by looking at the symbolism contained in the hieroglyphs that spell its name, *mesket*, which was written as follows: ⁸⁹

ms   k   t
= *mesket*, the Milky Way

The word *mesket* introduces three new hieroglyphs. The first is a depiction of three fox's pelts tied together and means 'to be born,' 'to give birth,' 'to make or create.' The hieroglyph probably refers to the Egyptian desert fox, the Fennec fox or *Vulpes zerda*. This tiny nocturnal creature has huge pointed ears which endow it with an especially cute appearance but, more practically, help to keep the animal cool and also provide it with a remarkable sense of hearing. The desert fox has soft, creamy-white fur which is much prized by hunters. Several pelts sewn together make a comforting mat or cover for a new-born and it is probable that the meaning of the hieroglyph derives from this. But there is a further level of symbolism in this attractive sign which suggests the three primary 'rays' or types of creative energy which are sometimes described as love, power and will. The hieroglyph appears in a number of words associated with birth: it is found for instance in the name of the goddess of childbirth, *Meskhenet,* and in words associated with the birthplace of the gods or with the home of the gods.

The second hieroglyph in *mesket* represents a hill. It indicates spiritual rather than temporal height, and describes something that has been 'exalted,' 'uplifted' or 'raised on high.' It is followed by the familiar feminine '*t*' and the final hieroglyph *niwt,* which is the determinative. The word *niwt* is often used as a determinative to specify a town, enclosure or walled settlement with intersecting streets but on a symbolic level it was used to indicate the coming together of diverse realities to form a coherent group, both in the outer and Inner worlds.[90] For example it was used in the phrase *niwt net neheh* meaning 'city of eternity' which was the necropolis or large cemetery attached to a town.

It is surprising that the word *mesket* does not include the hieroglyph of the star since it describes a celestial phenomenon composed almost entirely of stars. It does, though, suggest that the ancient Egyptians perceived the vast spiral galaxy that contains our universe as something more than, or different to, a collection of stars in the usual sense. The determinative tells us that the governing idea in this word is of a number of individuals who have grouped together to form a discrete entity, a body that is enclosed and clearly delineated by its boundary. There are many implications in this, and it could refer to individual beings, to new stars or novas, to universes yet unborn – or to all of these. The three preceding hieroglyphs tell us more about these 'individuals.' They are newborns, but the hieroglyph of the hill tells us that they have been uplifted or elevated from a previous state of existence before being born again within this celestial river. The stars of the Winding Waterway are not 'just' stars but are spiritual beings who have undergone a similar experience which now brings them together. The combined symbolism of these hieroglyphs suggests the esoteric belief in the 'second birth' or initiation into an enlightened state of consciousness which brings about an intuitive recognition of others who have shared that experience. All this, incidentally, adds to our understanding of the meaning of 'starriness.'

In the ancient texts, the questing soul crosses the Winding Waterway in order to reach the Imperishable Stars that lie on the far side of the Milky Way. "I will cross over to the side on which are found the Imperishable Stars so that I will become one amongst them." The Imperishable Stars or *ikhemu sek* were written in hieroglyphs as follows: [91]

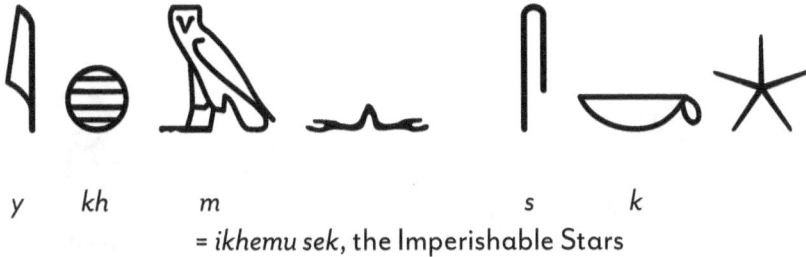

y   kh   m   s   k
= *ikhemu sek*, the Imperishable Stars

As mentioned earlier, there is much scholarly debate over which constellations the ancient Egyptians included in the group they called the Imperishable stars, so it would be helpful if the hieroglyphs gave us some clue to their identity. Unfortunately, this isn't so! But their overall meaning is evident because they combine a number of hieroglyphs whose symbolism is familiar to us from previous words. In the first word, *ikhemw,* the symbolism of the flowering reed and the sieve or placenta suggests the purifying effect that is experienced when the questing soul passes through the *sekhet iaru* or Field of Reeds. The third hieroglyph is of an owl. This sign is frequently used as the phoneme '*m*' but its underlying meaning is 'that which is within.' [92] The fourth sign is the determinative of the first word; it represents the universally recognised gesture in which the arms are extended from the elbows and the hands are turned upwards with the slight but expressive shrug of the shoulders that conveys total incomprehension. To the ancient Egyptians it also had the more succinct meaning of 'not,' which in this instance defines the word as 'not perishable' or in other words 'immortal,' 'everlasting.' The overall symbolism is of an internal purification in which the transient elements of the earthly life are filtered away, leaving only the undying spirit.

The second word, *sek,* is also spelt phonetically, starting with the folded cloth, a frequently used phoneme having the sound '*s*' but which could also indicate *seneb,* meaning 'good health' or 'soundness' in the sense of not injured, not diseased or flawed. The second sign is the shallow basket with a handle which represents the phoneme '*k*.' The final sign is the determinative of the star.

Moving on to individual stars and constellations, the following hieroglyphs spell *sAh* which was the name the ancient Egyptians gave to the constellation we know as Orion. [93]

sAh = sAh, Orion

The first hieroglyph gives the complete the word while the remaining three signs are determinatives: the star coupled as usual with the White vulture of sovereignty, then the seated figure of a god which completes the meaning as 'a divine figure in the stars which represents the immortal spirit.'

The first sign is generally agreed to be an illustration of three toes and is almost unrecognisably abstract in its design, although early examples are a little more naturalistic. It is interesting to compare this hieroglyph with the hieroglyph of an animal's spine, pronounced *Aw. Aw* means 'to stretch out,' or 'a long period of time or space.' [94] It shows the same 'loop' issuing from the lower edge which seems to be a representation of the spinal fluid and which the ancient Egyptians may have interpreted as the *kA*, the essential life-energy.

Aw = to stretch out; a long period of time or space

In *sAh*, the hieroglyph of the toes is puzzling! The 'toes' of the constellation as we now recognise it are represented by the brightest star in the constellation, Rigel, which forms Orion's left foot. The word suggests that the constellation might more accurately be translated as 'the Toes' or 'the Toe star' although we are perhaps naturally reluctant to identify one of the most striking constellations of the night sky with this lowly part of the human body. The same hieroglyph has many other meanings however, such as 'neighbourhood' and 'a grant of land.' It can be used as a determinative to mean 'to reach,' 'to arrive at' and 'to land from a ship,' all of which suggest the idea of a journey by water – and this brings to mind an image of the journey taken by the questing soul across the Winding Waterway towards the final destination represented by *sAh*.

We can also consider the possibility that to the ancient Egyptians *sAh* consisted only of the single 'toe star' Rigel, although the illustrations of the constellation such as those on the ceiling of the tomb of Senenmut at Deir el Bahri (see page 121) suggest a complete figure consisting of many stars. Perhaps Rigel symbolised a sort of celestial landing stage, the initial point of destination for newly arrived sky-travellers – a concept which makes more sense than the more difficult image of the traveller somehow managing to 'land' at the entire constellation. The name 'toe star' continued into later cultures: the word Rigel derives from the Arabic word meaning 'foot' or 'leg.' It is also worth keeping in mind that Rigel marks the place on the horizon where Sirius rises a little over an hour later, so of all the stars in the constellation it is the most closely linked with Sirius, just as Orion and Sirius are also closely linked in Egyptian mythology.[95]

sAh could also be written as follows:[96]

s   sA   A   h
= sAh, Orion

The first hieroglyph in this word is the folded cloth which as we have seen can indicate 'good health' and 'soundness.' The second sign means 'back.' It is infrequently used but its presence as a sound complement suggests that it has some significance in this word. The object it illustrates has not been conclusively identified and although 'a lid' and 'the cover of a quiver' have been suggested, these objects have no obvious connection with the symbolic meaning of *sAh*, and are not suggested by the use of the hieroglyph in any other known words.[97] For comparison, a later version of the hieroglyph *sA* is shown below,[98] followed by the hieroglyph *inr* which means 'block of stone'[99] and finally the similarly shaped hieroglyph *sabA* which means 'door' or 'pylon.'[100]

sA = back   *inr* = stone, rock, block or slab   *sabA* = door or pylon

It is possible that the object *sA* may represent a block of stone which has been specially placed at the back of the temple, perhaps in the rear wall of the innermost sacred precinct, a type of cornerstone. At any rate, the hieroglyph illustrates a rectangular shaped object which according to the conventions of hieroglyphic drawing is likely to be man-made or manually shaped rather than naturally formed. The hieroglyph has a number of interesting uses. Its primary meaning is 'back' in the sense of 'at the back of' or 'following after' but it is also found in words that mean 'to forcibly drive (into), 'to collect or gather together,' 'to be in charge of,' 'to prepare or recognise,' and in groups of hieroglyphs which mean 'to journey,' and 'to satisfy.' It can also mean 'to make wise' and 'a wise man.' With no great stretch of the imagination we can apply all of these terms to the constellation of *sAh* or Orion: as the stellar counterpart of Osiris, *sAh* is an exemplar of wisdom, one who oversees or is in charge of the process of transformation in which the questing soul transforms into the body of light, an experience which surely evokes a sense of fulfilment and satisfaction. We might also consider that *sAh* represents the coming together or unified presence of all those who have successfully reached this stage of enlightenment. And, further, that the meaning 'at the back of' or 'following after' is perhaps an oblique reference to the star Sirius which 'follows after' Orion, appearing above the horizon a few weeks after Orion. [101]

The word is completed with the White vulture, the twisted lamp wick which symbolises the perpetual flame, and the determinative of the star.

Coffin Texts 469 and 470 describe how the Pharaoh, searching for *sAh*/Orion, is guided towards a stairway which leads into the skies. Having ascended, he encounters the figure of *sAh* who is standing on the path before him and holding a staff or wand. *sAh* offers his staff to the Pharaoh, telling him that this will identify him as a son of *sAh*. The Pharaoh accepts it as a token of his spiritual progress which is such that he is now able to assume the qualities of the gods. He takes his seat in the shrine of the House of *sAh*, and having done so is able to call upon the powers of *sAh* at will.

However, before reaching the starry figure of *sAh* the questing soul passes through an important stage represented by the asterism we know as the Plough or Big Dipper, the part of the constellation of the Great Bear which is formed by the familiar group of seven stars. This constellation was known in ancient Egypt as *meskhetyw*, shown below: [102]

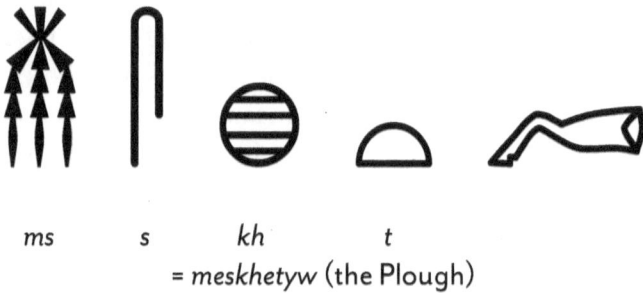

ms   s   kh   t
= *meskhetyw* (the Plough)

The determinative of this word is the hieroglyph of a bull's thigh or foreleg – the Egyptians interpreted this group of stars both as a bull's foreleg and as the entire animal – and the remaining hieroglyphs will be familiar from previous words explored in this chapter. The word begins with the hieroglyph of the three fox pelts tied together, meaning 'to be born' or 'to create.' The folded cloth indicates good health, the sieve or placenta represents the process of refining and purification, and finally the feminine '*t*' of the small offering-loaf. Here again are ideas associated with the symbolism of rebirth, of the absence of disease and the achievement of purity, but in this instance associated with a particular group of stars rather than the Milky Way.

The same word *meskhetyw* could also be written as follows, this time with the adze and star as determinatives.[103]

ms   kh   tyw
= *meshkhetyw*, the Plough

The adze, the bull's foreleg and the bull itself were variously used by the Egyptians as an image for this constellation. An instrument shaped like the adze was used in the Ceremony of the Opening of the Mouth which took place near the end of the process of mummification. The idea of the deceased or the magical initiate being 'given their voice' is readily understood, and when we find our true voice this is an indication that we have made an effective contact with our unique self and are able to give expression to its qualities.

Another star frequently mentioned in the ancient texts is the *neter dwAw* or Morning Star. The word derives from the root *dwA*, 'dawn.' [104]

ntr   dwA   A   y   y
= *neter dwAw*, the Morning Star

Towards the end of the journey into the stars, the questing soul is often referred to as 'Horus' or is said to have 'become like Horus' and is given the epithet 'Morning Star.' The orbit of Venus lies between the Earth and the sun, so from our point of view here on earth Venus appears to closely follow the orbit of the sun, which is why it is often visible just before sunrise, or at sunset. Because we now refer to the planet Venus as the Morning Star it is tempting to assume that the ancient Egyptians did likewise, and that the transfigured soul who had become like Horus was identified with the planet Venus as the visible image of Horus. The problem with this is that descriptions of the *neter dwAw* in the Pyramid Texts suggest that the celestial body in question moves freely about the sky, and one particularly problematic passage reads: "May you ascend the sky as Horus of the *dwAt* who stands before (or 'at the head of,' or 'as the foremost of') the Imperishable Stars." [105] This is unlikely to be a reference to Venus because the planet's orbit does not take it near the circumpolar stars. It seems more likely that 'Morning Star' is a generic term for all those who in life or after death have successfully undergone the challenges of the *dwAt*, have fully merged with the light of the spirit and symbolically risen, newborn, in the pale light of dawn just before the sun appears over the horizon. We saw the same idea earlier in the hieroglyphs that spell the word 'dawn.' This interpretation is confirmed by the hieroglyphs used in the words *neter dwAw* which as we have seen throughout this chapter are also used in many other words that relate to the stars. The hieroglyphs that spell *sabA wdjA*, Venus, written below, are significantly different to the hieroglyphs that spell 'Morning Star.' [106]

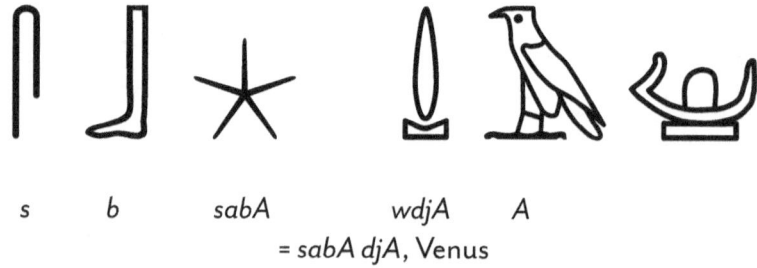

s   b   sabA   wdjA   A
       = sabA djA, Venus

The first hieroglyph is the folded cloth, followed by the hieroglyph of a foot and lower leg which is a frequently used phoneme '*b*' and also means 'to place.' This first word is determined by the hieroglyph of the star, presumably because the ancient Egyptians had no specific hieroglyph for 'planet.' The second word begins with the hieroglyph w*djA*. It represents a type of fire-drill in which a stick is lodged in a notch in a block of wood and rolled rapidly between the hands to produce a glowing ash which eventually ignites. The sign means 'strength,' 'to be intact' and 'to be whole,' and the symbolic meaning suggests the ability to create, kindle or initiate a spark of life. We have little knowledge of how the ancient Egyptians regarded Venus – or indeed any of the planets – but the symbolism of the hieroglyph suggests by analogy that just as we are able to create terrestrial fire so might Venus be thought of as the initiator of the creative flame of inspiration. It is interesting to note that many modern schools of esoteric thought regard Venus as the equivalent of the 'Higher Self' of the Earth, a view which is anticipated by this sequence of hieroglyphs.

The fifth sign is the familiar White vulture, and the final hieroglyph is the determinative. It represents the ceremonial boat or sacred barque that was used in ancient Egypt for sacred and ceremonial journeys, whether the last journey of the deceased Pharaoh along the Nile to the funerary temple or the orbit of the celestial bodies through the sky. It is worth noting that this hieroglyph is not used in words that refer to the stars.

Finally, we must mention a fascinating connection between the hieroglyph of the star and the sea urchin. The link between them has been described fully by Kenneth J. McNamara in his study of fossilised sea-urchins, '*The Star-Crossed Stone*.' [107] All species of sea-urchin display a five-pointed star formed by the 'ambulacral grooves,' so called because the sea urchin's 'feet' are extended and withdrawn from them. At the centre of the five grooves, the creature's mouth forms a distinct circular hole which looks very like the central circle depicted in many illustrations of the hieroglyph of the star. McNamara has amassed evidence of how these 'fossil echnoids' have been collected by humans from the Palaeolithic times. For example in Britain they have been found in a number of late Neolithic graves on the South Downs, and a hoard of them has been discovered in a Bronze Age burial on the Dunstable Downs, where over 200 were uncovered in a single grave. These fossilised sea-urchins are not easily come by, and the evidence suggests that they were painstakingly collected and highly treasured as if they had a significance far beyond that of curiosity or decoration. Fossilised sea-urchins are also found in Egypt, where they occur naturally in the limestone outcrops that were once at the bottom of the ocean but now form part of the desert.

One example is of particular interest to this study. When the Italian archeologist Ernesto Schiaparelli excavated at Heliopolis during 1903-1906 he found a sea-urchin in a group of objects which dated from the Old Kingdom (2686-2181 B.C.) The fossil was engraved with hieroglyphs that read: "Found in the south (or to the south) of the quarry of Sopdu by the god's father Tja-Nefer." As McNamara suggests, this recorded specimen may be the world's oldest curated object! [108]

Although we have focussed in this chapter on the stars as the visible manifestation of the shining spirit of each human being we must also consider the esoteric concept of 'the stars within the earth,' or in other words the ways in which the spiritual light indicated in *tA*, the earth, can be rekindled within the earth as well as within ourselves. It is fine and good to pursue one's destiny in the stars but even better to relate this gift to earth – and in the quest to find and release the light of the spirit in earth these star-shaped fossils are the perfect symbol. When all humanity has become one with the stars in the sky, then the stars will be kindled in the Earth, and the body of the Earth will be sacred among the stars.

Endnotes

74 *sabA*, star: Gardiner N14
75 A thorough exploration of possible correlations between Egyptian and modern constellations can be found at http://www.iac.es/proyecto/arqueoastronomia/media/Belmonte_Shaltout_Chapter_6.pdf
76 Lull, José and Belmonte, Juan Antonio, *A Firmament above Thebes: Uncovering the Constellations of the Ancient Egyptians: Journal for the History of Astronomy*; Nov 2006, Vol. 37 Issue 4
77 J.A.R. Legon, *The Orion Correlation and Air-Shaft Theories: Discussions in Egyptology Vol. 33* (1995), pages 45-56
78 *sabA*, a door: Gardiner N14, G1, O1
79 *sabAyt*, teaching: Gardiner N14, G1, M17, M17, X1, Y1
80 *sabA*, teaching: Gardiner N14, G1, A24
81 *Akh Akh*, stars: Gardiner G1, Aa1, G1, Aa1, N14, N14, N14
82 *Akh*, spirit: Gardiner G1, Aa1
83 *AkhAkh*, to grow green: Gardiner G1, Aa1, G1, Aa1, M2
84 *dwA*, to praise or worship: Gardiner N14, A4
85 *dwAt*, an area of the Inner worlds: Gardiner N14, G1, X1, O1
86 *dwAyt*, dawn, morning: Gardiner N14, M17, M17, X1, N5
87 *dwAt*, an area of the Inner worlds: Gardiner N15
88 *wnwt*, the priesthood: Gardiner N14, N5, X1, A1

89 *mesket*, the Milky Way: Gardiner F31, N29, X1, O49
90 see Maria Carmela Betro, *Hieroglyphs: the Writings of Ancient Egypt* (New York, Abbeville Press, 1996) p 190
91 *ikhemu sek*, the northern Circumpolar stars: Gardiner M17, Aa1, G17, D35, S29, V31, N14
92 The symbolism of the owl is discussed in greater detail in Chapter Ten
93 *sAh*, Orion: Gardiner D61,N14,G1,A40
94 *Aw*, to stretch out, a period of time or space: Gardiner F40
95 see John A.R. Legon, *The Orion Correlation and Air-Shaft Theories: Discussions in Egyptology Vol. 33* (1995), pages 45-56
96 *sAh*, Orion: Gardiner S29, Aa17, G1, V28, N14
97 Hans Goedicke, *On the origin of the hieroglyph* ⌂, *The Journal of Egyptian Archeology Vol 45*, 1959, pages 99-100
98 *sA*, back: Gardiner Aa18
99 *inr*, stone: Gardiner O39
100 *sbA*, door, pylon gateway: Gardiner O32
101 Raymond O. Faulkner's *A Concise Dictionary of Middle Egyptian* is especially useful in the interpretation of this word.
102 *meskhetyw*, the constellation of the Plough: Gardiner F31, S29, Aa1, X1, F23
103 *meskhetyw*, the constellation of the Plough: Gardiner F31, Aa1, G4, U21, N14
104 *neter dwAw*, the morning star: Gardiner R8, N14, G1, M17, M17, A40
105 Pyramid text 1301
106 *sbA wdjA*, Venus: Gardiner S29, D58, N14, U28, G1, P3
107 Kenneth J. McNamara, *The Star-Crossed Stone: The Secret Life, Myths and History of a Fascinating Fossil* (Chicago: The University of Chicago Press, 2011)
    My attention was drawn to this book following a dream in which I was travelling backwards, very fast, down a narrow path. Successful completion of this manoeuvre was rewarded by a gift of five fossilised sea-urchins although the source of the gift was not revealed.
108 Ibid, 173

The Pyramid

A brief survey of the seven hundred or so hieroglyphs listed by Gardiner in his catalogue of signs reveals that although many feature a square, a rectangle or a circle in their design, scarcely any include a triangle. There is no immediately obvious reason for this, although when we look more closely at the hieroglyphs that do contain a triangle it becomes evident that it symbolised something so significant to the ancient Egyptians that its use was deliberately confined to a few, special instances.

The first of the 'triangle' hieroglyphs is shown below: *spd,* or *soped.*[109]

spd = *soped*, sharp, skilled

This hieroglyph is the ideogram for 'thorn,' although it is primarily used as a determinative in words that mean 'sharp,' both physically sharp or pointed, and mentally sharp in the sense of keen and alert. It can also mean 'to restore to order' and 'to supply.' It is interesting that the modern English use of the word 'sharp' to indicate both a pointed object and an alertness of mind was anticipated by the ancient Egyptians! In fact the word 'sharp' contains numerous possibilities and the Thesaurus lists at least eighteen nuances of meaning including keen, intense, acute, piercing, strong, pointed, needle-like, distinct, abrupt, spirited, perceptive and intelligent. All of these describe a probably unexpected and perhaps uncomfortable burst of energy which can be experienced both physically and mentally: a sudden realisation, the 'aha' moment of inspiration, a flash of enlightenment which comes out of the blue.

It would be easy to overlook the apparently insignificant hieroglyph *soped* were it not that with the addition of the feminine '*t*' it forms the word *spdt* which is generally written as *sopdet*. *Sopdet* is the name the ancient Egyptians gave to the star we now usually identify by its Latin name Sirius, which is the brightest star in the sky. The hieroglyphs that spell the name of this star are illustrated below.[110] *Sopdet* was highly significant in ancient Egyptian magical belief, not least because of its association with the goddess Isis, with the inundation of the Nile, and with the funeral and mummification rites.

Some confusion has arisen around the word *sopdet* and it is worth pausing to clarify this before we look at the hieroglyphs in more detail. The Greek translation of the Egyptian word *sopdet* is *sothis*. The Latin translation of the word *sopdet* is 'Sirius,' which is customarily spelt with a capital 'S.' Consequently, many writers also give a capital letter to *Sothis* – even though there are no capital letters in the hieroglyphs. When *Sothis* is spelt with a capital 'S' it looks as if it must be the name of a deity, and so the star *sopdet/sothis* becomes the name of a goddess: 'Sothis, the goddess of Sirius.' For the ancient Egyptians, however, there was no such goddess.

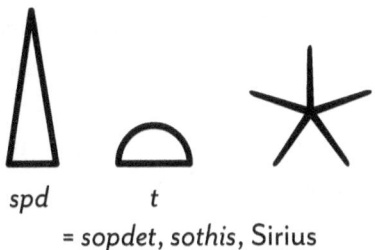

spd   *t*

= *sopdet, sothis,* Sirius

To add to the confusion, the same hieroglyph *soped* with the addition of the quail chick, '*w*' which confirms the word as masculine, followed by the determinative of a plumed Horus falcon, spells the name of a minor god associated with Horus: *Sopdw*, whose name, as we noted in the previous chapter, happens to appear in the inscription on the fossilised sea-urchin found in a quarry at Heliopolis. [111]

spd   w
= *spdw*, the god Sopdw

These words *soped*, *sopdet* and *sopdw* (or *sopdu*) are now used as if they are interchangeable, but this is not correct. Sopdw was a warrior-god, also known as the 'sharp-toothed one,' who was found mainly in the Eastern desert where he was responsible for the protection of the turquoise mines of Sinai. To summarise:

spd or *soped*	= a hieroglyph which means 'thorn' and 'sharp'
spdt or *sopdet*	= a star, which we now usually refer to as Sirius
Sirius	= the Latin translation of the word *sopdet*
Sothis	= the Greek translation of the Egyptian star *sopdet*
spdw	= the god Sopdw or Sopdu

Returning to the hieroglyphs which spell *sopdet*/Sirius, we must consider why an isosceles triangle has been chosen as the symbol for this star. If we contemplate the meaning of the isosceles triangle in the language of sacred geometry we can say that it consists of two lines which emerge from a single point and travel in different directions. These two lines are reconnected by a third line, which seems to represent 'something else' in that its point of origin is not the same as that of the first two lines and it appears to exist independently of them. However, it relates equally to both of the original lines and forms a bridge or relationship between them. Without the third line, the original two lines would continue to diverge into infinity.

A single point, or dot, represents the One, the wholeness of the Divine, the purest spark of spirit. From the One, two different energies emerge which follow increasingly divergent paths. In between these apparent opposites is a mediating or connecting energy which represents the human mind or consciousness. The mind can be thought of as both the outcome and mediator of the polarity between opposites and the means by which the polarity will ultimately be resolved into the One. The difference between the start and the end of this journey is that in the beginning there is spirit with no awareness of Self, while at the end of the journey the One now Knows Itself, or in other words God Knows God. We cannot comprehend the Absolute; it is necessary for us to perceive the two opposites in order to understand the nature of their source, and the triangle illustrates this process. There must be Three in One for the One to have meaning.

Unlike the fixed shape of the circle or square, the triangle can be drawn in a variety of ways, each of which expresses a different quality. In symbolic terms an equilateral triangle, having three equal sides and three equal angles, can be said to represent the three elements of spirit, matter and mediating consciousness in equal balance. A scalene triangle, which is formed of three unequal sides and three unequal angles looks odd, unbalanced, and is surprisingly difficult to draw. In a right-angled or Pythagorean triangle the square is already present in potential because "the square on the hypotenuse equals the sum of the squares on the two other sides." The isosceles triangle, of which the hieroglyph *soped* is an example, contains two equal but comparatively long sides, and two equal angles which are joined by a third, different angle. If you draw a triangle at random you will probably find that you have drawn either a right-angled or equilateral triangle, both of which have something satisfactorily balanced and complete about them.

Another example of the triangle in Egyptian symbolism is the stylised triangular apron which forms a prominent feature of ritual clothing shown in many bas reliefs and paintings, although it is not included in the hieroglyphs. The majority of these aprons appear to form an equilateral, or almost equilateral, triangle. They are decorated with a variety of symbols, although the most commonly seen is that of a splendid rayed sun which emerges from the apron's lower corner and suggests a symbolic connection between the equilateral triangle and the sun. A full study of the symbolism of Egyptian ceremonial aprons has yet to be undertaken but would prove invaluable.

What, then, is the connection between the star, the isosceles triangle and a thorn? It is relevant to consider what type of thorn is illustrated by the hieroglyph. The rose has inspired much symbolism, and roses were certainly grown in ancient Egypt, but the rose has short, curved thorns while the thorn of the hieroglyph is a long and slender isosceles triangle. The most likely inspiration is the *Acacia Nilotica,* the Acacia of the Nile or Gum Arabic Tree which is widespread in the Nile valley and in the desert oases. The tree is well adapted to prolonged periods of drought interspersed

The Nile Acacia Photo by the author

with periods of floods, so it is particularly suited to the local conditions. Its bark has many medicinal uses and its wood was used by the Egyptians to make furniture and temple statues. The tree displays an abundance of spherical, golden-yellow flowers along with distinctive slender, silvery-grey thorns which can grow up to three inches long. An unusual feature of the Nile Acacia is that its thorns grow in pairs, each pair emerging from the node where a twig joins the branch to form an approximate right-angle. The golden, spherical, rayed flowers can be seen as a symbol of the sun, and the slender, silvery thorns a pleasing symbol of rays of starlight.

The striking appearance of the Nile Acacia tree, the isosceles triangle of the *soped* thorn hieroglyph, the mental state of alertness and sudden 'wakefulness,' and the star *sopdet* or Sirius form a chain of symbolic meaning. The hieroglyph represents the qualities of readiness, quickness of mind and preparedness such as you experience when pricked by a sharp thorn. The sudden rush of adrenaline that floods through the body and stimulates it into a state of alertness with all senses awake, demonstrates on the earthly plane the state of Inner awareness that is initiated by the energy of the star. The energy from Sirius stimulates and rapidly awakens the higher intuition within the receptive human consciousness in a mindful initiation which permeates the entire being with inspiration, just as the rising of the star Sirius above the horizon – an event which at one time coincided with the dawning of the sun at midsummer – heralded the inundation of the Nile that created fertile and productive land.

The qualities of the isosceles triangle remind us further to consider all of this symbolism within the general context of *connectedness* and of the relationship between apparently different or opposing energies that is formed by the third, mediating element of the human mind. When we affirm the connection between *sAh/* Orion and *sopdet*/Sirius in our mind and imagination we are in effect completing the triangle – we are providing the link which brings them together in a creative and initiating relationship. As we have observed many times throughout this study, the principle of human mediation between two apparent opposites is fundamental to Egyptian magic, and the stellar relationship between *sAh* and *sopdet* is mirrored on earth in the inundation of the Nile upon the land.

The process of this 'triangular' exchange of energy is described in the Pyramid texts, where the star *sopdet* draws magical initiates onwards and upwards until they are transfigured into spiritual bodies of light exemplified by *sAh*, and take their place in the stars. "*Sopdet* has caused me to ascend into the sky among my companions who are the gods." [112] "You shall reach the sky as *sAh*, your soul shall be as effective as *sopdet*; have power, having power; be strong, having strength." [113]

Another use of the thorn hieroglyph is demonstrated in the word below which is usually translated as 'effectiveness,' a quality ascribed to the star in the quotation above. Here, the hieroglyphs that spell *sopdet* are determinative by the sealed roll of papyrus which indicates an abstract idea or concept.[114]

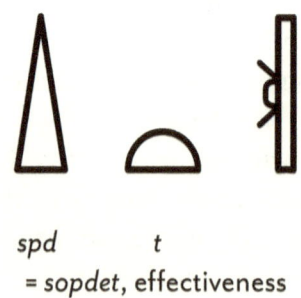

spd　　　t
= sopdet, effectiveness

'Effectiveness' is another difficult word to define precisely but it confirms the suggested symbolism of the triangle. For something to have effect, the initiating impulse must be carried through into a result; the originating thought or idea must achieve its purpose rather than become dissipated and lose its strength and identity. Simply to have an effect on something is not quite the same as 'effectiveness'; effectiveness is achieved when the result is obtained with a minimum expenditure of energy and within an appropriate period of time. The phrase "… your soul shall be as effective as *sopdet* …" suggests that the initiated soul will take on the stimulating, initiating effectiveness of the star and be able to pass on these qualities to others. This notion of 'effectiveness'

The Pyramid

appears to be enshrined in the symbolism of these 'triangular' hieroglyphs, all of which refer to the achievement of spiritual initiation or transfiguration which is perhaps difficult for us now to fully understand. The function of the Great Pyramid of Khufu at Giza whose connection with the stars of Orion and Sirius has been widely commented upon in recent years may have been to invoke or enhance this initiatory experience, either for individuals or perhaps for the land and people of Egypt.

Keeping in mind this chain of symbolism – triangle, thorn, *sopdet*, sharpness, initiation and effectiveness – we can move to the second hieroglyph that contains a triangle: *mr* or *mer*, the pyramid.[115]

mr = mer, the pyramid

Unlike *soped* which contains no reference to size or context, the pyramid hieroglyph *mer* rests on a rectangular base that symbolises the earth or a block of stone just as, for example, the Great Pyramid at Giza is built on a square of level stone. The appearance of this hieroglyph is not quite as we might expect, because none of the pyramids are shaped quite like this. The slope of the pyramids varies between one example and another, but they mostly fall within the range of 48 to 53 degrees, whereas the triangle of *mer* is much steeper. We must assume that the shape of this hieroglyph is the result of deliberate choice rather than careless draughtsmanship, designed perhaps to emphasise the connection between the pyramids and the stars, particularly the star *sopdet*. Or perhaps it is a symbolic combination of the equilateral sun triangle and the more slender star triangle?

The connection between the pyramids and the stars has been discussed by numerous scholars. Robert Bauval and Adrian Gilbert for example demonstrated that one of the 'air shafts' in the Queen's Chamber of the Great Pyramid would have pointed directly to the culmination of Sirius at around the time of the pyramid's construction. [116] Many of the pyramids were originally given names that emphasised the connection between the transfigured soul of the Pharaoh entombed within them and the stars: the pyramid of Pharaoh Djedefre at Abu Rawash for example is called 'Djedefre's starry sky.'

A third example of the use of the triangle in a hieroglyph is shown below. Pronounced *di* or *rdi*, it means 'to give.' [117]

di or *rdi* = to give

Here, the slender isosceles 'thorn' triangle *soped* has a smaller, identically proportioned triangle set inside it. *Redi* is usually described as a representation of the conical loaf depicted in numerous scenes of offering to the gods, and there is undoubtedly a connection between the hieroglyph, the loaf and the idea of offering or giving. But there is a further symbolic meaning to this sign which, at risk of stating the obvious, cannot simply be an illustration of a loaf of bread because one loaf cannot contain another loaf.

To the ancient Egyptians, the ritual offering of bread, fruit and beer to the deceased or to the gods represented more than a superstitious belief that regular supplies of bread and alcohol were necessary to fortify the inhabitants of the unseen worlds. The ritual act of giving was a symbolic representation of the real 'offering up' which was of one's self to the gods, or a raising up of the lower self into the light of the spirit. The process illustrated by the hieroglyph was of *revealing* one's self to the gods and required honesty and awareness; it was a learning process.

All that we have discovered in the symbolism of *soped* applies to *redi;* the same sense of keenness, alertness and skill is surely present when the act of giving to the gods is performed mindfully. *Redi* is used in words meaning 'to cause, permit or grant,' 'to put in charge of' and 'to command or show the way.' It describes a deliberate and positive action, not a casual or passively made gesture but an action which is designed to lead the way forward into something new: to *initiate*. The sense is that a significant change of state can be caused by *redi*.

The depiction of two *soped* triangles, one inside the other, symbolises a close relationship between two things which are essentially the same but which manifest on different levels of reality. The idea is similar to something we looked at earlier in the two pronunciations of the hieroglyph of the star, where *sabA* refers to 'starriness' as a transformative energy and an active source of wisdom, while *dwA* represents an attitude of dedication and devotion to the spiritual quest. In *redi,* the concept 'to give' can be understood within the context defined by the qualities of the 'thorn' hieroglyph that indicates a sudden jolt of energy which, on a higher level, is analogous to the initiating power of the star *sopdet* or Sirius. It is through the act of mindfully giving, in the sense of opening ourselves or revealing ourselves to the gods, that we are made ready to receive the initiating experience which may result from contact with the star. Equally, it may refer to a deliberate act of initiation, of contact with Sirius and Sirian energies being intentionally conveyed to another.

Redi could also be combined with the hieroglyph of the extended arm and hand, this sign having the same meaning as the previous example: 'to give.' [118]

redi = to make offering

The hieroglyph *redi* was often used as a determinative, for example in the phrase below which consists of the first four hieroglyphs of the 'Offering Formula' which was frequently used on coffins, tombs and stelae. The full text of the Formula gives precise details as to what is being offered, lists the gods to whom the offering is being made and gives the name of the Pharaoh who was said to be undertaking the offering – although for practical purposes the ritual was usually undertaken on his behalf by the temple priests.[119]

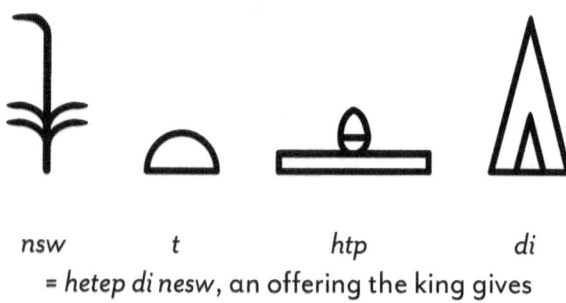

nsw   t   htp   di
= *hetep di nesw*, an offering the king gives

The phrase is spoken as '*hetep di nesw*' and not in the order shown above, because the sign *nsw*, meaning 'king,' is written first as a courtesy to the Pharaoh. The third sign is perhaps the most significant in this group: pronounced *hetep* or *hotep* it shows an offering loaf which has been placed on a mat of woven reeds. *Hetep* means 'offering' but also suggests 'peace,' 'rest,' 'to be at peace with,' 'to be happy, calm or content.' *Hetep* describes the serenity which arises when you are living in a state of harmony, when all internal conflicts and desires have been resolved and you experience a sense of alignment and integration with all aspects of yourself and your world. It relates to the concept of *zep tepi*, the First Time, when a perfect harmony was expressed through an exact mirroring between the stars and the earth. The phrase *hetep di nesw* suggests that this profound peace is achieved through *redi*, the act of offering or revealing one's self to the gods and, perhaps, of having received the implied initiation of *sopdet*.

The final example of the triangle can be seen in the hieroglyph of the obelisk, shown below.[120] It is pronounced *tkhn* or *tekhen*.

The Pyramid

tkhn = *tekhen*, obelisk

The obelisk is one of the most striking examples of Egyptian monuments although unfortunately its fame is now largely derived from the many examples that have been removed from Egypt and dispersed about the world. There are eight Egyptian obelisks in Rome for example, six of which came from the ancient city of *Innu* or Heliopolis.

The hieroglyph *tekhen* is mainly used as an ideogram or determinative. It contains three elements: the rectangular platform of the 'stone' hieroglyph which is also seen at the base of the hieroglyph of the pyramid, a tall pillar which represents the movement of energy between heaven and earth, and the small pyramid or 'pyramidion' at the summit. The tip of the obelisk was originally covered in shining metal, either gold or the gold and silver alloy electrum, and was positioned so that it would catch the first rays of the sun just before it became visible above the horizon. The obelisk was primarily a symbol of the sun: it linked the theology and magical symbolism of the sun with the power and earthly sovereignty of the Pharaoh. This is confirmed by the shape of the pyramidion which more closely resembles the solar, equilateral triangle featured in the apron rather than the slender, stellar triangle of *sopdet*.

An alternative spelling of *tekhen* is shown below.[121]

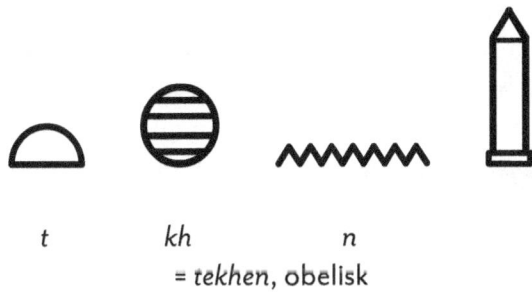

t   kh   n
= *tekhen*, obelisk

Here, the *tekhen* obelisk is the determinative for a sequence of three familiar hieroglyphs. The first is the small loaf of offering, used phonetically as the sound '*t*.' The second sign is the sieve or placenta which indicates a process of filtering, purification and refinement. The third is '*n*,' a hieroglyph which means 'belonging' and suggests the movement of energy between one thing and another. The signs are primarily used as phonemes, but there is background of symbolic meaning which indicates that the purpose of the obelisk is to transmit energy.

The pyramidion is also used in the sequence of hieroglyphs that describes the 'benben' stone, shown below. It symbolises the first mound of earth that emerged from the primeval waters and upon which the bennu bird alighted to herald the dawn of creation. It became the celestial pyramid in which the creator god Atum was said to dwell. The hieroglyphs of the leg and foot mean 'to place.' [122]

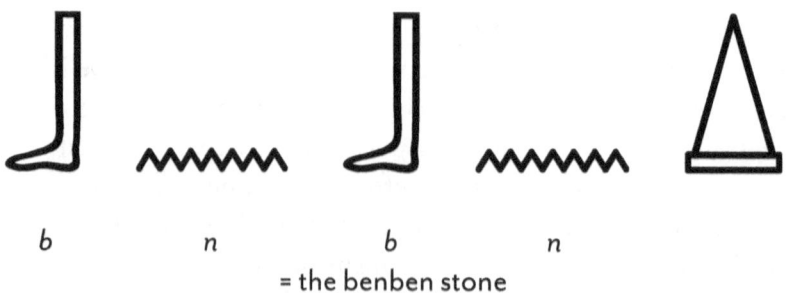

b   n   b   n
= the benben stone

As a final example we must mention the distinctive long, slender isosceles triangle that appears on the astrological ceiling of the tomb of Senenmut near the Funerary Temple of Hatshepsut at Deir el Bahri. Three stars in a row emanate from a schematised representation of a bull. The last of these stars is coloured red, and encircled by a red ring. A long isosceles triangle extends from the red star which has been tentatively identified as Alkaid, the end star of the 'handle' of the Plough, although the significance of this distinctive '*sopdet*' triangle has yet to be fully explained. [123]

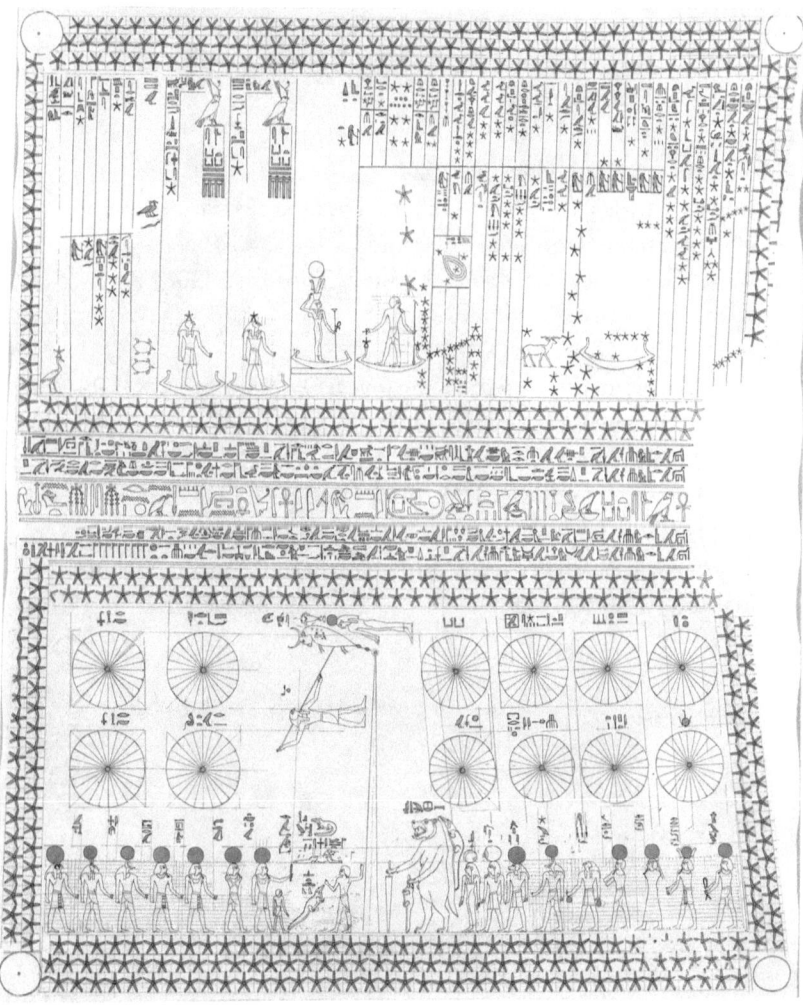

**The astrological ceiling in the tomb of Senenmut
near the Funerary Temple of Hatshepsut at Deir el Bahri**

Endnotes

109 *soped*, a thorn, sharp, skilled: Gardiner M44
110 the star *sopdet*: Gardiner M44, X1, N14
111 the god *Sopdw* or *Soped*: Gardiner M44, G43, G13
112 Pyramid Text Utterance 302
113 Pyramid Text Utterance 412
114 *sopdet*, effectiveness: Gardiner M44, X1, Y1
115 *mer*, the pyramid: Gardiner O24
116 Robert Bauval and Adrian Gilbert, *The Orion Mystery* (London: William Heinemann Ltd, 1994) and
 Mark Vidler, *The Star Mirror* (London, Thorsons, 1998)
117 *di* or *redi*, to give: Gardiner X8
118 *redi*, to give: Gardiner D37
119 *hetep di nsw*, an offering the King gives: Gardiner M23, X1, R4, X8
120 *tekhen*, the obelisk: Gardiner O25
121 *tekhen*, the obelisk: Gardiner X1, Aa1, N35, O25
122 ben ben stone: Gardiner D58, N35, D58, N35, O24
123 see José Lull and Juan Antonio Belmonte, *The Constellations of Ancient Egypt*: www.iac.es/proyecto/arqueoastronomia/media/Belmonte_Shaltout_Chapter_6.pdf

The *Ankh* and the House of Life

ankh = life

The *ankh* is probably the best known of all the hieroglyphs.[124] It was used from the earliest period of the Egyptian civilisation, where it appears not only in hieroglyphic inscriptions but in painted illustrations on the walls of temples and tombs, and in artefacts such as mirrors and libation vessels. It is generally agreed that the *ankh* stands for 'life' although there is no overall agreement as to what the hieroglyph actually illustrates, or how it symbolises 'life,' or indeed what is meant by 'life.' In the search for the origins of this enigmatic symbol many proposals have been put forward, some a little more convincing than others.

One of the first interpretations of the sign in modern times was made by Thomas Inman in his *Ancient Pagan and Modern Christian Symbolism* of 1875 where he observes: "It represents the male triad and the female unit, under a decent form."[125] The explanation perhaps raises more questions than it answers but his suggestion that the sign represents an exchange of polarised energy which leads to the creation of new life places it within the right field of speculation.

E.A. Wallis Budge suggested that the symbol originated as the belt-buckle of the goddess Isis. This is a hieroglyph in itself, sometimes referred to as the 'Knot of Isis' and shown below.[126]

tet - an amulet, the Knot of Isis

The two signs are certainly similar, and the downward-curving arms of the *tet* together with the suggestion of a robe or skirt between them gives the hieroglyph a feminine appearance which is absent from the *ankh*. The idea that the *ankh* represents the goddess Isis is certainly appealing, but the theory is largely based on a reference in Spell 156 of the Book of the Dead which gives instructions for making a *tet* knot of red jasper to be placed as a protective amulet on the neck of the deceased. The words to be spoken are: "Yours are the powers of blood, O Isis, yours are the powers of light, and the words of power belong to you. Here is an amulet of protection for this great being [i.e. the deceased] that will guard him against those who might injure him. These words are to be spoken over a *tet*-knot of jasper, sprinkled with the juice of the *imy* fruit, strung on a fibre of sycamore and placed at the neck of the blessed deceased on the day of burial. The powers of Isis will protect his body so that Horus will rejoice when he sees him and no paths will be hidden from him..." [127]

The evocative terms 'the Knot of Isis' and 'the Blood of Isis' are attractive, but the many available images of the *tet* and the *ankh* show that they retained a clear difference wherever they were used. The *tet* has a specific meaning which is different to the *ankh,* and the later appearance and comparatively infrequent use of the *tet* hieroglyph indicates that it did not inspire the *ankh*, although it may have derived from it.

In his 'Egyptian Grammar' of 1927 Gardiner describes the *ankh* as the ideogram for a sandal strap, the upper loop of the *ankh* representing the piece of leather that goes round the ankle and the 'stem' of the *ankh* corresponding to the strap that passes between the toes. The Egyptian word for the sandal strap is also spelt *ankh* and the Egyptians would certainly have been aware of the visual reference, but as Gardiner himself admitted it is difficult to discern any convincing symbolic connection between footwear and life. Common sense plays a part here: many illustrations show a stream of *ankhs* being poured by the gods over a recipient's head, a scene which becomes absurd if we envisage this flow of life and blessing as a rivulet of footwear.

An interesting argument for the *ankh* as the depiction of a thoracic vertebra of the bull is put forward by Andrew H. Gordon and Calvin W. Schwabe in their book *The Quick and the Dead*, a fascinating study of how the Egyptians interpreted and magically utilised the symbolism of the structure of the body of animals.[128] They include a photograph of a bull's thoracic vertebra for comparison with the *ankh*, although the visual analogy is not entirely convincing.

The hieroglyph has also been described as a symbol of the sun's journey over the River Nile, the stem of the *ankh* representing the river, the arms representing the land on the Nile's East and West banks and the oval symbolising the sun's path through the sky. Thus the three components of sun, river and land which represent the 'life force' of Egypt can also be linked to the three elements of the *ankh*.[129] Again, this is an attractive theory but it is difficult to relate it to the *ankh* in practice simply because the sun appears to describe a semi-circle through the sky between East and West while the upper portion of the *ankh* is an oval with a pointed end.

Later examples of the hieroglyph often anthropomorphise the sign: arms and hands sprout from it and the loop becomes a clear reference to the human head. Any symbol which contains an indication of arms, legs and a head will inevitably make a visual allusion to the human body, and many illustrations of the *ankh* do indeed look rather a human figure with outspread arms and a disproportionately large head. Such illustrations posit the equation *ankh* = the human body = 'life', although this in itself doesn't constitute an entirely sufficient explanation.

Earlier representations of the *ankh* contain details that are lacking in later versions and offer some useful clues as to its origin. The 'arms' often gently widen out towards the ends and are sometimes divided into two by a horizontal line. Similarly, the 'stem' broadens out towards the base and can also be divided into two, creating the suggestion of two legs and feet. More significantly, some examples illustrate a section of narrow vertical lines at the

From the Satet Temple of Montuhotep II, Dynasty XI, Elephantine Island

Photo by the author

junction of the loop, cross-bar and stem which look very much as if a length of thread has been wound around the three elements of the *ankh* to hold them together. This is clearly shown in the photo on page 126.

The most puzzling element of the *ankh* is the 'squashed loop' that forms its upper section. There is no inherent meaning in this shape; it isn't an oval or an ellipse; it has no sacred or geometrical significance and the shape doesn't occur naturally. In fact the easiest way to produce it is to take a piece of cord, fold it in half and pinch the two pieces together with your fingers approximately a third of the way down. If you try this, you will find that you have perfectly produced the loop of the ankh. You will also find that the ends of the cord naturally tend to splay out just as they do in many of the illustrations.

The proportions of the *ankh* are important. If you compare a number of illustrations – for instance those which appear when you type the word *ankh* into an online search function – you will find that some examples look right and others don't. Those that don't look quite right are usually modern versions of the hieroglyph which pay insufficient regard to the correct proportions. The satisfyingly 'correct' shape of the *ankh* is best produced by taking a length of cord and cutting it into two pieces, one of which will form the loop and stem, and the other forming the cross-bar. If you experiment with a piece of cord you will find that the most aesthetically pleasing shape is achieved if you make your initial cut according to the proportion of the Golden Ratio – in other words so that the ratio of the total length of the cord to the longer piece is the same as the ratio of the longer piece to the shorter piece.

For example, if the initial length of your cord is 21 inches, you will cut it into two pieces approximately 13 and 8 inches long.[130] The shorter piece that forms the 'arms' is then cut again, into two equal halves. If you lay the two shorter pieces across the longer, looped piece you will find that the arms tend to splay out a little towards the ends. Bind all the pieces together with some fine cord or cotton and will have made a *ankh* which looks very like that shown in the photo. There is no written evidence to suggest that the *ankh* utilises the proportions of the Golden Ratio or Golden

Mean, although many scholars have suggested that the Egyptians were aware of its properties and used them in the construction of the pyramids. Plato (c 428 B.C.-347 B.C.), one of the many Greeks who lived and studied in Egypt, was certainly aware of it.

The most significant symbolic element of the Golden Ratio is that it perfectly expresses how each part of the universe is a mirror of the whole; it demonstrates the microcosm as an image of the macrocosm. Its qualities can perhaps best be appreciated when it is presented as a spiral that has been defined by a series of squares and arcs, each forming a 'Golden Rectangle.' The proportions of the spiral resemble the patterns of growth found everywhere in nature from the leaves on a tree to the structure of crystals and the proportions of the human body. The symbolic meaning of this marvel of natural symmetry proclaims a universal order and pattern which is present in all living things and reveals their essential oneness.

If the *ankh* is indeed based on the proportions of the Golden Ratio this adds weight to the proposed equation *ankh* = the human body = life by suggesting that humans have a unique ability to manifest the One-ness of creation. If, for example, we define life as energy, or perhaps as 'spirit which is moving', we can readily symbolise this with a line – or in this instance a length of cord. Our ability to shape this cord according to the properties of the Golden Ratio is symbolic of our ability to manifest its properties in our own life. The *ankh* can therefore be seen as a type of 'shorthand' which symbolises not only a theoretical understanding of universal law but also its embodiment and manifest expression. The use of the *ankh* by the ancient Egyptians in their art and sacred writings demonstrates their belief that these abilities could not only be expressed by the individual but could also be given or communicated to others, hence the numerous illustrations of the gods, the Pharaoh and the priesthood conferring the gift of life upon others by holding the *ankh* towards them.

The use of the hieroglyph in other words supports this idea. The word below, which is also pronounced *ankh,* represents a mirror. [131] The second hieroglyph is the ideogram for copper.

ankh = a mirror

The *ankh* easily lends itself to the shape of a hand-mirror and many beautifully decorated examples survive, usually made from copper which when polished to a mirror-like sheen acquires a characteristic softness and depth. Here is another instance of the remarkable capacity of hieroglyphic symbolism to express complex ideas in a simple group of signs. If a mirror is shaped as a symbol of 'life,' then 'life,' it suggests, is enhanced by our observing, recognising and responding to what we perceive in ourselves and our environment.

Another interesting use of the *ankh* is found in the following phrase *ankh n niwt*, which means 'citizen.' [132]

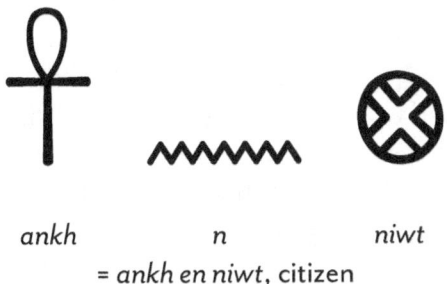

ankh   n   niwt
= *ankh en niwt*, citizen

All three hieroglyphs in this phrase have been discussed previously: the second sign '*n*' represents the idea of 'belonging to' and the final sign of the crossroads indicates a city, both as a physical entity and in the more abstract sense of a group of individuals. The presence of the *ankh* in this word instead of the more obvious choice of one of the many hieroglyphs that mean 'person' conveys the idea that being a citizen involves a higher level of shared experience than is found simply through the physical occupancy of a town or city. It confirms that the Egyptian understanding of 'life' is related to our relationship with everything around us.

To the ancient Egyptians, 'life' was not simply a description of something possessed by those in physical incarnation. The following hieroglyphs describe the *ankhu* or *ankhiu*, the eternally living ones, the blessed dead who have passed beyond the physical boundaries of the world.[133]

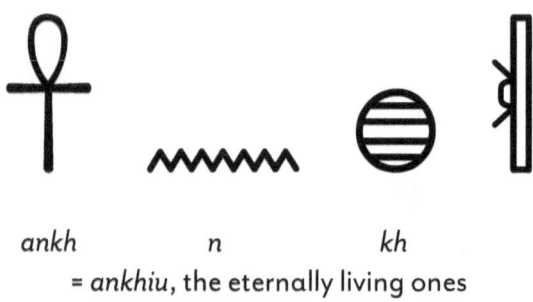

ankh   n   kh
= *ankhiu*, the eternally living ones

Here, the *ankh* is followed by two signs, both sound complements, which contribute to the overall symbolic meaning: the '*n*,' 'belonging to,' and the refinement and purification symbolised by the sieve. But the final hieroglyph of the sealed roll of papyrus tells us that the word refers to an abstract concept rather than to an actual being, whether alive or dead. The phrase refers to a purity of consciousness and expression of life-energy, a 'vibrant being-ness' which is naturally arrived at after the weight of the physical world has been left behind in death, but can equally be achieved by the living through a deliberate practice of the spiritual life.

In the next group of hieroglyphs the *ankh* is followed by two signs which develop its meaning: *wdjA* and *snb* or *seneb*.[134]

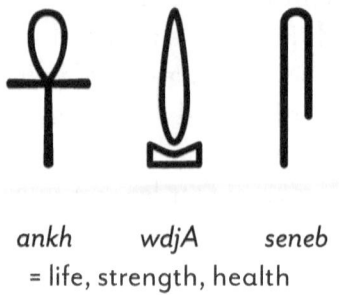

ankh   wdjA   seneb
= life, strength, health

These three signs were combined in an often used phrase which means 'life, strength (or prosperity) and health,' a popular epithet that concluded the list of names assumed by the Pharaoh and was also used as a salutation at the end of a letter. The *ankh* is followed by the hieroglyph of the fire-drill which means 'strength,' 'to be whole' or 'intact.' We first saw this sign in *sabA wdjA*, Venus, where it suggested the planet's initiatory relationship to Earth. The third sign is the folded cloth, an ideogram for 'health' and 'soundness.' These qualities were wished upon the Pharaoh, while simultaneously conveying the belief that Pharaoh was responsible for the preservation of those qualities within his land and people.

The concept of 'life' in its many possible interpretations was especially linked with the life, death and spiritual rebirth of the god Osiris, one of whose names was 'the Living One.' The title was written in hieroglyphs as follows: [135]

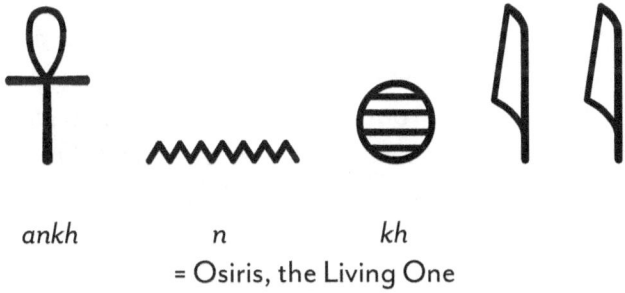

ankh   n   kh
= Osiris, the Living One

All four hieroglyphs in this word will by now be familiar to the reader, but their combination helps us to a fuller understanding of the significance of the *ankh*. Here, the '*n*' which suggests that life is pure moving energy that causes one thing to 'belong' to another is determined by the hieroglyph of the flowering reed. Where the waters of the Nile meet the desert, the first green and growing thing to unfold into life is the flowering reed that grows in profusion along its banks. Life, this word tells us, occurs when polar opposites come together to bring renewal, growth and regeneration and the foremost example of this process is found in the exemplary life of Osiris.

As a final example of the symbolic potential of the *ankh,* the phrase below, *di ankh,* means 'given life.'[136] The first sign was discussed in detail in the previous chapter; it refers to the hieroglyph *soped* and to the star Sirius. The phrase suggests that our experience of life-energy, particularly our ability to convey its properties and blessings to others, is fundamentally connected with the energetic and initiatory exchange we are able to receive from Sirius.

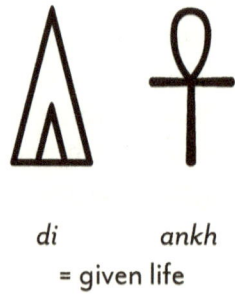

di   ankh
= given life

To the ancient Egyptians the concept of 'life' was profound and all-embracing. Indeed, the study of Life and 'the meaning of Life' constituted the very purpose of the schools of magical training known as *per ankh:* the House of Life. The hieroglyph for these schools combines the *ankh* with *per,* the house:[137]

per ankh = the House of Life

There were many Houses of Life in ancient Egypt and most if not all were attached to the temples. They formed an integral part of the temple's work and ensured that the serving priests received the necessary tuition in the skills needed to maintain the standards of the magical and spiritual work within the temple. The range of subjects studied within the House of Life was all-encompassing;

literally every aspect of life that is implied in the symbolism of the *ankh* was taught there. The knowledge of life after death and the reality of the Inner worlds was central to their teaching, not just in regard to the deceased's experience of the after-life but in the experience of living initiates of the Mysteries as they sought full knowledge and expression of their own Self.

Although little information as to the precise methods and techniques used by these schools has survived, the nature of the unseen realities and the means by which the questing soul can reach towards them remains much the same. There must be a thorough knowledge of the forms and principles of the Inner worlds combined with the practice of various techniques that enable the student to enter into those worlds. All of this is undertaken with reverence for the sanctity of the Mysteries and the desire to serve humanity. Central to the Egyptian Mysteries was the individual's ability to make real within themselves the birth, death and rebirth of Osiris who symbolised the principle of regeneration of matter and the raising up of the spirit within the physical body.

A number of references to the work of the House of Life are scattered throughout the ancient texts and many of these were brought together by A.E. Gardiner in his essay *The House of Life*.[138] Several different roles and official positions within the House of Life can be identified, including the frequently used title 'Scribe of the House of Life' which probably refers to the majority of the students or at least to those in their earlier stages of training. There are references to an 'overseer of writing' who, we assume, was in charge of the solemn task of teaching students how to inscribe and understand the significance of the hieroglyphs and their symbolic meaning. The job seems to have been recognised as central within the House, as an additional title refers to the overseer as one "to whom all sacred matters are revealed." An impressive job description!

The knowledge held within the House of Life was closely guarded. It was said of a book contained in it: "Thou shalt not divulge it. He who divulges it dies of a sudden death and an immediate cutting-off. Thou shalt keep very far away from it; by it one lives or dies. It is to be read (only) by a scribe of the workshop whose name is in the House of Life." We can recognise the same requirement for confidentiality in modern schools of magic, although sudden death is not normally prescribed for those who are tempted to indiscretion.

Medicine and healing were an integral part of the work. A fragment of text describes how Rameses II summoned help from a House of Life when his advice had been sought by a foreign envoy who was concerned about the illness of a princess in his native land. Evidently the reputation of the healers of this House had reached beyond Egypt's borders.

The inscriptions on a stele from the Ptolemaic Period record the owner as Ahmose, evidently a busy man who claimed the various titles of "... robing-priest who is in the chamber, *hesek*-priest, dancer, chief lector of Min, shaven-priest, overseer of the desert [i.e. the cemetery], overseer of pure-priests of Sekhmet, priest of Tehuti amid the House of Life."

A useful fragment regarding the nature of the magical training given within the House is mentioned in connection with Nakhthorheb who was "director of the masters of *hekA* in the House of Life." *HekA* is central to Egyptian magical thought, and although a difficult word to translate exactly, it can be thought of as the transformational power of sacred words and sounds when they are uttered correctly. The text suggests that these words have the same power when spoken by the living initiate of the Mysteries within a magical ritual: "... you are transfigured by the House of Life, your name is pronounced by the people of the House of Life..."

The House held its own rituals and ceremonies that were separate to the rituals held in the Temple. One of the inscriptions on the Ptolemaic Temple of Horus at Edfu records a procession to the hall of the House of Life where all the ceremonies were performed, including one in which "... the interpretation of the naming is made in the evening time." This suggests a regularly performed ritual which was based on the symbolic and magical meaning of certain words and phrases that had been written and studied that day. The opportunity for practical experience of the magical power of each hieroglyph after it had been mastered in theory must have been very effective.

Various levels of the priesthood are identified, one reference describing how the *wa'eb* priests or 'pure priests' were called upon by the Pharaoh Ptolemy IV who needed their help in identifying the markings that distinguished a sacred ram. There was also the 'robing priest' whose task was presumably to care for the ceremonial robes and to ensure that everyone was correctly attired. Other passages describe how the work of the House of Life involved the establishment of the names of the gods in the Temples, the overseeing of the daily offerings to the gods and ensuring the proper conduct of the festivals. Especial reverence was given to those gods who had particular connection with the work of the House. Tehuti was revered above all, but Isis also played a significant role and an inscription describes her as "… mother of the god, lady of the House of Life…" The god Khnum who was the creator of physical forms, and the goddess of writing, Seshat, are also named as being "foremost of the House of Life."

The drawing on page 137 is taken from a papyrus of the Late or Ptolemaic Period, known as Papyrus Salt 825 after the name of its collector, the early nineteenth century Egyptologist Henry Salt. The papyrus contains liturgical texts and a description of what was presumably the House of Life at Abydos, although the description is more metaphorical than actual, as if describing an envisioned ideal rather than an existing building.

"As for the House of Life, it shall be in Abydos. Build it in four bodies, the inner body being of covered reeds. As for … 'the living one,' he is Osiris, and the four houses are Isis, Nephthys, Horus and Tehuti. … These are the four sides. Geb is its ground and Nut its heaven. The hidden one who rests within it is the Great God. The four outer bodies [i.e. walls] consist of a stone that contains two wings [elsewhere translated as 'jasper'] and its lower part [i.e. its floor] is sand, and its outside has severally four doors, one south, one north, one west and one east. It shall be very hidden and very large. It shall not be known, nor shall it be seen; but the sun shall look upon its mystery. The people who enter into it are the staff of Re ['the sun's librarians'] and the scribes of the House of Life." [The manuscripts within the House of Life were known as the *ba* or soul of the sun god Re, hence the reference to 'the Sun's librarians.'][139]

To elaborate on this a little: the text describes a complex of four buildings arranged about a central fifth, each building dedicated to one of the named deities and each oriented to a cardinal direction while remaining under the overall jurisdiction of Osiris at the centre. This pattern of four quarters arranged about a central focus is frequently found in Western magical systems but, as mentioned previously, is rarely seen in ancient Egyptian temples and generally speaking this pattern was not part of Egyptian magical thought. The only other surviving ground-plan of a House of Life (from Armana) does not conform to this pattern, and the design outlined in the Salt Papyrus may have been a Late Period innovation. The illustration does not precisely depict the four-fold arrangement described in the text, and the statement that the House was very large yet hidden, unknown and unseen except by the sun, suggests that the text may relate to the structure of the teaching rather than to the buildings themselves. We might perhaps think of this structure as a graduated system of learning, each level coming under the aegis of one of the gods.

When we compare the written description with the diagram, some interesting details emerge. At the centre is the mummified form of Osiris holding the *uas* sceptre and facing an *ankh*. He is standing on the hieroglyph of the Nine Bows which represents the enemies of Egypt, both native enemies and those from foreign lands. He stands at the centre of a rectangle, around which eight hieroglyphs have been drawn. The rectangle is contained within a square, about which are placed four additional hieroglyphs.

If we look at the hieroglyphs immediately surrounding Osiris, in the top left hand corner we see an ibis on a standard which is easily identifiable as the emblem of Tehuti, the tutelary deity of the House of Life. [140] It is reproduced below:

The Sacred ibis: emblem of Tehuti

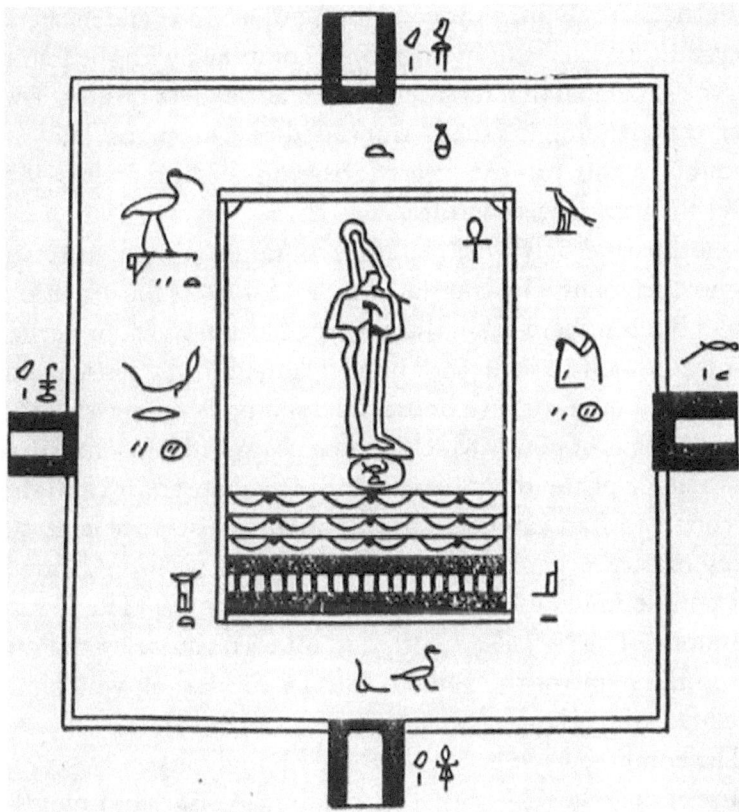

The temple of Osiris in the House of Life at Abydos

In the lower left hand corner is the hieroglyphic emblem of the goddess Nephthys.[141]

nbt hwt = *nebet hwt*, Nephthys

The emblem of the goddess Nephthys is a composite image of three hieroglyphs and serves to provide a useful indication of the attributes and qualities she represents. The large semi-circle at the top of the hieroglyph, *nb* or *neb*, represents a basket and means 'any, every, all.' [142] When this hieroglyph is combined with the feminine '*t*' of the small loaf that is placed just underneath to create the word *nebet*, the meaning is usually translated as 'Queen' or 'lady of all' although in this context refers to the universal female principle rather than to an earthly ruler.

The third hieroglyph is a rectangle containing a smaller rectangle, a sign which is usually translated as 'mansion.' It illustrates either a small building set within the corner of a courtyard, or perhaps a door leading into a courtyard or enclosure, but the sense in either case is of a 'house within a house.' The symbolism suggests a sacred centre, a focus of power which retains its own identity irrespective of its size or of the building in which it is housed. It can refer to the concept of an extended family, an administrative centre or a representative organisation, a term such as we would now use for example in 'The House of Plantagenet' or the 'The House of Commons.' The sign also referred to mines or quarries and can be seen in the name of the goddess *hwt hor* or Hathor, which means 'The Mansion of Horus.'

The combined symbolism of these hieroglyphs creates a useful picture of the role of Nephthys within the Egyptian cosmology. She represents the receptive stillness of the feminine creative principle which is the potential substance of all living things. The qualities of this principle – the polar opposite to the active, positive, directed energy of the masculine principle – are contacted and sustained within a sacred centre or by a dedicated group of priests within the temple.

Returning to the diagram, the hieroglyph at the lower right hand corner of the rectangle is that of the throne.[143]

st = the throne

This hieroglyph is the principle element in the names of *Aset*/Isis and *Ausar*/Osiris, although because Osiris is represented at the centre of the House of Life diagram we can assume that in this instance it refers to Isis. The meaning of the hieroglyph is 'place' or 'seat' and it indicates the presence of the god or goddess – who may appear for example in the form of a statue through which a living contact can be made. The hieroglyph of the throne is also used in words which refer to a state of being, such as a state of divinity or a state of purity in which an individual has 'become' that quality to the point where they are completely identified with it.

In the top right hand corner is another hieroglyph of a bird, rather sketchily drawn. The only remaining divinity associated with the four 'houses' is Horus, so by process of elimination we can assume that it represents the falcon-god Horus whose emblem is shown below.[144]

hr = the Horus falcon

The text describes two other temples: 'Geb is its ground and Nut its heaven.' Geb is the earth-god and the hieroglyphic emblem at the base of the rectangle is probably that of the White-fronted goose which was associated with Geb. [145]

gb = Geb, the earth-god

Of the six deities named in the text this leaves only Nut, who must therefore be indicated by the hieroglyph immediately above the figure of Osiris. Unfortunately the hieroglyph in the diagram is not clear; it looks like one of the signs for a loaf of offering (Gardiner X2) and does not resemble any of the hieroglyphs that spell Nut's name, which is usually written as shown below: [146]

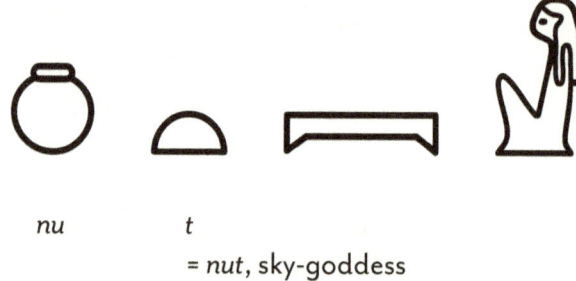

nu   t

= *nut*, sky-goddess

Nu, the vessel of the primeval waters, is followed by the feminine '*t*' and two determinatives of *pet*, the sky, and the seated female deity.

Two further groups of hieroglyphs are placed about the rectangle. To the left, between the emblems of Tehuti and Nephthys, are the following hieroglyphs: [147]

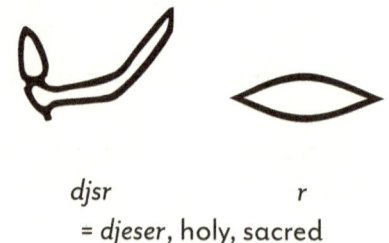

djsr   r

= *djeser*, holy, sacred

The word *djeser* is formed of the hieroglyph of an arm brandishing a mace-head, followed by the sound complement of the mouth. The word means 'holy' and 'sacred' and refers to a consecrated place that has been created by the ritual use of the mace-head to clear the area of unwanted influences. The hieroglyph of the mouth indicates that the ritual action has been achieved with the utterance of appropriate words of magical power.

Djeser is followed by a hieroglyph which is probably the sign associated with Nekhen or Hierakonpolis, the religious and political predynastic capital of Upper (southern) Egypt that was the centre of worship of an early hawk deity, Horus of Nekhen. Interestingly, the word can also refer to jasper, or to a shrine, both of which are mentioned in the text. [148]

nekhen = the ancient capital of Upper Egypt, jasper, a shrine

On the right of the central rectangle is a depiction of what is probably the hieroglyph shown below, although it is not clearly drawn. [149]

wab = to purify, to serve as a priest

This sign combines three separate hieroglyphs to produce something that looks quite odd to modern perception. The hieroglyph of the leg and foot we have seen before; it means 'to place.' Water is flowing from an urn or vase which hints at the hieroglyph *nw*, the primeval waters. The symbolic meaning pertains to the function of the *wab* priest which was to make real and bring about within himself and others the inward condition, or state of being, of purity. This hieroglyph complements *djeser*, the holy place, on the other side of the diagram.

Finally, four hieroglyphs are placed around the outer edge of the diagram to indicate the cardinal directions. The ancient Egyptians oriented themselves by facing south towards the source of the Nile and the direction of the sun at its greatest height. This means, for example, that the hieroglyph *imenet* which represents West also means 'the right-hand side' and the hieroglyph *iAby*,

East, means 'the left-hand side.' In the diagram of the House of Life, West is positioned at the top and the other directions are arranged accordingly. ¹⁵⁰

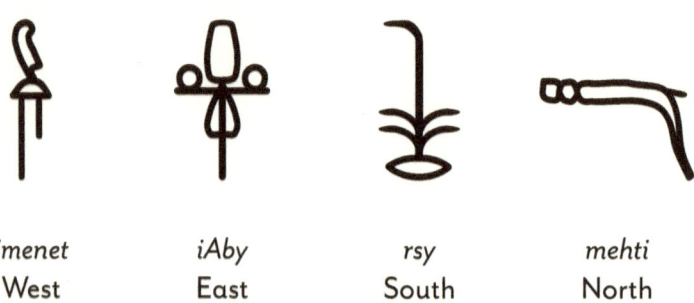

| imenet | iAby | rsy | mehti |
| West | East | South | North |

As we have mentioned before, there was no real equivalent in ancient Egyptian magic of the highly developed system of attributions and correspondences associated with the cardinal directions that is prevalent in modern Western magic, and these hieroglyphs for West, East and South do not convey much information. *Imenet*, West, consists of an ostrich feather perched on the hieroglyph of a folded cloth (*seneb*: health)¹⁵¹ and is a simplified version of an earlier emblem that also included a falcon. *Iaby*, East, shows a spear ceremonially 'decked out' and resting against a standard. *Rsy*, South, is the *swt* or *sut* plant, a type of flowering sedge associated with the kingship of Upper Egypt, which is shown as if growing out of the hieroglyph of a mouth. It is difficult to know what to make of this although it might have indicated the concept of giving voice to the qualities (of kingship) associated with Upper Egypt.

However, the final hieroglyph – *mehti*, North – a rope coiled around a stick or pole, is full of symbolic meaning. The direction of North predominated in ancient Egypt, and just as the waters of the Nile flow steadily towards the North so the movement of each individual life was perceived to 'flow' northwards towards the circumpolar stars that represented spiritual transfiguration. The symbolism of this hieroglyph is of a gradual coming together of two opposites: the moving, circling, spiralling length of cord, and the fixed pole. We can think of the stick as a symbol of the axis of the Earth and the rope as the 'string' of our lives which, as we evolve, gradually becomes aligned with that axis. It symbolises the alignment that we each make between our everyday personalities and the shining light of our spirit. It is interesting that the hieroglyph *meh* combined with the determinative of the roll of papyrus means 'to be full, complete, made whole, finished.'[152]

meh = to be full, complete, made whole

Here is the completeness that is achieved when the questing soul reaches the northern circumpolar stars, whether this is attained after death or through spiritual and magical achievement during life. The same idea is confirmed by the inclusion of *meh* in a word that describes the wholeness of the healed eye of Horus.[153] *Mehet*, shown below, makes an interesting connection that is often overlooked: that of the complex myth of the wounding and healing of the eye of Horus and the direction of North.

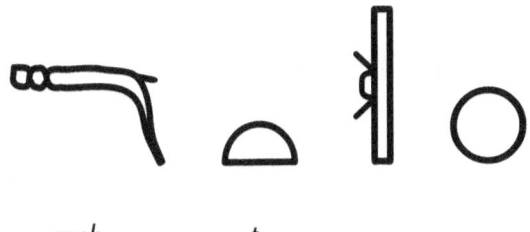

meh   *t*
= *mehet*, the completed or healed eye of Horus

The Eye of Horus is a fascinating hieroglyph in itself, and an exploration of its symbolism will be found in Chapter Nine.

To return to the *ankh* and the House of Life, what have we learnt of their meaning? The range of teaching and experience in the House of Life suggests that it encompassed every aspect of 'life,' of all things present, past and in the world to come. Life is All, Life is One. "... there exists in our manifested universe the expression of an Energy or Life which is the responsible cause of the diverse forms and the vast hierarchy of sentient beings who compose the sum total of all that is ... One life pervades all forms and those forms are the expressions, in time and space, of the central universal energy. Life in manifestation produces existence and being." [154]

Endnotes

124 *ankh*, life: Gardiner S34
125 Thomas Inman, *Ancient Pagan and Modern Christian Symbolism* (New York: J. W. Bouton, 1875), 44.
126 *tet*, the Knot of Isis: Gardiner V39
127 A.E. Wallis Budge, 'A Guide to the Third and Fourth Egyptian Rooms,' 32, no. 18; London, The British Museum, 1904
128 Andrew H. Gordon and Calvin W. Schwabe, *The Quick and the Dead: Biomedical Theory in Ancient Egypt* (Leiden: Brill, 2004)
129 Nicholas Buccalo: http://en.wikiversity.org/wiki/Ancient_Egyptian_Monuments_Project
130 Actually 12.98 inches and 8.02 inches
131 *ankh*, a mirror: Gardiner S34, N34
132 *ankh en niwt*, citizen: Gardiner S34, N35, O49
133 *ankhiu*, the dead, the eternally living ones: Gardiner S34, N35, Aa1, Y1
134 *ankh, wdjA, seneb,* life, health, strength: Gardiner S34, U28, S29
135 *ankh*, the Living One, Osiris: Gardiner S34, N35, Aa1, M17, M17
136 *di ankh*, given life: Gardiner X8, S34
137 *per ankh*: The House of Life: Gardiner O1a
138 A. H. Gardiner, 'The House of Life', in *Journal of Egyptian Archaeology* 24 (1) (1938) pages 157-179
139 ibid
    An earlier translation was made by Dr S. Birch, 'Egyptian Magical Text' in *Records of the Past, Being English Translations Of The Assyrian And Egyptian Monuments Published Under Sanction Of The Society Of Biblical Archaeology Volume VI,* 1873

140   the sacred ibis, emblem of Tehuti: Gardiner G26
141   *nebet hwt*, Nephthys: Gardiner O9
142   *neb*, any, every, all: Gardiner V30
143   *st*, the throne of Isis and Osiris: Gardiner Q1
144   *hr*, the Horus falcon: Gardiner G5
145   *geb*, the earth-god: Gardiner G38
146   *nut*, the sky-godess: Gardiner W24, X1, N1, B1
147   *djeser*, holy, sacred: Gardiner D45, D21
148   *nekhen*, the predynastic capital of Upper Egypt, jasper, a shrine: Gardiner O48
149   *wab*, to purify, to serve as a priest: Gardiner D60
150   *imnet*/West; *iAby*/East; *resy*/South; *mehti*/North: Gardiner R14, R15, M24, V22
151   *seneb*, health: Gardiner S29
152   *meh*, to be full, complete, made whole: Gardiner V22, Y1
153   *mehet*, the complete eye of Horus: Gardiner V22, X1, Y1, D12
154   Alice Bailey, *A Treatise on White Magic* (New York: Lucis Publishing Company, reprinted 2005) page 8

The House of the Net

From the House of Life we move to the more specialised work of the House of the Net which was the centre of hieroglyphic teaching in ancient Egypt. Although there were many Houses of Life, so far as we know there was only one House of the Net. It was located in the city of *Unnu,* also called *Khemenu* and Hermopolis, the capital of the fifteenth district or nome which marked the border between Upper and Lower Egypt. The House of the Net was known in Egypt as *hwt ibt* or *hwt ibet* (it is also sometimes written as *het abtit*), and although it was not often referred to, it was probably written in hieroglyphs as follows: [155]

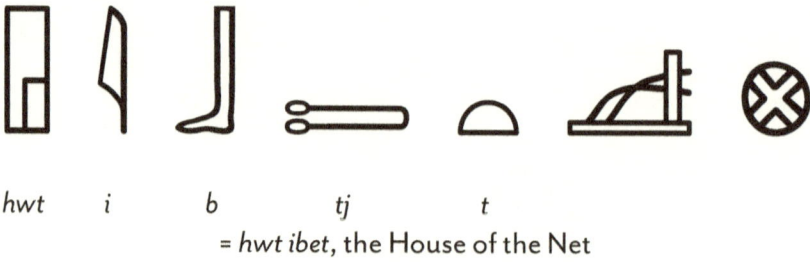

= *hwt ibet*, the House of the Net

We have already encountered most of these hieroglyphs, and their symbolism will by now be familiar. The first sign, *hwt* or 'mansion', was discussed in the previous chapter and indicates a sacred centre or focus of power which retains its identity irrespective of its physical location. The second sign, the flowering reed, has also been seen in many previous words and phrases; it symbolises the marshy borders of the Nile, the area between the river and the desert which represents the state of transition between the outer and Inner worlds. The third sign is the lower leg and foot which means 'to place or position.'

The fourth sign is not often used, so its appearance here is worthy of note. Pronounced as a soft '*t*' or '*dj*,' it represents the rope used to hobble animals by tethering one leg to another and thus restricting their movement. The symbolic meaning is of making a connection or relationship between two things while at the same time restraining them within certain imposed limits. These two concepts are fundamental to the practice of effective magic. First, the participants must be able to perceive and understand the connection between earthly and spiritual things – 'above and below' – and manifest these connections within, for example, a magical ritual. This requires a careful selection of words and invocations ('below') together with the active use of the imagination to create appropriate inner or astral forms which will connect with the 'above' of the spiritual worlds. At the same time, rather than invoking the entire and infinite potential of the universe which would result in an overwhelming diffusion, the law of limitation must be built into the magical work to give it a tightly structured form that limits and focusses the power that has been invoked.

There are two determinatives to *hwt ibet*: the first is the hieroglyph of a fishing net, which means 'to weave.' The second is the hieroglyph for a city which as we have seen previously can represent a group of individuals united by a shared purpose. The combined symbolism of these signs tells us that the House of the Net comprised a distinct group of individuals who had knowledge of the relationship between the earthly and spiritual worlds, of the law of correspondences, and of how effective magical power is achieved through the use of limitation and appropriate form. The hieroglyph of the net suggests a particular focus on the 'woven fabric of light' that forms the etheric body.

There are only a few written references to the House of the Net. One is found on a stele or engraved stone placed on the highest point of Sehel island, a rocky outcrop just to the south of Aswan in the section of the Nile known as the First Cataract. It is generally agreed that the stele was constructed during the reign of Ptolemy V (205-180 B.C.) although the hieroglyphs engraved on its surface refer to events that took place in the reign of the 3rd Dynasty Pharaoh Djoser (c 2560-2575 B.C.) who was responsible for building the Step Pyramid at Saqqara. The hieroglyphs describe how Egypt was afflicted by a famine because Hapi, the god of the Nile, had failed to appear for seven years, or in other words the flood waters of the inundation had not occurred for seven years. Djoser consulted his high priest and asked him to locate the birthplace of Hapi so that he could invoke the god of that place and ask for his help in restoring the inundation. The high priest replied that he would visit the House of the Net at *Unnu* and consult the sacred texts, so that he could be guided by their wisdom. He learnt that the inundation of the Nile was controlled by the god Khnum from Abu island (the modern Elephantine Island at Aswan), so Djoser built a temple to Khnum on the island, and the inundation was restored. The story suggests that the power and reputation of the House of the Net was held in high regard even at this late period and, incidentally, confirms the ancient Egyptian tradition that the symbolic source of the Nile was a cavern beneath the island of Abu.

The location of the House of the Net at *Unnu* was not a coincidence. One of the distinctive characteristics of the ancient Egyptian religion was that several major cities up and down the Nile appear to have promoted entirely different and apparently rival cosmologies, each with its own unique creation myth and family of deities. But in fact each was a part of the whole, each city focussing on a different stage of the complete and entire creative process. In the north of Egypt, in the city of *Iwnw* or Heliopolis, the deities of the Ennead who have now become the most familiar 'family' of the Egyptian pantheon were all descendants of the one god Atum, the creator god. The Ennead was divided into two generations: the remote gods of air and moisture, Shu and Tefnut, and the gods of sky and earth, Nut and Geb. They were followed by the well known figures of Isis, Osiris, Set and Nephthys.

A little to the south in the city of *Men-nefer* or Memphis, the focus of the creation myth was the stage of manifestation that was believed to have taken place before Atum came into being. Atum, it was said, had been brought into life by the god Ptah who was venerated above all for his creative power of mind. Ptah's ability to give creative utterance to thought, images and concepts and to bring them into manifest existence was evident throughout all creation, from the vast forces of the elements to the smallest creatures of the physical world. He was especially revered by craftsmen who, in imitation of the god, had the ability to give form to their creative thoughts.

Further south again, in the city of *Unnu*, the focus of belief was on the stage of creation that took place even before Ptah had created Atum and therefore before anything had come into manifestation. This is the condition that has been called the 'Unmanifest' and is very difficult for us to comprehend.

In *Unnu*, no fewer than eight different aspects of the Unmanifest were recognised, and were symbolised by a group of eight deities often referred to as the Ogdoad. They were Nu (male) and Naunet (female) who represented the formlessness and lack of organisation of the Unmanifest; Amun and Amaunet who represented its hidden and imponderable aspects; Kuk and Kauket who represented its darkness and obscurity (light has not yet come into existence) and Huh and Hauhet who represented its infinite, unending, limitless nature. According to the creation story of *Unnu*, these four pairs of deities eventually came together to produce between them a single egg (or in other versions a lotus) from which the Sun emerged on an island of flames in the form of a Bird of Light.

The city's emphasis on the uncreate realities lies at the root of its teaching and the image of the Bird of Light is appealing, even though it poses the conundrum of which came first, the bird or the egg! Are the eight deities themselves the creators of the egg, or are they the primal substance from which another, different, unidentified agent emerged and created the egg? The myth offers no clues but leaves it to the individual to come to their own understanding. Perhaps this very act of stretching the mind in an attempt to come to terms with such a conundrum formed part of the curriculum in the House of the Net.

The concept of the Unmanifest as 'pure existence' is also expressed in the name for the city and the nome in which it was situated: *Unnu* or *Wenu*, which means 'existence.' The word was written with the hieroglyph of the hare, *wn*, shown below, which was very often combined with the sound complement of the hieroglyph '*n*' that means 'belonging to' and suggests the moving energy that lies behind all things and characterises life. [156]

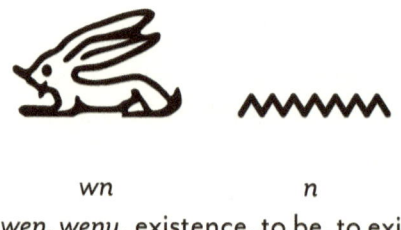

wn   n
= *wen, wenu*, existence, to be, to exist

The hare is the Cape Hare or *Lepus capensis* which is found in many parts of Africa. It is especially noted for its speed, and it can outrun most other animals. These two signs *wn* and *n* were evidently closely related and suggest that for the ancient Egyptians the concept of 'existence' was associated with the idea of movement rather than as something static or inert.

The following word uses the determinative of a pair of moving legs to indicate 'to hasten or hurry,' 'to pass by or pass away.' [157]

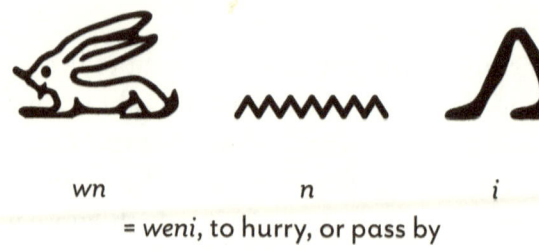

wn   n   i
= *weni*, to hurry, or pass by

The meaning of 'existence' is developed in the following words *wen mAi*, which mean 'true being' and 'reality.' [158]

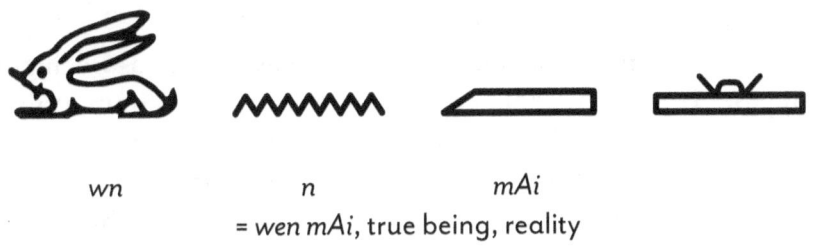

wn   n   mAi
= wen mAi, true being, reality

The third hieroglyph in *mAi* is rarely seen and has not been conclusively identified, although is usually said to represent a platform or plinth. Its symbolic meaning is 'truth,' deriving perhaps from the concept of a solid foundation, or a stable basis which, although sometimes insignificant in itself, is the bedrock upon which we build our understanding of how things are. Our concept of 'true reality' changes many times during our lives, yet somehow our intuitive sense that we do know what is real, proves sufficient for the moment.

This hieroglyph is an important element in the word *mAit* or Maat, the name of the goddess of truth and rightness whose title is shown below: [159]

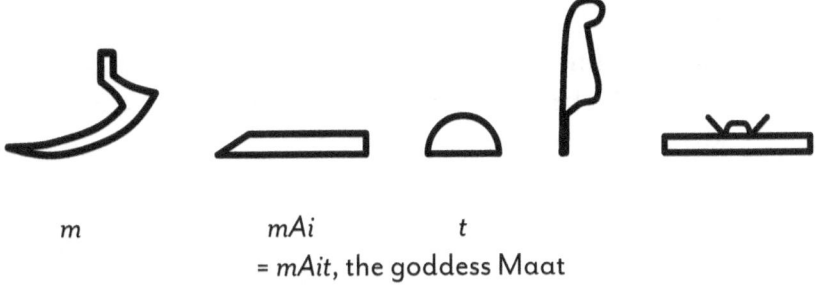

m   mAi   t
= mAit, the goddess Maat

Returning to the hieroglyph of the hare, a number of world mythologies associate the hare with the moon in the belief that the shape of a hare can be seen in the moon's markings. A myth widespread across Africa links the hare, the moon and the notion of immortality. The story tells how the moon wanted humanity to be immortal, and sent a hare to convey the message to humankind that just as the moon appears to die but rises again, so will humanity.

Unfortunately the hare got the message wrong, and the story he repeated was that just as the moon dies, so will humanity – and from then on this became true.

The meaning of the tale however is not as obvious as we might suppose. It poses a riddle concerning the nature of immortality and the relationship between what we believe to be real – or what we believe to constitute 'existence' – and what is 'really real.' At the time when the moon sent the message to earth, was humanity mortal or immortal? If mortal, then its condition was not changed by the hare's wrongly delivered message. If immortal, then the moon had no need to send the message that it would become immortal. The message seems to be that neither the hare nor the moon were responsible for humanity's mortality; it was humanity's *belief* that they had become mortal beings – because they had been told that this was so – that was responsible for their (apparent) loss of immortality. Perhaps we should not think in terms of *either* mortal *or* immortal; in many systems of esoteric thought the moon represents the etheric level of creation which precedes that of the earth plane of physical matter and is correlated with the 'body of light' or 'etheric double' which contains the perfect, immortal, living template of the physical body. Either way, the hare's message invites us to ponder what we understand to constitute our own 'existence.'

Humanity's immortality of spirit, if not of body, is represented in the story of the life, death and rebirth of Osiris, one of whose names, *wen-nefer*, links him to the hare. [160]

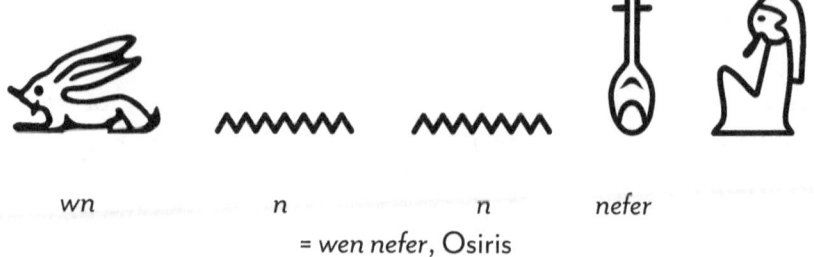

wn   n   n   nefer

= *wen nefer*, Osiris

The symbolic meaning of the hare is developed further through its association with Osiris. Hares (and rabbits) are exceptionally fecund; they can mate before they are a year old and the female produces up to four litters a year in a remarkable demonstration of regeneration in practice! The third hieroglyph represents the trachea and windpipe which, strange to our eyes, symbolises goodness, beauty and eternal youth with the implied sense that this goodness and youth derive from the perfection of the original creative impulse.[161] The final hieroglyph is the determinative for 'god.'

The symbolism of *wen nefer* develops our understanding of 'existence' by its association with the qualities of goodness and beauty that are an expression of the divine. Osiris embodies 'in truth' these divine qualities, and we can learn how to embody them ourselves through his mediation and example.

Wen is also used in words that describe the temple priests and priestly activities such as star-watching, time-keeping, service and duty, indicating that knowledge and awareness of the Unmanifest and the mediation of this remote source of creation was one of the especial roles of the priesthood, particularly for those working in the city of Unnu. The word *wenwt* or *unnut* means 'priesthood,'[162]

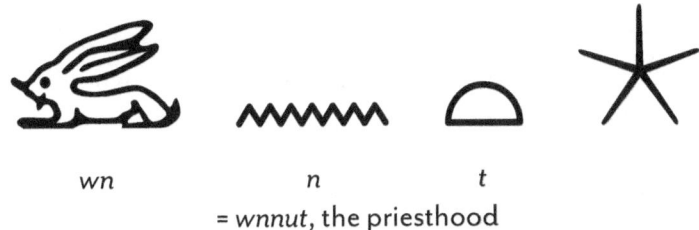

while the same group of signs with the addition of the hieroglyph of the water-pot that symbolises the primeval waters of the abyss, means 'duty' and 'service.'[163]

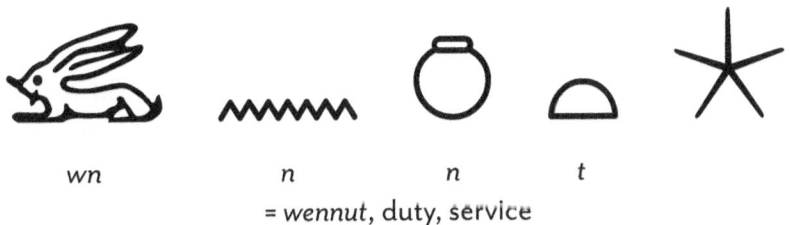

"I desire to know in order to serve" is the promise made by initiates of the Mysteries who vow that their search for the hidden wisdom and potential power of the unseen worlds will be used only for the greater good and not for their personal aggrandisement. The hieroglyphs suggest that this knowledge reaches back to the unknowable, inexpressible qualities of the Unmanifest as the ultimate source of all. When such knowledge has been attained and is given earthly expression, as was achieved in the life, death and rebirth of Osiris, this ultimate source of regeneration and renewal has been made real.

The name of the city of Unnu was written as follows: [164]

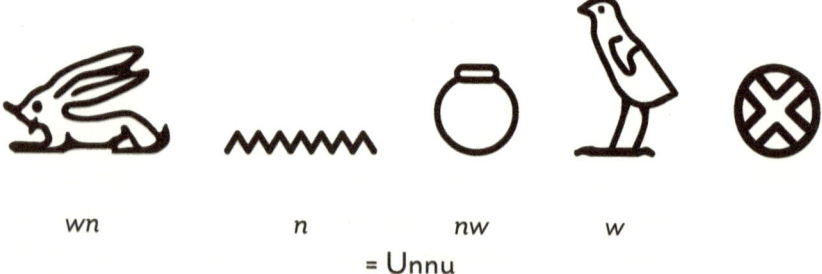

wn   n   nw   w

= Unnu

Here, the hieroglyph of the quail chick is used as a sound complement. If all the signs were pronounced they would produce something like '*wn-n-nw-w*' and there is surely significance in these soft, repeated sounds.

The work of the House of the Net was concerned with the connectedness of all aspects of existence: with the woven network of light that comprises the etheric body, with the shapes and forms of the astral plane, with the nature of the Unmanifest and its continued qualification of our earthly life, and especially with our own individual understanding of these Inner planes and forms. What is real? What is illusion? What really exists? How do we know the difference?

The journey through the 'net of illusion' is described in 'The Spell of the Net' that appears in chapters 153a and 154b of the Book of the Dead.[165] These two chapters tell how the deceased – or the magical initiates in their spiritual journey towards enlightenment –

arrive at the shore of the Milky Way, the celestial equivalent of the River Nile. Their challenge at this point is to demonstrate that they are able to distinguish between the outer world of appearances and the Inner worlds of qualities, principles and causes. The image presented to the aspirant is of a vast net which hangs between the earth and the sky, a symbol of the woven interconnectedness of all things. At the same time, however, it is a snare in which the attractive but illusory astral images of the Inner worlds can on the one hand be mistaken for the desirable things of the physical world, or on the other hand can be awarded a high spiritual status that they do not possess.

Those confronting this mysterious net must avoid becoming trapped; they must fly free from it like a bird escaping a snare. This is done by correctly describing each part of the net in mundane terms while at the same time demonstrating an awareness of its symbolic meaning – in other words, by proving the ability to distinguish between the outer appearance and the inner qualities of each constituent part of the net.

There are several available translations of the Book of the Dead, notably those by E.A. Wallis Budge which was originally published in 1909, and the more recent translations by Thomas Allen and Raymond Faulkner. These provide an accurate word for word translation, although the overall result can at times be somewhat cryptic and lacking in magical power. The 'spells' or 'utterances' of the Book of the Dead were intended to be given voice and would originally have been pronounced with powerful intonation, but most translations come across as rather pedestrian when read aloud. The exception is the inspiring but freely poetic interpretation by Normandi Ellis, which makes no claim to be an accurate word for word translation but nonetheless captures the spirit of the text.[166] The following translated excerpts from the Book of the Dead are an attempt to present the text in modern English while adhering fairly closely to the original.

The various stages of The Spell of the Net are presented in three sections, and we will take each in turn. The first few lines set out the nature of the challenge that confronts the questing soul who has arrived at the bank of the celestial river, the Milky Way.

Hail, oh thou God who looks backwards, you who have achieved power in your heart. You stand like a fisherman on the bank of the celestial river, to hold open the pathway between the worlds during the dance of the earth.

Oh you fishermen who travel through the astral waters, your nets might catch the wanderers and the earthbound, but you will not catch me. The weights of your net rest upon the earth and its floats are suspended in the sky, but I have flown free from it like a bird.

The 'God who looks backwards' is a reference to the constellation *sAh,* Orion, the stellar counterpart of Osiris. On the ceiling paintings in the temple of Denderah he can be seen sailing through the stars in his boat while turning to look back down over his shoulder towards the star Sirius, which rises above the horizon a little later. Osiris has achieved 'power in his heart' or mastery of his heart because he is the foremost example of one who has passed the test of the Weighing of the Heart. In this stage of the funeral rites, the heart of the deceased is symbolically weighed against the feather of the goddess Maat in order to assess its condition of truthfulness and light. Osiris/Orion presides over this stage of the soul's journey, holding open the pathway across the celestial waters that will take the initiate from the physical into the spiritual worlds.

The fishermen play an important role in this stage of the journey. The hieroglyph for 'fisherman' and 'fowler' is shown below, and interestingly the same hieroglyph also means 'to investigate.' [167]

wha = fisherman, fowler, to investigate

The sign portrays a boat with a high, curved prow and stern, and contains a pile of fishing nets. The symbolic meaning relates to the investigative skills of the fishermen and fowlers who carefully explore the waters and who, rather than casting their nets indiscriminately, have learnt how to make informed decisions about what to catch and what to leave. The same idea is also illustrated by the following group of hieroglyphs, which means 'to release,' 'to loosen fetters' and 'to return (home).' [168]

wha = to release, to loosen fetters, to return (home)

Only the first hieroglyph is pronounced. The hand and forearm means 'to give' 'to grant, permit or cause,' and the small spiral depicts a coil of rope which indicates 'to encircle or surround.' This is another of those evocative groups of hieroglyphs whose symbolism conveys a depth of meaning that can hardly be described in modern words. The fishermen and fowlers who stand on the far side of the river – and their name can be read in this context as a type of esoteric title – have demonstrated their ability to look into the astral waters and discriminate between reality and illusion. They are qualified to act both as guides and testers of those who are waiting to cross the river, although we must not assume that it is their deliberate intention to ensnare those who are still 'wanderers' or 'earth-bound.' There is no question as to the intentions of Orion who, also seen here, is the 'Fisher of Men' amongst the fishermen, and guides the seeker across the river and safely onto the path that lies on the other side.

The nets of the fishermen cover the whole of the astral plane between the earth and the heavenly river of stars: their weights rest on the physical world but their floats are drifting in the celestial waters. The same challenge of distinguishing reality from illusion applies to each successive plane of the Inner worlds: that which may appear as reality on one plane is revealed as illusion when viewed from a higher perspective.

The next stage for the questing soul is to demonstrate that they can name each part of the net and describe the symbolic purpose that lies behind its appearance, or in other words to demonstrate an understanding of the function of magical symbols.

> *I know that it is the hand of Re which holds the net.*
> *I know the name of the reel which pulls the mouth of the net tight: it is the finger of Osiris.*
> *I know the name of the wooden valve: it is the hand of Isis.*
> *I know the name of the knife which comes with the net: it is the knife which Isis used to cut the umbilical cord of Horus.*
> *I know the name of the fibres of the net: they are the sinews of Atum.*
> *I know the nature of the weights: they are made of iron from the sky.*
> *I know the nature of the floats: they are the feathers of the falcon.*
> *I know the name of the hill on which the gods stand and where the net is pulled tight: it is the Temple of the Moon.*
> *I know the name of he who receives the fish: he is the Servant of the Gods.*
> *I know the name of the table on which he places the fish: it is the table of Horus. He sits at the table but cannot be seen; he sits alone in the darkness.*

Initially, each part of the net is identified as part of the body of one of the gods: Re, Osiris, Isis, Horus, Atum. Here is expressed the idea that although the gods and goddesses are customarily depicted in human form they are in fact representations of universal powers and principles. However, their bodies of light can easily be visualised when we realise how these principles inform and inspire the things of the world. The net is held, metaphorically, in the hand of the sun god Re whose physical body is the visible solar system.

Another important part of the process of 'escaping' the net is to become aware of the links that exist between the particular function of each part of the net and the universal principles represented by the bodies of the gods. For example, the reel which tightens the net is equated with the finger of Osiris. The image here is of the gradual bringing together of the fibres of the net so that the spaces between them decrease in size; this is the process by which the insubstantial network which at first appears to be suspended between heaven and earth gradually takes on denser form until it becomes what we recognise as physical matter.

The wooden valve is identified as the hand of Isis. The valve is the means by which the flow in and out of the net can be controlled, so that fish which swim into the net cannot then return to the river. If you are a fish, the process is not a voluntary one! But for the questing soul the experience is of being drawn by the power of Isis into the spiritual worlds and into a growing awareness of their reality. When we have experienced the vibrant realities of the heavenly worlds we cannot 'return', because the outer world does not now appear to us as it did before our contact with the worlds of spirit. The analogy is extended in the next image: the knife that accompanies the net is the knife that Isis used to cut the umbilical cord of Horus. The closed net now becomes a symbol of the womb of Isis from which the initiate will symbolically be reborn as a child of the universe.

The next analogy likens the individual fibres of the net to the sinews or tendons of Atum. Atum or Atem was the first creator god in the Heliopolitan creation myth. The *tem* element of his name indicates 'finished, complete' and he can therefore be understood as the First and the Last, the One God from whom the entire cosmos emerged and to whom all will eventually return. In human and animal bodies the sinews connect the muscles to the bones, which makes the analogy between the net and sinews particularly apt. Sinew is a perfect fibre for net-making; it is strong, elastic, contains natural glues and shrinks when it dries, thus obviating the need for knots. Sinews store, release and recover energy efficiently, and it is their ability to contract which moves our muscles, which in turn move our bones. They are therefore the means by which impulses in the brain are translated into action in the physical world and are a remarkable symbol of how energy becomes action in the world through human consciousness and the human body. We can only marvel again at the knowledge possessed by the ancient Egyptians and their ability to perceive its symbolic potential.

Next are the weights and floats of the net, the weights symbolically resting on the earth while the floats drift in the astral waters. The "iron from the sky" is likely to be meteoric iron – iron ore was not smelted in ancient Egypt until 600 B.C. The floats of the net are identified as the feathers of the falcon, a reference to the falcon-god Horus.

This brings us to the Temple of the Moon. The next phrase refers to a 'Servant of the Gods' who receives and gathers up the 'fish' (the deceased or the spiritual seekers) who have not escaped the net, and presents them to Horus. Bearing in mind that the task of the questing soul is to avoid becoming ensnared in the net, these phrases seem to run counter to the idea that we must fly free of the net if we are to progress through the spiritual worlds, perhaps suggesting that even this belief is itself another illusion. But the masterstroke of the 'spell' is revealed here as the net itself is finally realised to be a tool by which we can ascend the spiritual planes, step by step, until we reach our destination. We may become ensnared at some point in our journey but, through the compassion of those who guide us from the spiritual realms we will eventually find our way to Horus.

The god is described as sitting alone at a table in the darkness. Perhaps this is the subjective impression of those who have been guided towards him whether they will or no, rather than having made their own way to his table. The point to keep in mind at this stage is that although our beliefs and assumptions about the nature of the spiritual worlds may be quite wrong, we will eventually reach our destination by one means or another.

This brief passage provides an interesting anticipation of the role played by the mysterious Fisher King in the Arthurian and Grail legends. The late 12th/early 13th century poet Robert de Boron, in his poems *Joseph d'Arimathe* and *Merlin*, describes how the Fisher King is part of a group of chosen companions who, after the crucifixion of Christ, accompany Joseph of Arimathea on his journey from the Holy Land to Avalon in Britain. During their journey, Joseph makes a table in commemoration of the table of the Last Supper, upon which he places a sacred chalice, later called the Grail, in which he has collected the blood of Christ at the crucifixion. The Fisher King places a fish next to the Grail, and although Boron does not offer an explanation of this mysterious character, he creates the impression that the Fisher King represents a sacred or magical tradition so ancient that its origins had either been forgotten or were considered too secret to disclose. In this context, Christ's epithet 'fisher of men' also comes to mind. The analogy between 'souls' and 'fishes' is not one that naturally comes to mind, so when this association is found in two esoteric contexts it may indicate a continuing thread of the Mystery tradition. We might go so far as to identify Horus as the first Fisher King, and although his function in the Spell of the Net is not elaborated he appears to play an enlightening and redemptive role for those who have found their way to him.

Having arrived in the presence of Horus, the questing soul is now able to say with confidence: "Here I am; I have come!"

I have come! I stand as a fisherman with my own net and reel, and with my own knife in my hand. I am able to find my way through the astral waters. I descended to the earth in the two great boats and have lived and ruled my life like Osiris. But now I have risen to take my place in the sun-boat of Re.

He triumphantly carries the net as an indication of progress achieved, a badge of recognition, and as a symbol that will help those who follow him along the same path. All those who have reached this stage are capable of making their own 'net.' They have demonstrated their ability to distinguish between reality and illusion and are able to use the reel and knife as magical tools, having control over the qualities they represent. The initiate pauses to recall the journey of descent into the earthly plane and a life that was lived in the spirit of Osiris. But now comes a new freedom and the ability to ascend to the higher spiritual worlds, embodying and radiating to others the life and light of the sun.

The next words are spoken to Horus and there is much symbolism behind them.

I have eaten the same food that has been brought to you. I too have brought you this food, and I too have eaten of it. It is the same food that Geb ate with Osiris.

Empowered to move through the astral waters without illusion, the initiate has now himself become a fisher of souls and takes on the responsibility of gathering up the 'fish' and placing them before Horus. The fish are 'consumed' by Horus and by the initiate. We are told that this food is identical to that which the god Geb consumed with Osiris, although the actual substance of the food and what it symbolises demands careful thought.

Geb is the god of the earth. The ancient Egyptians regarded the earth as male, thus retaining an essential element of polarity with the goddess of the sky, Nut. Geb represents the solidity of matter; he symbolises the earthly throne which supported Osiris as the first king of Egypt, and he was said to have been responsible for passing the rulership of the earth to Osiris. Even when describing the highest spiritual matters, the ancient Egyptian approach was always to connect them with earthly things. The relationship between Osiris (and by corollary all those who attempt to live their lives according to his example) and Geb is one of mutual exchange, in which the life and experience of one contributes to the life and experience of the other.

Geb is responsible for what is sometimes called the initiation of the nadir, the point at which each individual, having descended the planes into matter, realises the actual nature of that matter. This is a vital stage in the spiritual journey because until this realisation is made, the evolutionary journey of return to spirit cannot begin. The paradox is that this realisation is only achieved through a complete engagement with matter; in other words, you can't give something up until you have had it, or taken it in, or 'eaten' it. The food that Geb ate with Osiris and which the initiate now eats with Horus is undertaken as a ritual meal, a magical and transformational experience which symbolises a complete and final release from the limitations and imprisonment of matter. The metaphor applies equally to all levels of creation and, as the questing soul now realises: "I am sustained by the energy that sustains the gods." From here, there is no turning back.

My soul shines like the sun god Re. I take my seat in his boat as it travels across the sky and each day I am born into my own Being. My soul does not die but travels across the great sea to the northern sky. I am sustained by the energy that sustains the gods.

Endnotes

155 *hwt ibet*, the House of the Net: Gardiner O6, M17, D58, V13, X1, T26, O49
See Patrick Boylan, *Thoth or the Hermes of Egypt*, 1922, reprinted by Kessinger Publishing, Whitefish, Montana, page 152
156 *wen*, existence, to be, to exist, Gardiner E34, N35
157 *weni*, to hurry or hasten, to pass by or pass on: Gardiner E34, N35, D54
158 *wen mAi*, true being, reality: Gardiner E34, N35, Aa11, Y1
159 *mAit*, Maat, the goddess of truth: Gardiner U2, Aa1, D36, X1, H6, Y1
160 *wen-nefer*, a name of Osiris: Gardiner E34, N35, N35, F35, A40
161 The hieroglyph *nefer* is discussed more fully in Chapter Eleven
162 *wennut*, the priesthood (of Unnu): Gardiner E34, N35, X1, N14
163 *wennut*, duty, service: Gardiner E34, N35, W24, X1, N14
164 *wenw*, Unnu: Gardiner E34, N35, W24, G43, O49
165 The Spell of the Net is also found in Utterances 473-481 of the Coffin Texts
166 trans. Normandi Ellis, *Awakening Osiris: The Egyptian Book of the Dead* (Grand Rapids, MI, Phanes Press, 1988)
167 *wha*, fisherman, fowler, to investigate: Gardiner P4
168 *wha*, to release, to loosen, to return (home): Gardiner P4, D36, V1, D36

The Eye of Horus

The *wedjAt* eye or Eye of Horus is a widely recognised symbol, and has much in common with the image found in many cultures of an all-seeing eye or Eye of Providence that represents the power of the Supreme Being. The hieroglyph of the Eye of Horus is still frequently used in Egypt, often painted in bright colours on the prow of the feluccas, the tall-masted sailing boats so skilfully navigated along the Nile. [169]

wdAt = *wedjAt*, the healed or uninjured Eye of Horus

The Eye of Horus was used only as an ideogram and as a determinative, illustrating the healed eye of the falcon god Horus which, according to legend, had been injured or removed by the god Set and was later discovered and restored by Tehuti. The hieroglyph combines three distinct elements: the human eye and eyebrow, the vertical stripe underneath the eye which replicates a distinctive facial feature of the falcon, and the symbol of a spiral which emerges from where the human and falcon eyes conjoin. The eye itself, *ir* or *iret*, also forms a separate hieroglyph. [170]

ir = to do, create or achieve

It means 'to make,' 'to create or beget,' 'to do or construct,' 'to achieve, provide or act.' It represents a positive act of accomplishment, not just the initial idea but something that has been put into action and carried through to a tangible result.

It is worth pausing to consider why the ancient Egyptians considered the eye to be a symbol of 'doing' and achievement. As we now understand the function of the eye, it does not create, but observes what has already been created as a visible object. The creation of something new on the physical plane is brought about through the use of the mind and the body, and when we are able to *see* what we have created we enter into a new relationship with it because we can begin to bridge the gap between subject and object. As a result of this relationship both we, and what we have created, may be changed by the experience. This interaction between subject and object is the basis of the third principle of creation, the development of consciousness or the 'mediating intelligence.'

The 'Observer Effect' has been well documented in scientific thought of recent years, not least in areas such as the 'Heisenbug' of computer programming and the paradox revealed by the Schrödinger's cat thought-experiment. Looking a little further back in time we can find the same idea hinted at in the first Book of Genesis, where on the sixth day of creation "God saw everything that He had made and, behold, it was very good." The creation of the world according to the authors of Genesis was completed at the conclusion of the sixth day, at which point God observed what God had created and a relationship between God and God's creation began. The seventh day of rest therefore represents in cosmic terms the beginning of a new phase of creation.

The hieroglyph of the eye was combined with others in a number of words that describe someone who achieves, constructs or acts, for example in the word below which adds the determinative of a human figure to indicate 'a doer,' someone who gets results and actively causes positive achievement.[171] The implication seems always that the accomplishment is positive and beneficial.

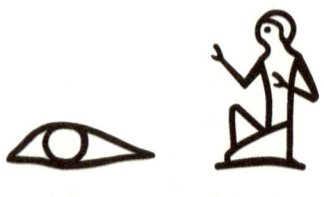

ir = doer (of good)

The following phrase, *ir hemet*, means 'to marry,' 'to take a wife.' [172]

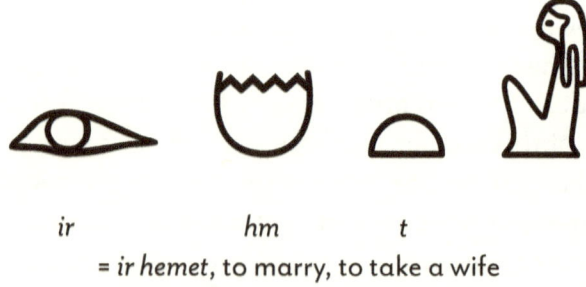

ir   hm   t
= *ir hemet*, to marry, to take a wife

The second hieroglyph *hm* or *hem* indicates a well, a pool or a marsh. It was related to a similar sign that represented the uterus, and it could also refer to copper. The word is completed by the feminine '*t*' and the determinative of the hieroglyph of a woman. The symbolism likens marrying a woman to the creation of a new well, or to mining a precious mineral. The sense is of a deliberate and positive action which causes something to be brought up out of the deep earth into the world (figuratively speaking!) bringing potential into actuality and causing the invisible to become visible. The phrase adds to our understanding of *ir* by suggesting that the act of seeing something not only refers to visible objects but also indicates a far-sighted, intuitive grasp of what is yet to be. The *wedjAt* eye painted on the prows of boats not only offers protection to the boat and its occupants but its power provides the captain with an intuitional insight into the condition of the river ahead and of possible dangers that lie beyond the range of normal sight.

The eye could also be combined with the *ankh*, 'life,' to indicate 'providing' for someone or making provision for them, again with the sense that this is a deliberate and positive act. [173] The symbolic meaning of these two hieroglyphs suggests that rather than being a simple gift, such provision may also consist of 'looking out' for someone by anticipating their future needs and smoothing the way for them.

ir   *ankh*
= to provide for someone

One of the most significant uses of the hieroglyph of the eye is in the name of the god *wsir* or *asir*, more familiarly known by the Greek translation of his name: Osiris.[174]

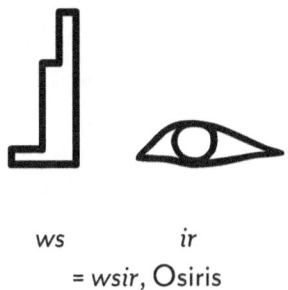

ws   *ir*
= *wsir*, Osiris

The first of these two hieroglyphs is usually said to represent a throne, although it bears little resemblance to any known examples of Egyptian chairs. It may perhaps have evolved from the image of a stepped dais or platform that indicates authority as the hieroglyph can also mean 'state,' 'office' and 'place or position.' Its combination with the hieroglyph of the eye suggests that it is the ability of the individual thus enthroned to bring potential into actuality which constitutes the real power of the throne. Here again is the idea of 'seeing' as a far-reaching act of intuitive perception which is brought through into present actuality by the sovereign, and through the relationship between the Pharaoh, the land and people.

Keeping this symbolism in mind we can move to the second element of the *wedjAt* hieroglyph, the vertical stripe beneath the eye. This is often referred to as a 'teardrop' but in fact is an accurate reproduction of one of the facial markings of the Egyptian *Falco biarmicus* or Lanner falcon. This species of falcon is beautifully illustrated in Egyptian wall paintings as a portrayal of the god Horus. In common with other species of falcon, the Lanner falcon's eye is encircled by a ring of bright yellow which readily becomes a symbol of the 'eye' of the Sun.

This combination of human and avian features is visually appealing, but the underlying symbolism is of an integration between different types or levels of consciousness within the human psyche, and thus of different ways of perceiving and interacting with the forces of the universe. The combination of human and falcon eyes represents the creative power of the sun, its manifestation through the actions and achievements of the Pharaoh, the ability to look ahead and to turn potential into actuality, all of which are desirable qualities in a leader. This is in addition of course to the protective power of the Eye, and to the implied links with the god Horus who was miraculously conceived, and whose all-seeing powers were exemplified by the Pharaoh.

This union of the best of human and falcon qualities is confirmed by the third component of the hieroglyph: the spiral that emerges from where the human and falcon eyes meet. The spiral of the *wedjAt* hieroglyph looks rather like the spiral that emerges from the top of the Red Crown or *deshret* of Lower Egypt. A fine example of this can be seen on the reverse or 'serpopard' side of the Narmer Palette (see page 20). No examples of the *deshret* crown have survived, so we can only speculate on how they were made, although a long curling reed could easily be coaxed into this shape.

We can perceive a spiral either as a curving line which emerges from a central point and travels outwards, or as a curving line which emerges from an infinite distance and progressively turns inwards to a central point into which it is finally subsumed. To those on the spiritual path, both of these movements are often perceived as one and the same: the further out you travel in your consciousness the nearer you reach to the centre of spiritual reality. And many will be familiar with the feeling of seemingly going round in circles but with a dawning awareness that each time the circle is completed it is realised to be a higher turn of the spiral.

Another interpretation of the hieroglyph suggests that it relates to number, time or volume. A widely accepted theory links the Eye to the *heqat*, the ancient Egyptian measurement of grain and beer. Crucial to this theory is the notion that each part of the Eye represents a fraction of one whole, this being demonstrated in the familiar diagram of the division of the Eye of Horus into six component parts, each part representing a numerical value which is half of the previous part. The diagram also reveals the fascinating conundrum that if you add these fractions together they come to 63/64s, not 1.

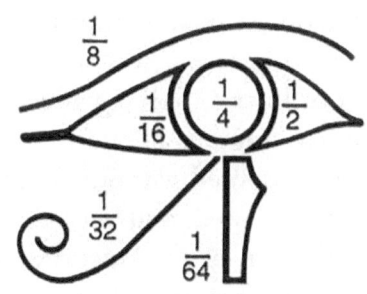

There is much that appeals in this theory. It could be said that the secret of the relationship of the part to the whole is the ultimate Mystery of creation, and if we can comprehend this Mystery then we have in effect 'healed' or 'made whole' the Eye of Horus. If we can see beyond the veil of illusion which represents our belief that everything is separate and disconnected, we realise that ultimately all is part of the One. Through this realisation we ourselves become part of the at-one-ment, and part of the evolutionary process of return to the One. The healing of the Eye thus becomes a metaphor for our own evolution.

The idea makes such good sense on a symbolic and allegorical level that it is unfortunate that there is almost no evidence that the ancient Egyptians actually made this connection between fractional divisions of the *heqat* and the symbol of the Eye of Horus. The idea was first put forward by Georg Möller in 1911, in a study of hieratic script in which he correlated each hieratic sign according to what he considered to be its original hieroglyphic form.[175] His evidence for the Eye of Horus fractions came from only two stone votive cubits dating from the New Kingdom or later. These slender, engraved cubit-long artefacts were sometimes placed in tombs and temples, probably as sacred offerings or for symbolic or ceremonial use. They were usually engraved with hieroglyphs, but Möller found two on which some hieratic signs for fractions appeared in proximity to what seemed to be the hieroglyphic signs for parts of the Eye of Horus. He suggested that this could be taken as evidence that the complete hieroglyph of the (right) Eye of Horus comprised a series of fractions which symbolised the myth of its injury and healing.

His discovery was largely ignored until it was repeated by Gardiner in his *Egyptian Grammar* together with the now familiar diagram of the Eye of Horus fractions, although these were transposed without comment to the left eye. The claim was widely accepted, and was reproduced for many years along with the diagram of the fractions, until 2002 when Jim Ritter in his thoroughly researched article *Closing the Eye of Horus* re-examined the original evidence and concluded, convincingly, that although tantalising, it was tenuous and inconclusive.[176]

Nevertheless, considerable symbolic meaning is ascribed, and with good reason, to the power of the *wedjAt* eye through its association with the story of the injury and healing of the Eye of Horus. Many fragments and variants of this story appear throughout the ancient texts and although it is difficult to discern a single, original narrative behind them, two fairly consistent ideas emerge. First, that Horus is a god of light whose face represents the sky and whose eyes are the sun and the moon; the left eye usually being identified with the moon and the right eye with the sun. Earlier versions of the story tend to focus on the left eye (the moon) which is said to have disappeared, or to have been lost, but is discovered and restored by Tehuti. A close link between the moon and Tehuti is one of the most significant aspects of this god, who at times was almost synonymous with the moon and acknowledged as the representative and interpreter of the moon's powers. Tehuti was not the 'god of the moon' – that was Khonsu, or the earlier Iah – but he was responsible for communicating knowledge and understanding of the moon's properties to humankind. His many titles included such epithets as 'the brightly shining,' 'the silver sun,' 'Lord of Time,' 'Reckoner of Time.' [177]

The hieroglyph of the sacred ibis of Tehuti is shown below, a sign which reveals his function. [178] The sacred ibis is still widespread in sub-Saharan Africa, although it no longer breeds in Egypt.

hb = *heb*, the sacred ibis

The striking appearance of the *Threskiornis aethiopicus* derives from the bold contrast between the black and white areas of its body. Its body is pure white except for some black feathers on its rump, and the black tips to its wings, which are only visible in flight. Its legs are a dense black, as are its bald neck and head, its eyes and beak. The juxtaposition of white and black together with the long curved beak like the crescent moon suggest a correlation between the ibis, Tehuti and the moon. The ancient Egyptians did not consider the moon in the same way as it is regarded in modern Western magic, but viewed it primarily as the governing influence in cyclic patterns of growth and in the measurement of time.

We take for granted the accurate measurement of days, months and years, so it is difficult to imagine what life would be like without access to mechanically accurate clocks and instant verification of the time in any part of the world with a glance at our smartphones. In fact, dividing the solar year into manageable portions is not easy.

Our year of 365.25 days is defined by the earth's passage around the sun, but 365 cannot be divided by any numbers except 5 and 73, neither of which are useful units of measurement. Measuring the passage of time by the moon is a viable alternative, and the notion of a year divided into 13 'months' or moon periods of 28 days is an attractive theory, although unfortunately it doesn't work all that well in practice. The moon orbits the earth to arrive back at the same sidereal position – that is to say the same position when measured in relation to a 'fixed' star – once every 27.32 days. However, because during that time the earth has also progressed in its own orbit around the sun, the moon has to travel a little further before it returns to its original position in relation to the earth, so it actually takes 29.53 days for the moon to complete a full 'lunation' – or in other words, what we perceive as one Full Moon to the next Full Moon. In a complete solar year there are 12 Full Moon cycles with 10.87 days left over – another awkward number. Most calendars are based on the lunar cycle in their division of time into manageable chunks but incorporate a variety of means by which it can be brought into synchronisation with the solar year.

    The ancient Egyptians solved the problem by dividing the year of 365 days into twelve months of thirty days, each month being further divided into three groups of ten days or decans. This makes 360 days, so the year had to be completed with the addition of another five days, the so-called 'Epagomenal' days which were said to have been won by Tehuti from the moon during a game of *senet*. "... playing at draughts with the moon, [Tehuti] won from her the seventieth part of each of her periods of illumination, and from all the winnings he composed five days, and intercalated them as an addition to the three hundred and sixty days. The Egyptians even now call these five days intercalated and celebrate them as the birthdays of the gods." [179] The maths are almost exact: if we take a complete lunation as 29.53 days, divide this number by 70 and multiply by 12 (there are 12 complete lunations in a year), we arrive at 5.06 days, making 365.06 days in a calendar year. This may all seem a little academic, but knowledge of the exact numbers associated with the moon as the chief measurer of time on earth was vital to all ancient civilisations, not least because it created the potential to predict and explain cosmic events such as eclipses of the sun and moon, an ability which seems to be featured in the earlier stories of the disappearance, discovery and return of the Eye of Horus.

Later versions of the story tend to emphasise the right eye of the sun, or refer to both eyes which are said to have been injured or removed by the god Set. The right eye is described in terms of fire and light; it is said to have come into being "... in the flame of the sunshine ..." [180] These later variants bring the story closer to earth and describe the conflict between Horus and Set in terms of two brothers fighting for the inheritance of their father Osiris's throne, rather than as opposing gods or as cosmic principles. The conflict, though, is clearly symbolic of cosmic forces in a relationship of polarity, and depicts the same balance of opposites that we have seen demonstrated throughout Egyptian magical thought. Tehuti remains a vital figure in the story because he functions as arbitrator and conciliator. And so to the overall symbolic meaning of the *wedjAt* or healed Eye of Horus we can now add the ability to maintain a point of balance between opposites. The restoration of the Eye restores it to its original condition of Wholeness, but it is the *process* of doing so and the effect it has on the healer which is significant. This process causes changes in the consciousness and perception of those who find and maintain the place of balance that enables the Eye to be made whole. The healed Eye thus becomes a symbol of an achieved change of consciousness which supports evolutionary growth, rather than being the cause of that change. The difference is real understanding rather than superstitious belief.

The story is found in full in the New Kingdom tale *The Contendings of Horus and Set*, where the two gods each claim to be the rightful successor to the throne of their father Osiris. Many wild battles develop as they fight it out, and the story is full of vivid and often violent symbolism whose subject matter is the interplay of powerful cosmic forces embodied by the sun and moon. These cosmic forces are often described in terms of the sexuality and life and death of the gods, but for our present purpose the relevant passage occurs when Set finds Horus lying in the shade of a tree in the 'land of the oasis.' Set seizes Horus, throws him upon his back on a mountain, removes his eyes and buries them in the mountain. The eyes eventually become lotus plants, a symbol of regeneration. In this version of the story Horus is discovered by the goddess Hathor, who is referred to here as the Lady of the Southern Sycamore. She captures a gazelle and milks it, then pours the milk (perhaps a reference to the stars) on Horus's eye sockets, healing them and restoring his sight.

In the earlier story of Set and Osiris, Set's imprisonment of Osiris in a coffin and Osiris's rebirth in the stars sets the pattern for an initiation into the Mysteries which can be emulated by those who follow Osiris's example. Similarly, we can think of the loss and restoration of creative vision as a form of initiation for Horus which also has a wider relevance. In the Pyramid and Coffin Texts, the Eye of Horus is said to have been 'made small' by Set's finger, or to have been torn out and swallowed by Set. The texts are unanimous in their recognition of the magical power of the Eye once it has been restored and healed, and the first hundred or so Utterances of the Pyramid Texts are devoted to praise of the universal powers of the healed Eye which appears to be capable of almost every possible protective and restorative function.

As we have seen, one of the basic tenets of Egyptian magic is that the universal forces which can be experienced in every aspect of our universe are equally present within our own selves, so that 'out there' is the same as 'in here'. To fully understand the symbolism of the Eye of Horus we must find a way in which to relate these apparently remote cosmic battles to our own lives. *The Contendings of Horus and Set* comments that Set's intention, once he had removed and buried the eyes, was that they should now provide 'illumination for the earth.' Just as Set is the catalyst for Osiris's imprisonment within the confines of the earthly plane symbolised by the coffin, so he is the catalyst for the transference of the creative powers symbolised by the sun and moon into the world of humanity, the mountain being a symbol for the whole earth. The 'contending' can be understood as a process of balancing that takes place between the creative, constructive forces of the sun and Horus, with the raw, limiting powers symbolised by the desert and Set. As we have commented throughout this study, the unique magical significance of the land of Egypt comes from its manifestation of polarity as a universal creative principle and of the generative power that arises from the coming together or 'contending' of positive and negative, spirit and matter. The essence of this relationship is that it is not static; it is constantly changing, adapting and developing, and the basis for the most profound magical work is the ability to work creatively with the Inner tides of this perpetual change and rebalancing.

So far, we have looked at the symbolism of the healed or whole Eye of Horus as a symbol of the completed relationship between the sun, moon and earth – or between the sun, moon and observer as it can be understood in terms of number, quantity and time. There is a further level to the relationship between them however, which is that of the effect of the sun and moon's energy in ourselves, both within our physical bodies and our subtle bodies or aura. Eastern esoteric wisdom offers a comprehensive understanding of this concept, particularly in the various Yogic practices that focus on the development and balance of the two channels of energy that rise and intertwine about the central column of the spine. One channel, the Pingala, represents active, positive, warming solar energy, while the other channel, Ida, represents receptive, cool, nurturing lunar energy. When both are flowing freely, the central channel or Sushumna becomes fully active and energised. The same symbolism can also be seen in the Caduceus of Mercury and in the glyph of the three pillars of the Qabalist Tree of Life and the serpent that intertwines about the Sephiroth.

As so often happens when we try to define how the ancient Egyptians perceived the world about them, we find that their uniquely integrated perception of the wholeness of life was so very different from our habitual practice of reductionism. We are analytical; they were analogical. We focus in on the detail; they expanded their consciousness to the whole. The hieroglyph of the healed or whole Eye is itself symbolic of the Egyptian way of seeing things. Its combination of human, bird and abstract symbolism demonstrates an integrated understanding of the created universe, and while we can profitably contemplate the Eye either as a symbol of the sun or of the moon, or of the mysteries of time, number and volume, or of the relative cycles of the celestial bodies, or of healing, or of rulership, or of the wholeness of human understanding, all we can say for certain is that the power of its magic is more than the sum of our understanding.

Endnotes

169 *wdAt,* the *wedjat* eye, the healed eye of Horus: Gardiner D10
170 *ir,* to do, create or achieve: Gardiner D4
171 *ir,* a doer (of good): Gardiner D4, A1
172 *ir heme*t, to marry a woman, to take a wife: Gardiner D4, N41, X1, B1
173 *ir ankh,* to provide for someone: Gardiner D4, S34
174 *ws ir,* Ausir, Osiris: Gardiner Q1, D4
175 Georg Möller, (1911) *Die Zeichen für die Bruchteile des Hohlmaßes und das Uzatauge. Zeitschrift für ägyptische Sprache und Altertumskunde,* 48: 99-101
176 Jim Ritter, *Closing the Eye of Horus: the Rise and Fall of 'Horus-Eye' Fractions.* In *Under One Sky; Astronomy and Mathematics in the ancient Near East,* ed. J. Steele and A. Imhausen, (Münster: Ugarit-Verlag, 2002) pages 297-323.
177 see Patrick Boylan, *Thoth or the Hermes of Egypt,* (Whitefish, Montana: Kessinger Publishing, 2010, reprint of original edition 1922) pages 180-200
178 *heb,* the sacred ibis of Tehuti: Gardiner 26
179 trans Frank Cole Babbitt, *Plutarch, Isis and Osiris* from *Moralia,* Volume V of the Loeb Classical Library edition 1936, http://penelope.uchicago.edu/thayer/e/roman/texts/plutarch/moralia/isis_and_osiris*/a.html
180 Coffin Text 316

Birds, Animals and Insects

Egypt offers a perfect habitat for a wide variety of birds and animals. The majority make their home along the Nile valley and in the delta, but a surprising number can be found in the desert. They are well represented in the hieroglyphs, and in Gardiner's classification no less than seven categories are devoted to birds, mammals, fish, invertebrates and insects.

Until the construction of the Aswan Dam in the south of Egypt, the floodwaters and rich silt brought down from the mountains of Ethiopia by the yearly inundation of the Nile attracted birds in their millions. The Nile's floodwaters are now almost entirely controlled but the country still supports over seventy species of resident and breeding birds, and in addition some three hundred species of migratory birds make an annual or bi-annual visit, stopping over on the long haul between Europe and Africa to rest and feed by the Nile. Birds are a particularly inspirational source of symbolism because they pass freely between the three elements of land, water and sky, thus becoming a perfect representation of humanity's aspiration to leave the confines of the earthly plane and soar into the heavens. In ancient Egypt, as in many other cultures, birds were regarded as messengers or representatives of the gods, bringing guidance from the heavenly worlds to humanity. This belief was affirmed by the large population of migratory birds whose land of origin and ultimate destination was not always known. Migratory birds also symbolised 'foreigners' or 'invaders' to the ancient Egyptians: the skylark for example, a visitor from Europe, was regarded from predynastic times as a symbol of enemy forces that had either attempted unsuccessfully to invade Egypt or had been overcome in battle.

Birds were also seen as symbols of protection, specifically of the protection offered by the gods to humanity and consequently by the Pharaoh to his people. As described in Chapter One, the words *sA re*, son of the Sun, are regularly used in hieroglyphic inscriptions next to the cartouche of the Pharaoh's name to illustrate the duty of care that the Pharaoh provided to the land and its people. [181]

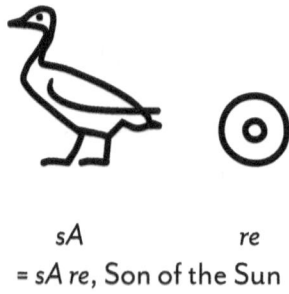

sA   re
= sA re, Son of the Sun

The word 'son' is used here in a wider sense than simply 'male offspring.' It conveys the idea of an earthly representative or exemplar of a higher level of being, an idea which can be seen again in the hieroglyphs below which define the snake, *sA tA*, as 'the son of the land' or 'son of the earth.' [182]

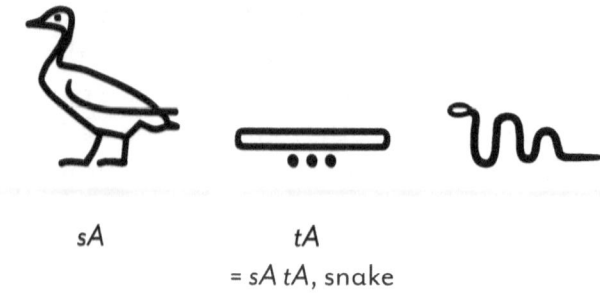

sA   tA
= sA tA, snake

These hieroglyphs tell us that the snake exemplifies qualities that might be considered some of the essential characteristics of *tA* – the land, the country or the earth. The snake's most widely recognised symbolism derives from its ability to shed its outgrown skin in a demonstration of transformation and renewal. The symbolism was used to great advantage by the Pharaohs, whose traditional headdress of an erect uraeus serpent was worn to confirm the legitimacy of their rule and authority as mediators of the powers of regeneration and renewal. But the symbolism of *sA tA* also suggests that if the snake is the 'son of the earth' then the earth too has a natural and inherent power of restoration and renewal. In our present time of acute concern over finite resources, sustainability and climate change, this concept seems ever more significant.

The hieroglyph *sA* did not refer only to male offspring; the addition of the feminine '*t*' links the idea of 'earthly representative' to a daughter. This can be seen in the following word *sA ty bt ty*.[183]

sA　　　　ty　　　　bt　　　　ty
=*sA ty bit ty*, Shu and Tefnut

Here are the 'Royal Twins' Shu the god of air, and Tefnut the goddess of moisture. They are represented by the paired hieroglyphs of the duck and the honey-bee (the sound '*ty*' indicates a plural) followed by the feminine '*t*' and the determinative of a seated deity. The emblem of the honey-bee probably originated in the delta of Lower Egypt but was adopted by the Pharaohs as one of the signs of sacred royalty. Shu and Tefnut were part of the Heliopolitan Ennead, being the first offspring of the creator God, Atum. They did not walk the earth as recognisable beings but remained in the background as remote universal powers. The notion of 'son or daughter' could, it seems, be applied to any of the stages in which new forms of life unfolded from the first spiritual principles downwards into dense physical matter. The link with the causal spiritual principles was maintained through the performance of sacred and magical work, and by the mediation of the Pharaoh and the priesthood.

This expression of 'cosmic filiation' is reflected in the title of one of the priestly offices: *sA meref*, 'the loving son.' [184]

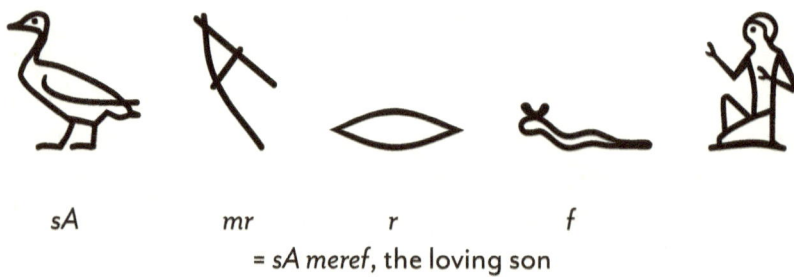

sA　　　mr　　　r　　　f
= sA meref, the loving son

The title *sA meref* was reserved for the priest responsible for mediating the presence of Horus in a magical ceremony or ritual, and the nature of his duties is explained in the symbolism of the hieroglyphs that spell his name. The second hieroglyph is *mer*, the hoe, which means 'to love, will, desire, or wish.' [185] It is followed by the hieroglyph of the mouth, '*r*,' whose primary meaning is of giving voice to thoughts or ideas but which can also refer to the more abstract ideas of purpose, intention and futurity. The fourth hieroglyph is the venomous horned viper, *Cerastes cerastes* which is found throughout the Sahara desert. Herodotus describes the horned viper as sacred to the ancient Egyptians, and many of them were embalmed in the temple at Thebes. The sign is here used phonetically but it also functions as an ideogram for 'father.' It appears in the names of a number of early Pharaohs – Khufu, for example – although was overtaken by the cobra as a symbol of sacred kingship.

There is a depth of symbolism in these two words which is inadequately expressed by their English translation. The Priest of Horus is the loving son or earthly representative of the father-god, who in this instance is Horus. His role is to mediate the power of Horus to humanity through his words and aspiration, and just as the hoe is used lovingly to prepare the land for the seed, so the role of the priest is to 'make ready' the hearts and minds of humanity for the incoming power of Horus. The final sign is the determinative which means 'humankind' and reiterates that the work of the priest is undertaken on behalf of all humanity: in potential we are all the loving sons and daughters of Horus.

Another bird frequently seen in hieroglyphic inscriptions is the vulture. Five or more different species of vulture existed in ancient Egypt, of which two are featured in the hieroglyphs. In Chapter Five we looked at the Egyptian or White vulture, whose primary use is in the word *Akh* and symbolises the pure, white spiritual light of the stars. By way of contrast, the hieroglyph of the Nubian or Lappet-faced vulture shown below is quite different in both appearance and meaning, and stands for *mwt*, 'mother.' [186]

mwt = mother

The goddess Mut, wife of the god Amun, was frequently portrayed as a vulture, as was the goddess Nekhbet, and a symbolic connection between the vulture and motherhood seems to have been obvious to the ancient Egyptians even if it evades our current understanding. The vulture's bald head and the fleshy folds of skin or 'lappets' on the sides of the vulture's neck are particularly unattractive, as is its habit of eating the decaying flesh of dead animals. Detailed illustrations such as those found in the tomb of Tutankhamun clearly identify the bird in the hieroglyph as the Nubian vulture *Torgos tracheliotos*, the largest of all the vultures and having a wing-span of nearly three metres. It is remarkably strong; its beak can tear the hide of an elephant, so it can easily tackle carcasses that other birds are unable to cope with. A strange belief recorded by both Horapollo and Plutarch was that vultures were virgin born. According to these writers there were no male vultures, only female, and their method of conceiving was to stand with their nether regions exposed to the North wind. It is difficult to imagine quite what this image signified to the ancient Egyptians, although presumably it formed an important element in the vulture's association with motherhood and the feminine. Perhaps the significance lies in the direction of the wind, and as the North was regarded as the region of the eternal spirit that abided in the Imperishable Stars, so the direct impregnation of the vulture from the spiritual realm of the north would perhaps signify an especial quality in both the mother and its offspring.

The Nubian vulture builds a large and untidy nest of sticks at the top of a tree – usually an Acacia tree – which means that its young are directly exposed to the sun. The parents therefore take it in turns to provide shade for their chicks by standing over them with their wings outstretched. Their stance is accurately illustrated in many reliefs and paintings and is probably responsible for the vulture's association with qualities of protection and nurturing, especially from the harmful and destructive powers of the sun.

Another frequently seen hieroglyph is that of the owl, shown below. The fine detail of many illustrations enable us to identify it as the barn owl. [187]

m = the owl

The hieroglyph of the owl was rarely used as an ideogram, but its phonetic value 'm' makes it one of the most frequently seen signs in hieroglyphic inscriptions. It could also be used as the prepositions 'with', and 'of', and to indicate 'that which is within'. When a hieroglyph is primarily used phonetically its symbolic value becomes less significant, but there are some interesting features about this sign. It has the distinction of being one of only two hieroglyphs that are shown in full face rather than in profile, the other being the human face.[188] The convention of Egyptian illustration was that each part of the body was drawn in its most typical and easily recognisable form, so the rare exceptions to this rule are significant. The direct stare of the owl and the fine detailing of many illustrations give it a remarkably human appearance as if inviting the observer to contemplate the analogies that can be made between the human and the owl.

There is something of the 'visitor' about the barn owl: it does not build a nest but lodges in whatever suitable shelter it can find. Its time on earth is brief; most barn owls breed only once, producing on average fewer than three chicks in a lifetime. Another curious fact is that although the owl can be seen everywhere in hieroglyphic inscriptions it is noticeably absent from every other aspect of Egyptian magical practice; it is not associated with any of the gods or goddesses, and there is no record of the name by which it was known to the ancient Egyptians. On a symbolic level we can think of the owl as indicating that which is hidden, or a representative of the unseen worlds, or of 'that which is within.' The analogy is seen in the owl's behaviour: it hunts mainly at night and has developed the most sensitive hearing of any creature, allowing it to locate its prey in complete darkness. The unique structure of its wing feathers means that its flight is virtually silent. Its direct and uncompromising stare is challenging; it prompts us to look beyond the world of appearances, to stop relying on our eyes and to use our inner senses, attuning our awareness to the unseen worlds.

With this in mind, here is the combination of the owl with the hieroglyph of the mouth that forms the word *mer*, the pyramid. [189]

m   *r*

= *mer*, pyramid

The symbolic meaning of these signs suggests that the pyramid represents something which is hidden, or at least which cannot be detected by our outer senses. It is not concerned with the things of the everyday sun-lit world but 'speaks' or gives voice to the Mysteries of darkness, the night sky and the stars. The hieroglyph of the mouth can also suggest the ability to prophecy, of seeing or sensing the future and of bringing remotely abstract ideas into conscious awareness and definition, a concept which is certainly manifested by the remarkable properties inherent in the structure and design of the pyramids.

Less frequently seen than the owl, and not so easily identifiable, is the hieroglyph of the swallow which is shown below.[190] The Egyptian name for the swallow was *mnt* or *menet,* but the sign was mainly used as a phoneme to represent the sound *wr*.

wr = wer, the swallow

It is not possible to identify the exact species of swallow from the hieroglyph, and its unremarkable appearance means that is it easily overlooked in hieroglyphic inscriptions, yet the swallow stands for 'greatness' and was used symbolically to represent the highest potential of the human spirit. Swallows are well-known for their agility of flight and their preference for feeding on the wing; they scarcely touch the earth and even take their sleep while in the air. They pass through Egypt twice a year: once as they fly north from South Africa to Europe for the warm summer days of the northern hemisphere and again as they return to South Africa for summer in the southern hemisphere. Their remarkable navigation skills allow them to return to the same nest year after year. It is probable that neither of these destinations was known to the ancient Egyptians, so the bird symbolised an ability to travel to remote and mysterious locations *and* to return safely. The North was the direction of the circumpolar stars and the ultimate destination of humankind, while the South represented the immediate and present world, so the swallow's ability to fly between the two may have been regarded as symbolic of the soul's return to earth in each new incarnation, bringing with it the wisdom of the spiritual worlds.

The hieroglyph of the swallow was often followed by the hieroglyph of the mouth used as a sound complement. For example *wer*, shown below, indicates 'much', 'the eldest', 'the most important', 'great in size' and 'a chief or ruler.' [191]

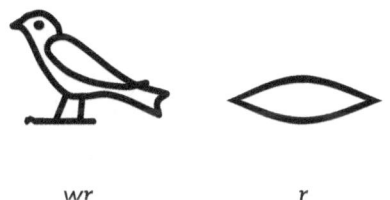

wr   *r*

= *wer*, the eldest, the most important, the chief

If the swallow is followed by *two* 'mouth' hieroglyphs, the meaning becomes 'too much'! The combination of these hieroglyphs suggests that the 'greatness' symbolised by the swallow was linked with an ability to give voice to those qualities upon which the title depended.

In illustrations, the swallow can often be seen perched unobtrusively on the prow of the sun-boat, as if the herald of the dawn. There are a number of interesting references to the swallow in the Pyramid Texts. In Utterance 626, for example: "The King has flown up like a swallow ... the King has alighted like a falcon." The swallow was also identified with the circumpolar stars. Utterance 519 says "I have gone to the island in the Field of Offerings on which the swallow-gods come to rest; the swallows are the Imperishable Stars." Chapter 86 of the Book of the Dead contains instructions for transforming into a swallow or 'becoming' the swallow, and concludes with the advice that if the deceased follows this guidance he or she will not be refused passage through any gate in the Inner worlds.

The Coffin Texts also describe how the deceased ascends into the heavenly worlds like a swallow: "I flew up as a swallow, I cackled as a goose, I came to rest on the great shore of the island to the north of the horizon of the sky. I came to rest upon it and I appear as a god." [192] The goose or 'Great Cackler' was the cosmic goose that brought the universe into being by uttering a single hoarse cry. These quotations from the Coffin Texts identify the swallow as the soul that has flown in vision to the shores of an island in the far north of the sky, this island perhaps representing the qualities of the first mound of creation that has newly arisen in the primeval waters. The meaning seems to be one of renewal and rebirth experienced at a profoundly spiritual level. Even this, though, is but a step further in the journey towards the ultimate destination in which the soul becomes identified with the 'Great Cackler' whose harsh cry initiates the start of creation.

The swallow represents a positive and joyful expression of the ability of every human soul to journey towards an increasing identification with the light of the spirit before which all shadows and obstacles fade away. There is a transcendent quality to this hieroglyph, whose symbolic meaning incorporates, yet surpasses, that of other hieroglyphic birds such as the falcon, the duck and the white vulture. It is interesting to note that there appears to be no specific link between the swallow and the Pharaoh; the qualities it represents are apparently not reserved for the few but are attainable by all humanity. Its 'greatness' is our essential spirit which enables us to fly into immortality.

The hieroglyphs of the swallow and mouth can be seen again in the following word which indicates the *wrrt* or *weret* crown, an epithet which was used of both the white crown of Upper Egypt (as shown) and the red crown of Lower Egypt.[193]

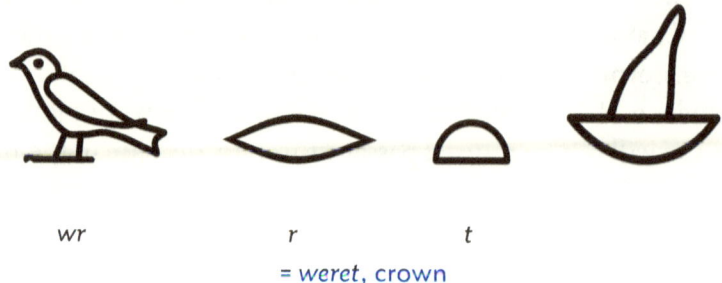

wr   r   t

= *weret*, crown

The power represented by the *weret* crown is spiritual and magical rather than temporal; it represents the illimitable qualities of the human spirit. The same concept is developed in the phrase shown below: *wr hekA,* which means 'Great of Magic,' an epithet given to many of the gods and goddesses, although was particularly reserved for the goddess Isis. [194]

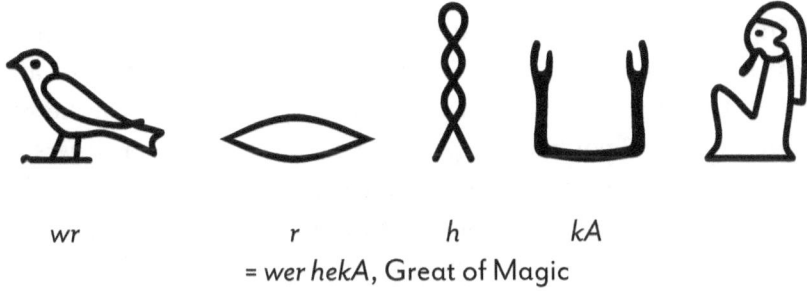

wr   r   h   kA
= *wer hekA*, Great of Magic

Here, the swallow and mouth are followed by the hieroglyphs of the coiled lamp-wick which is associated with the notion of eternity, and the raised arms that spell *kA,* a word which is usually translated as 'spirit.' [195] The word is determined by the hieroglyph of a seated god. The phrase can be read simply as a description of the mysterious powers of the gods but our knowledge of the symbolic meaning of the swallow tells us that while the properties of *hekA* are indeed spiritual and transformational, they are possessed in potential by all humanity. When we turn this potential into actuality then we become like the gods.

Birds' feathers were an important symbol in their own right. The hieroglyph *swt,* a feather, is shown below.[196]

swt = feather

The hieroglyph depicts a white ostrich feather which displays the characteristic 'flopping over' at the tip. It represents the idea of lightness, of being empty, of something missing or lacking; the absence of something. None of these are easy concepts to represent visually but the floating, virtually weightless strands of the ostrich feather which are moved by the slightest breath of air are as good a symbol as any. The reason for the apparent weightlessness of the ostrich's feathers is that they do not have the tiny hooks which, in flying birds, lock the separate strands of the feather together so that it pushes through the air efficiently to provide forward and upward thrust. These are the little 'sticky hooks' that can be felt quite strongly if you try to separate the strands of most feathers.

The absence of something is not the same as 'nothingness.' If something is absent or lacking, the implication is that it was once present but has now disappeared. The positive use of the ostrich feather in Egyptian iconography tells us that this lightness and emptiness is regarded as beneficial because an undesirable weight or encumbrance has been relinquished. The feather was a symbol of the god Shu who is often described as the god of 'air,' although the sense is not so much of 'atmosphere' but of light, heat and dryness – or in other words a quality or condition characterised by lack of moisture.

The feather was also the emblem of the goddess Maat who represented the qualities of truth, order and universal balance. In the funerary ceremony of the Weighing of the Heart, the deceased's heart was balanced in the scales against a single feather of Maat in order to reveal the extent to which the heart had become 'weighed down' by worldly error. Something of this can be found in our expression 'light-hearted,' by which we mean joyful and carefree, having trust in the future and an acceptance that all will be well. Against this can be contrasted the heavy-heartedness that results from persistent anxiety, regret or foreboding. While we may not be aware of a physical sensation of lightness or heaviness in our hearts, the phrases ring true.

The feather of Maat also represents the notion of 'righteousness,' a spiritual state of being which was revealed by the symbolic lightness or emptiness of a heart unencumbered by the immorality, greed, dishonesty and general transgression against the natural laws of universal order that are described so clearly in the words of the prayer known as the 'Negative Confession.' The ceremony of the Weighing of the Heart was not punitive but an affirmation of the enlightened state that can be achieved through the positive practice of good will, integrity and honesty. Maat also represented the state of perfect balance that could be achieved in a proper synchronicity between the earth and the cosmos. Her role in the Weighing of the Heart ritual reveals how humankind's ability to live in righteousness is not just a matter of morality but depends also on our ability to achieve a balance and alignment between our selves and the natural forces of the universe.

The following hieroglyph represents an egg, and could be pronounced as either *swht* or *imy*.[197]

swht, imy = the egg

This hieroglyph was rarely used except as an ideogram, although a notable exception is its inclusion in one of the many spellings of the name of the goddess *Ast* or *Aset*, better known in the Greek translation Isis.[198]

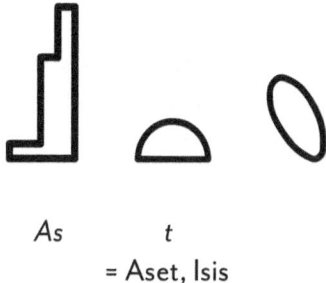

As   t

= Aset, Isis

The history of the goddess Isis is long and complex. Her role changed and evolved more than was usual in the fundamentally conservative Egyptian approach to the sacred, and during the Greek and Roman occupations of Egypt her identity was merged with that of the Greek Athena, and the Roman Hera. It is now difficult for us to discover the 'original' Isis, but the unusual group of hieroglyphs that comprise one version of her name (it could be spelt in several ways) is a good place to start. The first sign, usually described as a throne, has the phonetic value of either *st, as, htm* or *ws*. Its meaning is metaphorical rather than literal: it signifies 'the place of' or 'the seat' in the sense of a symbolic or representative focal point of power or authority. It could also indicate a state of being in which an individual is so identified with a certain quality or condition that they can be said to embody it. The idea is expressed in modern phrases such as 'a state of purity,' 'a state of disarray' or 'a state of enlightenment.' The throne represents the presence of this quality or condition which is exemplified by the person who is seated upon it and which is so strong that it becomes influential throughout their sphere of influence.

The second sign is the familiar '*t*' which denotes the feminine, and the hieroglyph of the egg therefore becomes the determinative. The expected determinative of the seated female deity was not always included in this word and its absence, as shown in the example, places more emphasis on the symbolic qualities of the egg as an indication of the nature of the goddess.

The symbolic meaning of the egg is perfectly expressed in the conundrum: 'which came first, the chicken or the egg?' The phrase speaks of the ultimate Mystery of Life and of the cosmos that produces the egg which gives birth to the god who creates the cosmos. The symbolism of *Aset* suggests that the goddess is the very embodiment of this Mystery; she engenders and supports our awareness of the enigmas of creation that preceded the first 'egg,' and she maintains their presence within our consciousness. Without our sense of Mystery we would not enquire further into the meaning of our world, and the hieroglyphs that spell her name make a significant contribution to our understanding of the goddess.

Birds, Animals and Insects

If the impression has been created thus far that the world of the hieroglyphs is all sweetness and light, this is counteracted by some of the hieroglyphic representations of animals. Here, for example, are the hippopotamus and the crocodile.[199]

db = *deb*, hippopotamus

msh = *meseh*, crocodile

Both creatures were feared for their aggressiveness, dangerous strength and voracious appetite, yet each was acknowledged as a deity. They were often combined in images of the goddess Tawaret. Known as 'the great one' and the goddess of fertility, pregnancy and childbirth, Tawaret is usually depicted as a hippopotamus, standing on her hind legs and with a crocodile (the god Sobek) forming her back and tail. The same composite figure is found on a number of the 'astronomical ceilings' of the temples and tombs, where it forms one of the largest of all the star groups. It is not possible to correlate it precisely with any modern constellations – it has been identified for example as a sizeable group of stars that stretches from the modern constellation of Lyra towards Boötes, with its head approximately coinciding with the head of Draco – but it was almost certainly one of the circumpolar group of 'Imperishable Stars.'[200] On the astrological ceiling of the tomb of Senenmut at Deir el Bahri (c1470 B.C.) this great figure places a hand on another constellation, the *menet* or 'Mooring Post.' (See illustration on page 121.) The 'Mooring Post' suggests a connection with the North celestial pole (the imagined line projected into space which is a continuation of the axis of the earth) around which all the stars of the northern hemisphere appear to rotate.

Another animal seen frequently in ancient illustrations is the lion, which formed a significant symbolic presence in Egyptian magical thought. It is depicted in two different postures in the hieroglyphs, the first being the standing lion, *mAi*.[201]

mAi = lion

The connection between this king of the beasts and the qualities of powerful authority in human leadership was recognised in ancient Egypt as it is now, and the hieroglyph was often followed by the word *hsA* which means 'ferocious.' [202] We can also be reasonably confident that the group of stars the Egyptians called *mAi* were the same as the modern constellation of the lion, Leo.[203]

The recumbent lion, *rw* or *ru*, is shown below. [204]

rw = crouching lion

The best known example of the recumbent lion is of the course the Sphinx that crouches in front of the great pyramid of Khufu on the Giza plateau – although the identity of its human face is still open to debate, as is the date of its construction. Recent research suggests that the Sphinx is a representation of the constellation of Leo, and serves to emphasise the significance of this constellation as the visible background of stars at the time of the heliacal rising of Orion and Sirius at the Summer Solstice. In ancient times, this stellar configuration coincided with the inundation of the Nile and marked the start of the New Year. [205] The close physical proximity of the three pyramids at Giza as an earthly representation of the three stars of Orion's belt, the Sphinx as a representation of Leo, and the Nile as the equivalent of the Milky Way together form a remarkable composite symbol of one of the most fundamental principles of Egyptian magical thought: that of balance or *mA'at* between heaven and earth.

A full exploration of this vast area of symbolism is beyond our remit but as is so often the case the hieroglyphs throw some interesting light on the subject. For example, a combination of the lion and the feather produces the word *rswt*, which means joy.[206]

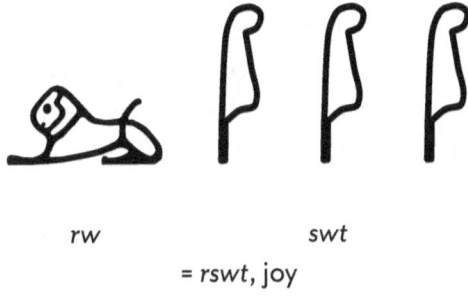

rw   swt

= rswt, joy

The association of a lion with a feather is unexpected, least of all as an evocation of joy, and reminds us that the ancient Egyptian way of perceiving the world was quite different to ours. But as we have noted, the feather indicates a lack of something in the sense that something which was present and probably undesirable has been removed. Its absence brings 'lightness,' both lightheartedness and the realisation of increased light within a previously dark situation or state of mind. To this, the lion adds the qualities of strength, will and purpose, suggesting that an experience of joy is also likely to bring an increased sense of power and purpose; of human will aligned with spiritual will. *Rswt* uses the feather of Maat to define 'joy' as the strength that is attained when a perfect balance is achieved between the earthly and spiritual worlds such as that symbolised by the pyramids, the sphinx and the Nile at Giza. Even more remarkable is that these two hieroglyphs describe the quality of 'joy' more lucidly than an entire paragraph of modern English.

The front and hind quarters of the lion were also used as hieroglyphs.[207]

hAt = the first, foremost

The front quarters of the lion indicate the concept of 'first' in the sense of the beginning or initial occurrence of something, such as the first words in a book. They could also indicate 'the finest, the best or foremost,' 'the prow of a boat,' 'the vanguard or leader of a group,' and 'a herdsman.' Interestingly, the sign was also used to represent the heart. The Egyptians believed this organ not only to be the primary seat of the emotions but also of the will and the intelligence. Our modern understanding of the human brain leads us to assume that the brain, rather than the heart, is responsible for these functions and that the heart merely serves to propel blood around our body, but given the ancient Egyptians' remarkable understanding of themselves and the universe we might be justified in wondering if they knew something that we have since forgotten. This spelling of 'heart' is shown below. [208]

hAty = the heart

The hieroglyph of the hind quarters of the lion was generally used to mean 'to finish, to end, to reach or attain.' The hieroglyph, which could be pronounced in several different ways, is shown below. [209]

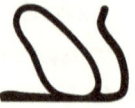

phwy or ph = to finish

Surprisingly, this hieroglyph has a more emphatic emphasis than that of the forequarters and could imply that the end or finish of something had been deliberately caused, or that something had been intentionally contained or restricted. It was associated with the idea of moral or discretionary boundaries and when combined with the hieroglyph of the heart meant 'trustworthy,' offering a thoughtful comment on the meaning of trustworthiness. [210]

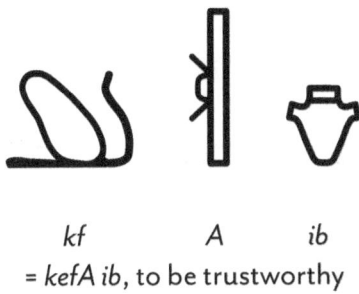

kf   A   ib
= *kefA ib*, to be trustworthy

Another familiar animal to appear in the hieroglyphs is the Anubis jackal, *inpw* or *anpu,* shown below. [211]

inpw = *anpu*, Anubis

There is still some uncertainty as to whether the animal represented in this hieroglyph is a jackal, a wolf or a dog, but from the earliest times it was associated with the rites of the dead that were overseen by the god *anpu* or Anubis, probably because the animal was known to frequent the desert cemeteries on the West bank of the Nile. It is usually shown as above, stretched out protectively as if along the top of a sarcophagus. The meaning of the hieroglyph is 'secret, confidential,' 'a sacred mystery,' and 'to make inaccessible,' acknowledging the profound nature of the rites of the afterlife and particularly the long and complex process of mummification. There is also the sense in which Anubis is the guardian of these secrets, rather like a door-keeper or watchman, and many will be aware of such a presence guarding the secrets of ancient Egyptian wisdom. There are some aspects of Egyptian magic which are in danger of becoming trivialised but there is much which still lies beyond our comprehension.

A similar canid is found in the next group of hieroglyphs which spell the name of the god *wp uAt*, *Wepwawet* or *Upuat*, although again the exact species of animal is not known.

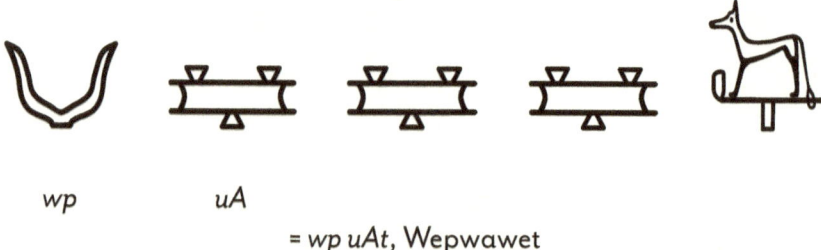

wp   uA

= *wp uAt*, Wepwawet

The meaning of this word is made clear only by the determinative hieroglyph which is the deity Wepwawet. The first hieroglyph depicts the long horns of a cow or bull and symbolises the idea of dividing or separating, just as the cow's head is divided by a distinct ridge where the horns emerge from the cranium. Symbolically, its meaning extends to the more abstract notions of discriminating and distinguishing, and for students of the esoteric these qualities hold especial relevance as the virtues of Malkuth, the lowest sphere on the Qabalistic Tree of Life.

The three repeated hieroglyphs are discussed in detail in Chapter Three. This sign is the ideogram for a road or path, which has the symbolic sense of 'far away,' 'long ago,' 'to begin or prepare for a journey,' and 'to take someone's example.' The overall meaning of the word identifies the god Wepwawet as a significant tutelary deity who has the ability to guide the seeker along the spiritual path, to prepare them for the journey, perhaps identifying relevant karmic events from the past and also setting an example for the future. It is surprising that this god has not become more widely known, because his qualities are certainly very useful to all seekers of wisdom. An early appearance of Wepwawet can be seen on an ivory label (c 2900 B.C.) found in the tomb of the 1st Dynasty Pharaoh Den, which shows the Pharaoh slaughtering the 'foe from the East.' Here, Wepwawet perches on the top of the Pharaoh's banner and seems to indicate a role which is related to a victory over a threat from foreign invaders, or perhaps to Den's successful navigation of the illusions of the Inner worlds.

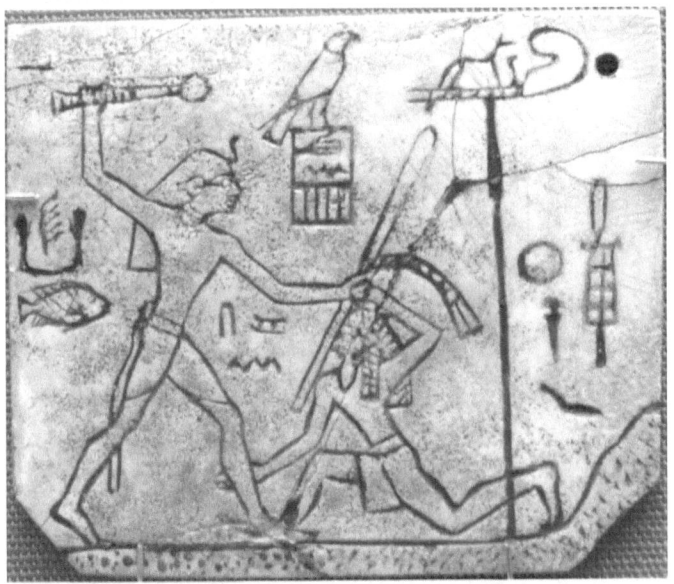

The ivory label depicting the pharaoh Den, found at his tomb in Abydos, circa 2900 B.C.

The final example in this chapter is the hieroglyph of the *kheper* beetle or scarab.[212]

khpr = *kheper*, the scarab beetle

The *Scarabeus sacer* or dung beetle symbolises the concept of 'becoming' or of 'bringing into being' which was fundamental to ancient Egyptian magical thought. The symbolic significance of the scarab beetle derives from its habit of gathering its own dung together, rolling it into a ball and then laying eggs inside it before burying it in a hole. The larvae feed from the dung during gestation, later hatching in a seemingly miraculous expression of life emerging from dead matter as if they had created themselves or brought themselves into existence. In one of the creation myths the scarab-headed god Khepri says: "I brought myself into being from the primeval matter which I made." The ancient Egyptians also recognised an association between the ball of dung that appeared to regenerate itself and the daily cycle of the sun which appears as if from out of the earth each morning before rolling across the sky during the day. Recent research provides a fascinating affirmation of this belief in the discovery that dung beetles manoeuvre their balls of dung at night by starlight and are even able to navigate solely by the light of the Milky Way. [213]

The concept of *kheper*, 'becoming,' is as enigmatic as that of *wen*, 'existence,' but we can suggest that 'becoming' is a more dynamic and energetic state than that of 'existence.' 'Becoming' involves perceptible movement, growth and change; it is a visible unfolding of potential into actuality which presupposes the ability to regenerate and renew. It takes place against the background of the comparative stability of existence and implies the involvement of the will. It might be said that 'becoming' is what happens between one state of existence and the next.

The word also describes a way of perceiving the world which involves the ability to take on or get inside the qualities of other life-forms such as the birds and animals, the landscape, the elements or the gods. This is not to suggest that the ancient Egyptians literally attempted to become dung beetles or grains of sand or trees: 'becoming' doesn't mean 'the same as' but describes a process by which we can realise our shared life-energy with all things. This leads us to the realisation that ultimately all is One and provides the means by which we can transcend our habitual experience of duality. Because we have consciousness, we are aware of both ourselves and the object – both this, and that – but if we are able to become 'that,' the duality disappears; there is only 'this' or 'I Am.' Also implied in 'becoming' is the important spiritual practice of acting 'as if,' in which we adopt as real and immanent those transcendent spiritual realities that are merely glimpsed or intuited.

This is expressed more fully in the phrase below, *kehper djes f*, which means 'who came into being of him/herself.' [214]

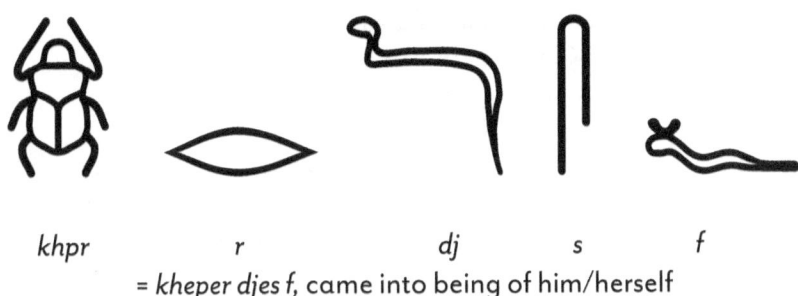

| khpr | r | dj | s | f |

= *kheper djes f*, came into being of him/herself

In this phrase the *kheper* beetle is followed by the hieroglyph of the mouth which indicates the act of giving voice to something, with a sense of purpose, intention and futurity – of 'becoming.' The third hieroglyph is the cobra which symbolises eternity and renewal. The fourth sign is the folded cloth which means 'health' and also stands for the pronoun 'her.' The final hieroglyph is the horned viper which means 'father' in both an immediate and familial sense and as a sacred or divine ancestor, and stands for the pronoun 'his'. The overall symbolism is of the inevitable process of evolution and creative renewal which is brought about through the desire of all beings to achieve the fullest knowledge of the 'Self' just as God desires to know God.

Endnotes
181 *sA re*, son of the Sun: Gardiner G39, N5
182 *sA tA*, snake, son of the land/earth: Gardiner G39, N16, I14
183 *sA ty bt ty*, Shu and Tefnut: Gardiner G39, G39, L2, L2, X1, A40
184 *sA meref*, the loving son: Gardiner G39, U7, D21, I9, A1
185 *mer* is discussed more fully in Chapter Three
186 *mwt*, mother: Gardiner G14
187 *m*, the owl: Gardiner G17
188 The god Bes was also shown in full face.

189 *mer*, pyramid: Gardiner G17, D21, O24
190 *wer*, the swallow: Gardiner G36
191 *wer*, the eldest, the most important, the chief: Gardiner G36, D21
192 A free translation of Utterances 278, 287, 581
193 *wrrt*, the weret crown: Gardiner G36, D21, X1, S2
194 *wer hekA*, Great of Magic: Gardiner G36, D21, V28, A40
195 the word *kA* is discussed more fully in Chapter Twelve
196 *swt*, the feather: Gardiner H6
197 *swehet*, the egg: Gardiner H8
198 *Aset,* Isis: Gardiner Q1, X1, H8,
199 *deb*, hippopotamus: Gardiner E25 and *meseh*, crocodile: Gardiner E13
200 José Lull and Juan Antonio Belmonte, *The Constellations of Ancient Egypt* www.iac.es/proyecto/arqueoastronomia/media/Belmonte_Shaltout_Chapter_6.pdf
201 *mAi*, the standing lion: Gardiner E22
202 see Maria Betro, *Hieroglyphics: the Writings of Ancient Egypt* (New York, Abbeville Press, 1996) page 98
203 Lull and Belmonte, *ibid*
204 *rw*, the crouching lion: Gardiner E23
205 see for example Robert Bauval and Adrian Gilbert, *The Orion Mystery* (London, William Heinemann Ltd, 1994) pages 146-147
  In *The Egypt Code* (London, Century, 2006) Bauval pinpoints this date as 11,451 B.C.
206 *rswt*, joy: Gardiner E23, H6, H6, H6
207 *hAt*, the first or foremost: Gardiner F4
208 *hAty*, the heart: Gardiner F4, X1, F34
209 *phw*, the hind quarters of a lion: Gardiner F22
210 *kfA ib*, to be trustworthy: Gardiner F22, Y1, F34
211 *inpw*, Anubis: Gardiner E15
212 *hpr*, the kheper or scarab beetle: Gardiner L1
213 Marie Dacke, Emily Baird, Marcus Byrne, Clarke H. Scholtz and Eric J. Warrant, *Dung Beetles Use the Milky Way for Orientation: Current Biolog* 23 (4): 298-300. doi:10.1016/j.cub.2012.12.034. PMID 23352694.
214 *khepher djes f*, came into being of himself: Gardiner L1, D21, I10, S29, I9

Hieroglyphs of the Human Body

The famous words of the Emerald Tablet: "That which is above is like to that which is below, and that which is below is like to that which is above, to accomplish the miracles of the one thing," (often reduced to 'As above, so below') form the core of Hermetic teaching whose origins can be traced back to ancient Egypt. A similar phrase: 'As within, so without,' is worth considering alongside its more familiar counterpart, particularly in regard to Egyptian magical thought, because it emphasises the connection that exists between the forms and energy systems of the human body and those of the universe. An awareness of this correspondence is more usually associated with Eastern spiritual traditions, but in ancient Egypt the link between the physical body, the subtle bodies or aura, and the energetic principles operating throughout the universe was well understood. Starting with what we know – our own bodies – and applying the same rules to what we don't know, can lead to a better understanding of both, and the practice of this theory soon becomes evident when we look at the rich symbolism of the hieroglyphs that depict the human body and its various parts.

First, the face. The hieroglyph below was used mainly as an ideogram for the face (as opposed to the entire head) or to indicate 'the head' in the sense of 'chief,' 'foremost' or 'that which is in the front.' [215] It is of particular interest as it is one of only two hieroglyphs of living creatures that are illustrated full-face rather than in profile, the other being the hieroglyph of the owl.

hr = *her*, the face

Modern depictions of this sign tend to be quite basic in style and don't compare well with the original illustrations which are finely detailed and boldly naturalistic, although the protuberant ears are always present.

The second hieroglyph of the human face, *tep*, shows the head in profile, and in terms of symbolic meaning it is the more interesting of the two. [216]

tp = *tep*, the head

Tep has a number of related meanings. It indicates 'the first, the best, the finest, the earliest' and, like the previous sign, is also found in words and phrases that mean 'foremost,' 'head,' 'high priest,' and 'taking precedence.' The hieroglyph could be used to indicate the head of an organisation just as we would now use the word 'head' to refer to the leader of a group. We are 'ruled' or 'governed' by the head to the extent in which our lives are directed by the activity of our mind. *Tep* was used in legal documents where it indicated the capital on which a new enterprise could be launched.

But *tep* also contains an important temporal element. It can refer to the first identifiable instance or occasion in which something occurred, with the suggestion that this first occasion was the perfect ideal that set the standard against which later instances should be compared. *Tep* appears in groups of hieroglyphs that refer to ancestors, predecessors, those who lived in a previous era. The sense of this can be appreciated in the phrase *zep tepi*, 'the First Time,' a concept that was of particular significance to the Egyptians and which has in recent years been the subject of much discussion. It has been speculated that the phrase might refer to a remote golden age when gods walked the land, or to an alien race of beings who visited Earth in order to communicate their wisdom to a fledgling humanity. A more persuasive explanation has emerged from the research made possible by modern computer technology which enables us to look at accurate images of the night sky as if from any place on earth and at any time in the past. As mentioned in the previous chapter, in an earlier epoch there was a close mirroring between the configuration of prominent constellations and the natural and man-made features on the Giza plateau such as the sphinx, the pyramids and the River Nile. The Egyptian New Year was fixed in a perpetual recreation of this moment of perfect equilibrium between heaven and earth, even though, due to the effect of the precession of the equinoxes, this exact 'mirroring' between heaven and earth gradually slipped away.

Zep tepi therefore refers to an original 'golden' time in which the powers of heaven and earth came together in a state of perfect balance and harmony, or *maat*. But the quality of this moment can be recaptured and recreated, and the essence of the First Time can be brought into the present moment by the ability of the human mind and imagination to recreate its perfection through knowledge, contemplation and sacred ritual. *Tep* expresses the idea that the first occasion on which something happens is the finest and purest because it is the nearest to the spiritual impulse of its birth. We can become part of this thread of being if we 'use our heads' to recreate our journey into spirit, raising and expanding our consciousness as we do so. A recreation of the spiritual power of a time of harmony between heaven and earth was one of the main reasons behind the strict conservatism observed in Egyptian magic for three millennia, and it was this, rather than any nostalgic veneration of a previous golden age of 'Atlantis,' which inspired them.

Zep (or *sep*) *tepi* was written as follows: [217]

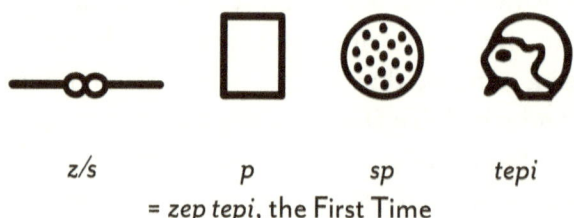

z/s   p   sp   tepi
= *zep tepi*, the First Time

The first hieroglyph in this phrase represents a door-bolt; the second is the woven mat; the third sign, which represents a threshing floor and means 'time' and 'occasion', is used here as a sound complement, and the final sign is the determinative, *tep*, the head.

The hieroglyph of the door-bolt is an illustration of the great double doors of the inner sanctuary of Egyptian temples, where a wooden or bronze bolt was mounted on one door between two loops and drawn through a similar loop on the other side to hold the doors fast. The drawing is quite stylised and focusses our attention on the symbolic potential behind the mundane object. It evokes the idea of two equal forces that have travelled towards each other from opposite directions and are presently held in equilibrium. The layout of Egyptian temples represents the stages of the soul's journey from the earthly plane into the stars, starting at the great pylon entrance that was shaped like the hieroglyph of the *Akhet* horizon, then through the courts of pillars that represent the Field of Rushes or *sekhet iaru* that feature prominently in the texts of the afterlife, and culminating in the inner sanctuary at the far end of the temple. The double doors across the entrance to this sanctuary and the door-bolt itself are described in the Pyramid Texts as the final barrier encountered by the deceased, or by spiritual seekers, as they near the end of their journey through the Inner worlds of creation. When the individual is ready, the bolts of the doors slide back, the 'doors of the sky' swing open and the breathtaking view of the night sky filled with stars is revealed. For example, in Pyramid Text Utterance 355: "The doors of the sky are opened to you, the great bolts are drawn back for you, the brick is drawn out of the great tomb for you."

Interestingly, the same hieroglyph could also mean 'man,' 'someone' or 'anyone', and makes an interesting correlation between the symbolic function of the door-bolt and our own psyche. In the physical building the door-bolt represents a barrier between one part of the temple and another, but in the metaphysical world it represents the 'veil' which is perceived to exist between different levels of reality and different levels of consciousness. The symbolic meaning of the hieroglyph suggests that the door-bolt which separates one level of reality from another is not only 'out there' but also 'in here,' a part of our own consciousness. In the end, we discover that only we can open these doors. There is no mysterious, external doorkeeper or guardian of the threshold to pull back the door-bolt for us; the hieroglyph tells us that we ourselves are the keepers of the door.

The second hieroglyph in *zep tepi* is the small rectangle. This is the ideogram for a mat and was also frequently used as the sound '*p*.' The mat of woven reeds was an important household item in ancient Egypt where the lack of hardwood trees meant that wooden furniture was a comparative luxury; woven mats were used for sitting and sleeping on rather than as decorative floor-coverings. The mat also played an important role in sacred buildings, and in the earliest temples it was used as an altar on which the offerings of bread and beer were placed. Later, the offering-mat was replaced by a stone altar, but surviving examples show that the hieroglyph of the mat was often engraved upon it, so that it retained the symbolic presence of the original.

The third hieroglyph, *sep* or *zep*, is usually said to illustrate a threshing floor, although the connection between a threshing floor and the hieroglyph's meaning of 'time,' 'occasion,' 'deed' and 'matter' is not immediately obvious. [218] The threshing of grain is now mostly achieved by mechanical means, so it can be useful to know what the original process involved when we consider the symbolic meaning of the hieroglyph. Threshing floors in ancient Egypt comprised a large circular depression four meters or so in diameter, lined with clay to produce the necessary hard surface, and sometimes ringed by a low wall. Examples found in some of the early predynastic settlements in the delta region still contain remnants of the reed mats that had once been placed over the clay. The purpose of threshing the grain is not to separate the wheat from the chaff as is often assumed, but is the preliminary stage in which the ears of grain are detached from the stalk. In Egypt, as in many other cultures, this was achieved by piling the scythed corn onto the threshing floor and driving a team of oxen or donkeys backwards and forwards over it so that the animals' hooves broke the ears from the stem. Illustrations of this can still be seen on the walls of Egyptian temples and tombs. Once the ears of grain had been severed from the stem, the straw was swept away and used for animal bedding, and for binding the mud and loam mixture that was shaped into bricks for building.

R.O. Faulkner gives a comprehensive interpretation of this hieroglyph in his *Concise Dictionary of Middle Egyptian* and lists a number of variations on the concept of time, such as 'repetition, duplication, reciprocity, similarity and succession.' *Zep* is also defined as 'matter, affair or case,' as 'deed, act or conduct,' 'occasion, chance or mishap' and as 'venture,' 'success' or 'condition.' The overall symbolic meaning is not of the passage of time as such, but of a particular occasion on which something occurred that was thereafter remembered as significant, and which initiated a succession of events whose essential quality was attributable to that occasion.

If we link these various definitions to the activity of threshing grain, the hieroglyph seems to indicate one particular occasion on which grain was threshed that became in effect *the* occasion, the archetype behind all similar and subsequent events. The hieroglyphs which comprise the phrase *zep tepi* are linked to the story of Osiris and his death and rebirth in the stars, a sequence which became the model for all humanity. Harvesting the grain involves a series of deaths: the cutting down of the whole plant, the separation of the head from the stem and the final winnowing to separate the grain from the chaff. All these 'deaths' are necessary to produce fertile grain for food and viable seed for the next year.

Osiris was identified as a god of grain, and legend describes how the god of the desert, Set, brought about his death and dismembered his body into fourteen parts, thus beginning the process which would culminate in Osiris' rebirth as *sAh*, Orion. The Ramesseum Papyrus, which dates from c 1980 B.C. (it is the oldest known surviving illustrated papyrus roll), identifies Osiris with barley and the god Set with a donkey, and refers to the activities of 'beating' or 'threshing' the grain and hacking the god to pieces. The same link between Osiris and grain is seen in the various 'body of the god' models that have been discovered in a number of tombs from the period of Rameses II, Tutankhamun and Akhenaten. A model of the body of Osiris, fashioned in clay and filled with fertile silt from the Nile valley was placed on a wooden 'bed' and planted with grain. The symbolic significance of the sprouting grain within the tomb, of life emerging from death and of the god-man who carries the seed of his own beginning makes a clear reference to the symbolism of the threshing floor, in which the fertile grain is separated from the body of the stalk in order to provide the seed for the future.

If we put together the symbolism of the four hieroglyphs of *zep tepi* we arrive at a useful understanding of their magical significance. The first occasion or 'birth' of each new life on earth 'heads' its future development, influencing its unique quality throughout all subsequent growth. The essential qualities of this first perfection may become gradually obscured over time, but they are not lost. Our return to the conditions of the First Time can be achieved by a re-membering of the symbolic death on the threshing floor, in which the lower is relinquished to the higher. The journey back to the First Time is often experienced as a series of barriers or doors which, we discover, can be opened by 'using our heads.' In taking this journey we become involved in a ritual re-enactment of the resurrection of the scattered fragments of the earthly body of Osiris into a transfigured body of light through the attractive, universal powers of synthesis embodied by Isis. Thus from the imperfect and destructible emerges the perfect and immortal, and the circle of the threshing floor is finally revealed as a symbol of the star-filled sphere of heaven.

From the head we move to *ib*, the heart.[219]

ib = *ib*, the heart

Gardiner includes this sign in Section F: 'Parts of mammals' and its shape is indeed more like a sheep's or cow's heart than that of a human. There may be significance in this or it may simply be that the irregular form of the human heart did not appeal to the ancient Egyptians who probably found the comparative symmetry of the animal heart aesthetically more pleasing. The hieroglyph's symmetrical form also gives it the appearance of a stoppered container or a vase with handles, a visual relationship which adds to its symbolism and was obviously appreciated by the Egyptians, who created vases in the shape of the hieroglyph.

The surviving medical texts demonstrate that the Egyptians had a fair understanding of anatomy and physiology. They knew for example that the blood supply runs from the heart into all the organs of the body, but they also made a distinction between the functions of the 'outer' physical heart or cardiac muscle and its 'inner' energetic qualities or attributes. We might describe these qualities as belonging to the etheric body, or perhaps to the heart chakra, rather than to the physical body. They also seem to have been familiar with a form of 'taking of the pulses' which is now generally thought to be the sole province of Chinese acupuncture. Acupuncturists detect a number of different pulses in the wrists which indicate the condition of the organs of the body and reveal the patient's general levels of energy, making their diagnosis through an assessment of the quality of energy of each pulse. They recognise twelve principle and two additional channels of energy or 'meridians' running through the body, and their treatment of the patient is based on restoring a full and balanced flow of energy to each meridian. A remarkably similar system is described in the Egyptian Ebers medical papyrus of c 1550 B.C. which refers to the concept of ten functions or organs, and twelve plus two *metou* or channels of energy which were detected by assessing the patient's pulses. [220]

In medical texts, the Egyptians tended to use the word *hAty* when referring to the physical organ of the heart, while the word *ib* was more often used in sacred writings. They believed the heart to be the centre of three essential human qualities: the will, the emotions and the intelligence. If we were now asked to identify the location of these qualities within our body we would probably associate the heart with the emotions and the head with intelligence, although we might hesitate in defining the position of the will. But to the Egyptians, the heart was not only the physiological centre but also the seat of consciousness, and the centre of the sense of self or 'I am' within each individual. Such was the heart's symbolic importance that after death, although the brain and other internal organs were removed during mummification, great care was taken to preserve the heart within the mummified body, as if for eternity.

These three qualities of will, emotion and intelligence are of symbolic significance within the human energy system because they are expressions of the three universal spiritual principles referred to variously as the three 'rays,' or the 'Trinity,' or as the triple attributes of Deity. The same triplicity is manifested in the human being as the originating Divine Spark, the Soul or Higher Self, and the Lower Self or Personality, described in various traditions as representing Power, Love and Mind, or Strength, Wisdom and Knowledge, or as the Father, Son and Holy Spirit.

These three qualities of life-energy were central to the funerary rite of the Weighing of the Heart. The many surviving illustrations of this ceremony (there are surprisingly few textual references) show how the heart, indicated by the heart hieroglyph, is placed upon one pan of the scales and balanced against the feather of Maat which rests in the other pan. At risk of stating the obvious, the scene is symbolic, not actual. The Egyptians did not remove the heart in order to weigh it, and however exemplary the life of its owner, a human heart will always weigh significantly more than a feather.

Keeping in mind that the ceremony not only represents a stage experienced by the soul after death but was also a process that could be experienced during life, we can perhaps best understand it as a form of personal and intuitive self-assessment of spiritual progress. It reveals the extent to which aspirants have progressed in the Great Work of gaining mastery of their lower self and integrating the light of the spirit into their waking consciousness. If it was performed as a magical ritual, the various characters depicted in the illustrations would represent the roles that were undertaken by members of the officiating priesthood, but equally we can interpret each aspect of the scene as an aspect of ourselves. Thus the role of Tehuti symbolises the 'observer,' the soul or higher aspect of our consciousness which dispassionately watches over our achievements and intuitively knows whether we have measured up to our potential. The scales are a symbol of the extent to which we have balanced spirit and matter within ourselves, and the menacing figure of Ammit, part crocodile, part lion and part hippopotamus (all man-eating animals!) who crouches by the balance ready to devour the heart if it was not sufficiently 'light,' represents the state in which we are consumed by our own baser nature if we allow ourselves to be overtaken by our so-called 'animal' instincts.

Moving down the body, the next hieroglyph, *nfr* or *nefer*, illustrates the heart combined with the trachea or windpipe.[221]

nfr = nefer, the heart and trachea, goodness

Nefer means 'goodness,' 'beauty,' 'kindness' and 'happiness.' As an anatomical drawing the hieroglyph lacks a certain finesse, but early illustrations make it clear that it does indeed represent these organs. The trachea conveys air to and from the lungs and divides into the right and left bronchi at the level of the fifth thoracic vertebra which is probably hinted at in the hieroglyph by the small horizontal line near the top of the drawing. The sign is included by

Gardiner in the category 'Parts of Mammals' although again there is no obvious reason why it should not be considered as part of the human body.

A stylised anatomical drawing would not normally impress us as an illustration of goodness or beauty, but the beauty here is more than skin deep. The symbolism lies in the combination of the heart and the trachea which, together with the larynx or voice-box, play an essential role in human speech and are largely responsible for the uniquely individual quality or *timbre* of our voice. The sign therefore describes our ability to express in words the essential qualities of our heart – our will, emotion and intelligence – that are responsible for our state of goodness, kindness and happiness.

Surprisingly, *nefer* also means 'zero' and 'there is not,' and three *nefer* hieroglyphs in a row indicate 'the end (of a period of time.')' This qualifies our understanding of what the ancient Egyptians meant by 'beauty' and 'goodness.' Zero is a state of neutrality or harmlessness which lies between positive and negative; it represents a condition of potential and suggests that goodness, and the natural beauty that arises from goodness, emerge when a person is unswayed by external or internal conflict and is able to maintain the point of balance between them. One of the names of the Pharaoh was *neter neferu*, 'the good god,' an allusion to his unique position between the gods and his people, neither one nor the other but able to hold the place of mediation between them. Here again is the idea of reconciliation between two opposites, and *nefer* indicates how the 'lack' of something and the relinquishing of undesirable and 'heavy' accumulations in the heart are a positive achievement.

Nefer was used in combination with a number of other hieroglyphs, for example with the hieroglyph for 'desert hills' to indicate the necropolis: [222]

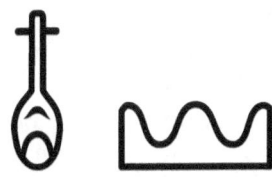

nfr = *nefer*, the necropolis

Here, beauty and goodness are an expression of the blessedness which emanated from the souls of the deceased and was communicated to the land and people about them. The desert hills on the West bank of the Nile were hallowed by the abiding presence of those who had passed into eternal life and maintained the connection between heaven and earth.

The trachea appears in another hieroglyph, *smA*, where it is attached to what looks like a heart but is actually a representation of the lungs. [223]

smA = *sema*, the lungs

The hieroglyph was used as an ideogram for lungs but its symbolic meaning is 'to blend,' 'to join or unite.' A typical example of its use is found in the phrase *semA tA*, which means 'to unite the Two Lands' – in other words Upper and Lower Egypt. [224]

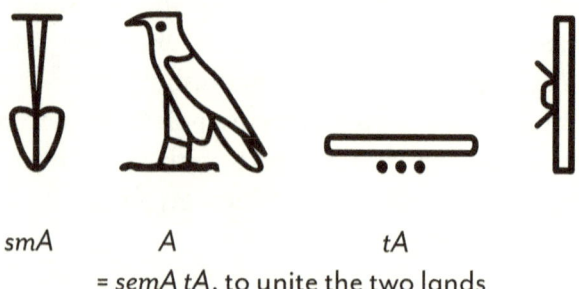

smA   A   tA
= *semA tA*, to unite the two lands

The symbolic division of the land into Upper and Lower Egypt was one of the foremost examples of the polarity expressed in the landscape of Egypt. The ability of the Pharaoh to unite the 'two lands' was a measure of his magical and spiritual ability as well as his physical and mental strength, but the achievement was as much an internal and symbolic act as an actual one – and in fact there is little evidence to suggest any real existence of two separate states. The inclusion of the White Vulture in the above word, representing the pure spirit shining like starlight, confirms that the ability to unite the two lands was more than a physical accomplishment, as does the determinative of the papyrus roll which indicates that the phrase describes an abstract or symbolic concept. *SmA tA* also meant 'internment,' suggesting that the unity or synthesis is achieved by the deceased, whose body is committed to the earth but whose spirit is united with the stars.

SmA was also used in words meaning 'to associate with,' 'to partake of,' 'to join a group' and 'to be a companion,' indicating that when we unify or blend two things this initiates a continuing process of synthesis. The Two Lands of Upper and Lower Egypt are symbolic of a bigger picture; their unity is not an end in itself but the practical demonstration of a creative and evolutionary activity.

The hieroglyph below is the ideogram *r*, the mouth.'[225]

r = the mouth

This sign has appeared in a number of words discussed previously, where its meaning has been described as 'to give voice to.' But it is one of those hieroglyphs whose design appears to be not quite right, and therefore prompts us to think further. If you didn't know that this sign represented a mouth you would probably not have guessed. It isn't obvious because the upper and lower lips are identical; it lacks the distinctive curve of the 'cupid's bow' along the top of the upper lip which enables us to identify it as a mouth.

The hieroglyph was used in a number of different ways. It could simply illustrate a mouth, and function as a phoneme having the sound '*r*.' It was used as a preposition meaning 'at,' 'by,' or 'near' or 'towards.' It could represent a door, an opening or entrance.

It could also indicate 'futurity' in the sense that when we use our mouth to speak or give utterance to something, we are – whether deliberately or unconsciously – having an effect on what will happen in the future. We are clothing an idea with definition, reducing the possibilities and targeting an energy towards one direction rather than another.

More detailed illustrations of the hieroglyph reveal it to be a single line which is in the process of dividing into two but has not yet become completely separated. The slight extension of the line at the corners of the mouth, a feature which appears in some of the original bas reliefs, hints at the continuation of the single line into infinity in each direction, as if it reaches into both past and future. The symbol is dynamic: an energetic tension exists between the two parts of the bifurcated line like a drawn bowstring. The symbolism is expressed in its meaning: it can also indicate 'a cleft or fissure,' or 'the act of causing something to separate into two parts.'

The potential power of giving voice to something is found in words such as *rn* or *ren*, 'to name,' which combines the mouth with the hieroglyph describing the movement of energy, '*n*.'[226] The same idea is expressed in the Bible: "In the beginning was the Word …"

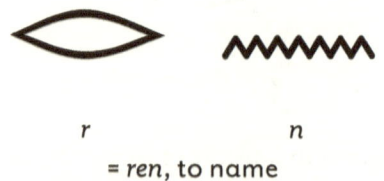

r   n

= ren, to name

A further example of '*r*' is found in the word below, *rnn* or *renun*, which means 'to rejoice' or 'to praise.'[227]

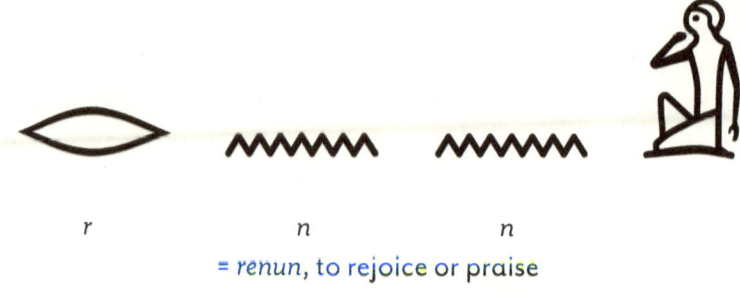

r   n   n

= renun, to rejoice or praise

Renun reveals that giving voice to the qualities of moving energy, or life-energy in its most remote and abstract sense symbolised by the hieroglyph '*n*' is an act of rejoicing, of experiencing joy in those qualities, which in turn becomes an expression of praise. And there is more, because the repetition of '*n*' implies that a reciprocal action is occurring between the mouth and the human figure. The concept involves taking the mind back to the remotest beginnings of life-energy and our own connection and involvement with those remote beginnings. There is no overt religious reference in this word and the hieroglyphs do not refer to a Deity, but the clear indication is that the existence or continuation of this energy is equally dependent upon the opposite ends of the pole: that which gives voice to the energy and that which returns it by voicing praise, which in itself then becomes a creative act.

The hieroglyphs below spell *rekh keht*, 'wisdom.' [228]

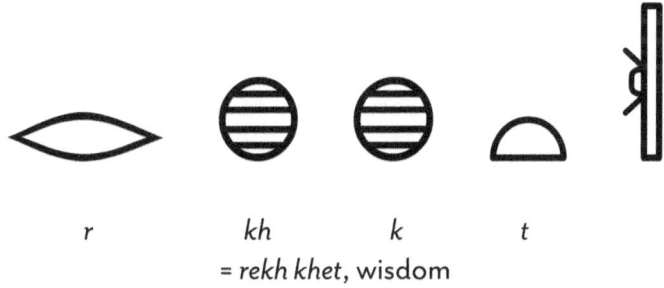

r   kh   k   t
= *rekh khet*, wisdom

The combination of the mouth with the hieroglyph of the sieve provides a marvellous definition of wisdom as the ability to filter out unwanted information in order to get to the essence of something – and then to give voice to it, so that it will have a positive effect for the future.

The hieroglyph below is the spinal cord, *Aw*, which means 'long' in the sense of a length of time or space. [229]

Aw = the spinal cord, long (in time or space), venerated

Aw also means 'to honour or venerate' and 'gifts.' In their study of the symbolism of biomedical knowledge in ancient Egypt entitled *The Quick and the Dead,* Gordon and Schwabe identify this hieroglyph as a representation of four thoracic vertebrae of a hoofed mammal, and suggest that the fluid issuing from the spine indicated by the 'droplets' at each end of the hieroglyph was probably thought of by the ancient Egyptians as both bone-marrow and as semen, and was regarded as a source of life.[230] Certainly the meaning of the hieroglyph suggests longevity, even perpetuity, and is used in the phrase *im Ahyw* which means 'a revered one' and 'one who has been made a living spirit.'

The hieroglyphs we have explored so far in this chapter illustrate the symbolic potential of parts of the human and animal body to express universal truths. Behind this symbolism there is often the implication that the body referred to is that of Osiris, the perfected human being. This connection is made explicitly in the *dd* or *djed* shown below, a hieroglyph which is often identified as the backbone of Osiris.[231]

dd = djed

The hieroglyph is widely reproduced, but over the millennia its appearance has become stylised to the extent that we cannot now be sure what it originally represented. The word *djed* means 'stability,' and 'enduring.' These two qualities are similar but not quite the same: stability suggests balance, steadiness and strength, while endurance has more to do with stamina and staying power, the ability to keep going in spite of obstacles and challenges. It might be said that our endurance depends upon our balance and steadiness.

The sign has become widely identified as the emblem of the living Osiris: a pillar, a tree and the backbone of the god combined in a single glyph. In many of the original illustrations the lower section of the pillar is divided into wide, brightly coloured horizontal bands of red, green and blue which contrast with the narrow vertical stripes of the upper sections. The four upper sections often broaden out towards the top like a stack of truncated cones, and convey the impression of vigorous organic growth and of new life emerging from existing forms.

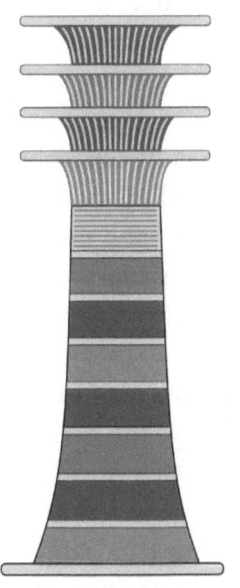

The *djed* pillar, representing the backbone of Osiris.

The lively and organic feel of earlier illustrations confirms the belief that the sign represents a tree, the four horizontal bars representing branches which have been lopped from the trunk. The symbol of a tree as a representation of Osiris is appealing, although there is not a great deal of textual evidence to support the idea. The Pyramid Texts contain only one clear reference, Utterance 574 which begins: "Hail to you, you tree which encloses the god, under which the gods of the lower sky stand, the end of which is cooked, the inside of which is burnt, which sends out the pains of death ... Your tomb, O Osiris, the shade which is over you, O Osiris, which repels your striking-power, O Set..."

The basis of the myth is certainly here: the tree which has become the tomb of Osiris and is venerated by other gods also serves to protect him from the power of Set. There is a reference to 'burning' which might refer to a ritual cutting down of the tree, or perhaps to the scorching power of Set as god of the desert. But this is an isolated reference and there is very little else, so far as we know, that connects Osiris with a tree until Plutarch's *De Iside et Osiride* written in the 2nd century. Plutarch's account is the fullest available version of the myth, and contains a number of elements that are absent from earlier, briefer, versions. He describes how the god Set imprisoned Osiris in a coffin which he then threw into the Nile. The coffin floated downstream to the Delta where it entered the Mediterranean Sea, eventually coming to rest at the ancient Phoenician city of Byblos a few miles north of the modern city of Beirut. A tree grew up around the coffin, and after many years it completely obscured the coffin from sight. The King of Byblos was attracted by the size of the tree, so he cut it down, chopped off its branches and used it as a pillar to support the roof of his palace, curiously unaware that it contained the coffin of Osiris inside its trunk. If we were to take the story literally we would assume that the tree was a large, local species such as the Cedar of Lebanon, and as it happens Egypt did import Cedar of Lebanon from Byblos in exchange for mineral wealth.

We have no means of knowing whether Plutarch was recounting an original version of the narrative that he had learnt in Egypt or whether this part of the tale is his own invention, but given the scarcity of large trees in Egypt it seems unlikely that there was ever a strong connection between the *djed* pillar and a tree. In the end, it has to be said that the hieroglyph doesn't look very much like a tree. The concept of the World Tree is found in many other cultures but it was not a strong feature in Egyptian mythology.

The earliest examples of the *djed* are two small amulets carved in ivory discovered in a First Dynasty tomb at Helwan, on the East bank of the Nile, opposite the stepped pyramid at Saqqara. These amulets are finely detailed and contain all the principle features of later examples of the hieroglyph: a single column from which emerge four layers of sprouting growth, with an indication of twine or binding that secures the bundles of vegetation to each other and to a central column. The vegetation looks most likely to be four sheaves of corn, of graduated lengths and having full and pendulous ears of grain. The main purpose in binding together these four bundles of corn seems to be to emphasise the significance of the number four within the whole meaning of the hieroglyph, and this numerical element of its symbolism is preserved in almost all later examples. To the ancient Egyptians the number four represented completion, entirety, the whole, so the composite sheaf of corn represents the entirety of the fertile corn throughout the whole land of Egypt. As we have noted earlier, the association between Osiris and corn became increasingly well-established. It was believed that the heavenly worlds were supported on four pillars, so the hieroglyph can also be understood as a representation of the whole world.

However, keeping in mind that a hieroglyph is a symbol of inner realities as well as a depiction of an actual object, the question remains as to how four sheaves of corn tied together can symbolise stability and endurance. The term 'stability' is not often used today, perhaps because steadiness and durability are no longer regarded as desirable qualities. Stability is not the same as 'staying the same' but is achieved by continual adaptation to change and the ability to make appropriate adjustments to new developments and evolving circumstance. If this ability is lacking, the result is stagnation and degeneration rather than renewal and regeneration. The *djed* represents the principle of renewal and regeneration symbolised in the cycle of life, death and renewal of the grain, which even as it is cut down, contains the living seeds of its own rebirth. The hieroglyph therefore represents the idea of continued adaptation and the emergence of new and viable forms from the seeds of previous forms: not just life but eternal Life.

The concept of renewal was central to the Sed Festival, a ritual which dates from the earliest dynastic times. The Festival involved a long ceremony in which the Pharaoh undertook a symbolic renewal of his own life and vitality which was then transmitted to the land. Scenes from the Sed Festival are depicted on the walls of the Temple of Seti I at Abydos and illustrate how part of the ceremony involved the ritual raising of a *djed* pillar from a prone to an upright position. The symbolic meaning of the action is clear: the fertile power of the 'risen' Osiris fecundates the land, and continues to do so even when – especially when – Osiris has taken his place in the sky as *sAh*, Orion. At the culmination of the ritual the Pharaoh shot an arrow to each of the four quarters of the land.

There are a number of written references to the *djed* as the backbone of Osiris. For example, Spell 155 of the Book of the Dead, a 'Spell for the *djed* of gold,' reads: "Raise yourself, O Osiris, place yourself on your side that I may put water beneath you and that I may bring you a *djed*-pillar of gold so that you may rejoice at it." [232] Pyramid Text 271 contains the same idea: "The two *djed* pillars stand erect even though the broken steps (rungs?) have fallen. I ascend this ladder which my father Re made for me." The association of the *djed* with the backbone also makes good sense, and the four horizontal bars on the hieroglyph can certainly be read as a representation of the vertebrae.

However, while the *djed* was increasingly linked with Osiris as he gained pre-eminence in the Egyptian sacred tradition, it was originally associated with Ptah, the Memphite god of Creation who was known as 'The Noble *Djed*.' Ptah has remained one of the least anthropomorphised of the Egyptian gods and can best be understood as the god behind all other gods, representing the Thought and Word that characterise the early stages of creation that later became more clearly manifest in the better-known deities of the Heliopolitan Ennead. He is often shown grasping between his hands a unique staff, not found in any other context. It combines the *uas* wand which represents magical power, the *ankh* which represents life-energy, and the *djed* of stability and endurance.

There is something of an understatement in this symbol which places responsibility for the three principles of creation into the hands of Ptah. The spine gives us stability and endurance, it is the central pillar of our body and, like the *djed*, is divided into four divisions: the cervical, thoracic, lumbar and sacral sections of the spine. In his *From Fetish to God in Ancient Egypt,* E.A. Wallace Budge gives especial weight to this interpretation and includes an illustration of Ptah standing with his back resting against a *djed* whose four divisions exactly correspond with the four divisions of the spine.[233] We can also make a correlation between the four divisions and the four systems in the human body: the skeletal, muscular, cardiovascular and nervous systems.

However, any attempt to reduce the symbolism of the *djed* to *either* a backbone *or* a tree *or* as bundles of corn is confounded by the beautiful example shown below. The illustration is of a frieze of *djed* pillars constructed from blue-green faience tiles, originally located in the tomb of Pharaoh Djoser inside the stepped pyramid at Saqqara, but now housed in the nearby museum. Creating an extraordinary *trompe l'oeil* effect, the pillars recede into the background, and it is the space between them that draws our attention. The pillars support the arch of heaven but their real significance is that they form a series of gateways through which

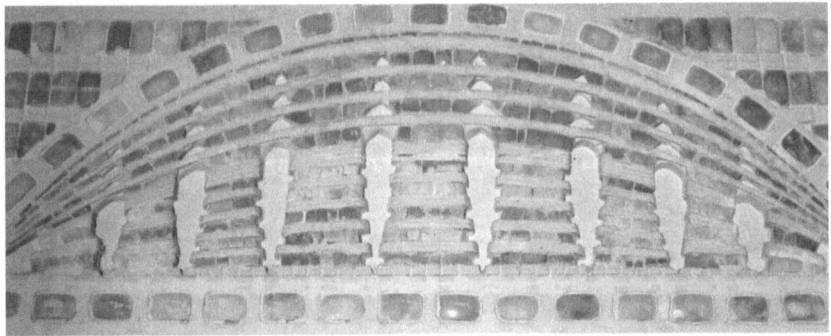

The frieze of djed pillars from the tomb of Pharaoh Djoser in the pyramid at Saqqara (now in the nearby museum)   Photo by the author

we can glimpse the heavenly worlds into which the soul of Djoser has ascended. It is the metaphysical rather than the physical which is revealed here.

When considering such primary symbols as the pillar and the tree of life or world tree, useful parallels can be made with other esoteric systems. An interesting correlation can be made for example between the four emerging components of the *djed* and the Four Worlds of the Qabalah which are symbolically represented as four interlocking Trees of Life, each rising out of a shared central pillar. In Qabalist thought, these four Trees represent the gradual materialisation of the created world in stages which are characteristically described as Emanation, Creation, Formation and Action, all four being an aspect of the One Unity.

An interesting comparison can also be made between the *djed* and the two great pillars that stood in the entrance porch of the Temple of Solomon. The original temple is generally agreed to have been constructed c.1000-950 B.C., by which time the hieroglyphs had already been in use for at least 2000 years. One of the pillars was named Boaz, which means 'in strength,' and the other was Jachin, meaning 'to establish' or 'Jah establishes.' The association of strength and stability with symbolic pillars topped by vegetation strongly suggests an Egyptian origin, although there is little direct evidence of this.

To conclude this chapter, here is a group of hieroglyphs which form the word *phrt* or *pehret*. *Pehret* includes three hieroglyphs of parts of the body, and forms a succinct description of the transitory state which is our life on earth.[234]

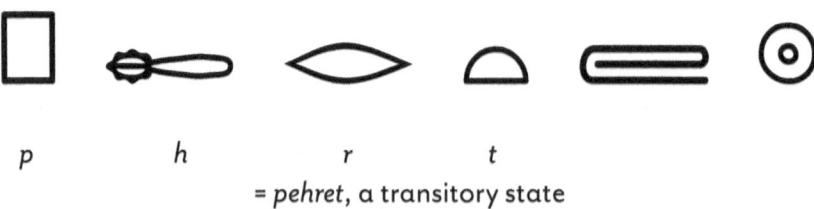

p   h   r   t
= pehret, a transitory state

The first sign is the mat used in early temple for placing offerings of bread and beer. The second sign is the ideogram of a belly or womb. The third sign is the mouth, and the fourth is the feminine '*t*' of the small offering loaf. The fifth sign is the ideogram for 'intestine' which indicates 'to turn and turn about' or 'to travel,' and the determinative is the sun which tells us that the whole word refers to the Solar Logos as the primary source of life energy within our universe, and to the passage of time. The symbolism needs little further explanation; the hieroglyphs speak for themselves in whichever order you read them.

Endnotes

215 *her*, the face: Gardiner D2
216 *tep*, the head: Gardiner D1
217 *zep tepi*: the First Time: Gardiner O34, Q3, O50, D1
218 The connection between the hieroglyph and the threshing floor was originally made by the archeologist Hermann Junker, who excavated a threshing floor at Merimde to the northwest of Cairo in the 1930s.
219 *ib*, the heart: Gardiner F34
220 See 'Ancient Egyptian Medicine and Traditional Chinese medicine,' a paper by Abelle Vinel and Jacques Pialoux available at www.cornelius-celsus.org
221 *nefer*, heart and trachea, goodness: Gardiner F35
222 *nefer*, the necropolis: Gardiner F35, N25
223 *semA*, the lungs: Gardiner F36
224 *semA tA*, to unite the two lands: Gardiner F36, G1, Y1, N16
225 *r*, the mouth: Gardiner D21
226 *ren*, to name: Gardiner D21, N35
227 *renun*, to praise: Gardiner D21, N35, N35, A2
228 *rekh keht*, wisdom: Gardiner D21, Aa1, Aa1, X1, Y1
229 *Aw*, the spinal cord, long, venerated: Gardiner F39
230 Andrew H Gordon and Calvin W. Schwabe, *The Quick and the Dead: Biomedical Theory in Ancient Egypt* (Leiden, Brill, 2004), 95 - 100
231 *djed*, stability: Gardiner R11
232 trans Raymond O. Faulkner, *The Egyptian Book of the Dead: The Book of Going Forth by Day* (San Francisco, Chronicle Books, 1994) plate 32
233 E.A. Wallace Budge, *From Fetish to God in Ancient Egypt* (Oxford: Benjamin Blom, 1972 reprint) 13
234 *pehret*, a transitory state: Gardiner Q3, F32, D21, X1, F46, N5

Hieroglyphs of the Subtle Bodies

Throughout this study we have explored how the symbolic content of the hieroglyphs makes a link between the physical appearance of the world about us and the qualities or energies of the Inner realities that lie behind outer appearances. This chapter looks at some of the hieroglyphs that are particularly concerned with the higher levels of our consciousness, and with our subtle bodies or aura.

The ancient Egyptians had a well-developed understanding of the human subtle bodies, and of the different levels of consciousness. Two of the best-known examples are the *bA*, which is generally agreed to correspond with what we now refer to as the soul, and the *kA* which is usually identified as the human spirit. In recent years there have been a number of attempts to explore a more detailed correlation between our current understanding of the elements of human consciousness such as the Higher Self, the spirit, the aura and the shadow with their counterparts in ancient Egyptian belief. It is a fascinating subject, although there is no overall agreement as to what is meant by the spirit, the soul or the aura and we cannot assume that our understanding of these concepts corresponds to that of the ancient Egyptians. Added to which it is unusual for scholarly Egyptologists to possess a thorough understanding of the esoteric theory of the subtle bodies and the creative energies of the universe, while those versed in the dynamics of the human subtle constitution rarely benefit from an academic knowledge of ancient Egypt, so there are plenty of opportunities for confusion.

To take one example among many, here is the description of the *kA* given by E.A.Wallis Budge in his *A Hieroglyphic Vocabulary to the Book of the Dead*. "The double of a man or god, the personality of a man or god, the being of a man which is associated with the heart-soul *bA* and is independent of the spirit-soul *akh*." [235] There is confusion here between the personality, the soul, the spirit and the 'being' of a man, while references to the 'double' and the 'personality of a god' are given without further explanation. Similarly in Gardiner's *Egyptian Grammar*: "Modern concepts to which that of the *kA* occasionally corresponds are 'personality,' 'soul,' 'individuality,' 'temperament' …" [236]

Equally, many esotericists demonstrate a happy disregard for known facts. The occult writer Dion Fortune, although influential in formulating a comprehensive system of magical training for subsequent generations within the Western Mystery Tradition, is a little incautious with factual accuracy in her Egyptian novel *Moon Magic*. This story of magical work undertaken between a modern priest and priestess is presented as an authentic reconstruction of Egyptian temple magic, but the purportedly accurate account of a temple of Isis on the West bank of the Nile that is central to the novel is in fact a description of the vast temple dedicated to the god Amun at Karnack on the East bank. While some poetic license might be attributed to a lack of available information at the time (the 1930s) the same provision cannot be granted to more recent writers.

Our understanding of the subtle levels of the human psyche and the energies of the Inner worlds changes with each generation, and current thinking owes much to the work of Helena Blavatsky, Alice Bailey, Rudolf Steiner and others who opened up the wisdom of Eastern traditions to the West. Broadly speaking, we now tend to follow their example in identifying three main components within the human subtle constitution: the Personality or Lower Self which is how we present ourselves to the world in our current body and character, the Higher Self or Soul which is the immortal part of our Self that endures throughout our lives on earth, guiding and overseeing the experiences of each incarnation, and finally the innermost light of the Spirit, the spark of the Divine flame which is at the centre of our being.

Surrounding our physical form are 'layers' of energy which are usually said to be seven in number, although some identify twelve or more. Many schools of thought emphasise the importance of the etheric body that closely surrounds the physical body, describing it as a web of life-force or *prana* which streams towards us from the sun and which is woven around the subtle substances of space to form a sort of template for the physical body. The etheric body is said to contain seven primary centres of energy or *chakras* which resonate with, and connect us to, the seven-fold manifestation of our universe.

The problem with transferring this model to ancient Egypt is that it is an attempt to describe the unseen and the invisible, and our current theories on the subject are not the same as those of even a hundred years ago. For example the term 'astral' body, which a century ago was generally used as an all-inclusive term for the whole of the human aura, now tends to be applied only to a single, discrete level of our subtle constitution. Similarly, the term 'astral plane' once referred to the entirety of the Inner worlds but is now generally used only in reference to the plane which corresponds with the emotional level of the human psyche.

And there is also the likelihood that our consciousness has changed over the last few thousand years because we are evolving, or perhaps it would be more accurate to say that we are evolving as a result of the changes that have occurred in our consciousness. Surrounded by technology, driven by consumerism and with our immediate perception of the world usually obscured by a computer screen or smartphone, it is unlikely that we relate to our world in the same way as the ancient Egyptians who lived in a machine-free, pollution-free environment under the sun and the stars, had reached old age by the time they were thirty-five but were capable of building the pyramids with their bare hands.[237] However, keeping these reservations in mind, the hieroglyphs of the subtle bodies offer some fascinating evidence of how the ancient Egyptians thought about these things.

The word below represents the physical body and immediately challenges any assumptions we may have as to its actual substance. It is usually translated as *kha*, or *khat* with the addition of the feminine '*t*.' [238]

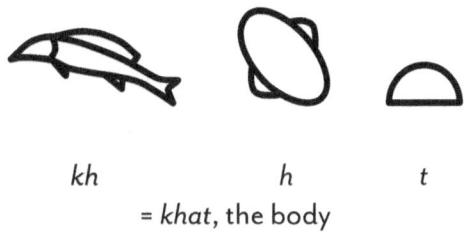

kh   h   t
= *khat*, the body

The first sign represents the Oxyrhynchus fish, also known as the long-snouted, sharp-nosed or elephant-nosed fish. It is believed to have a complex social structure but because it lives in the muddy water at the bottom of rivers where the light does not penetrate, very little is known about its habits. It has poor vision but senses its environment by generating a weak field of electricity and then interpreting the reflected energy waves in a process rather like radar. Interestingly, the ratio of the weight of its brain to its body is considerably greater than that of humans.

The symbolic significance of this fish in connection with the human body arises from the Egyptians' belief that after the dismemberment of the body of Osiris by Set, Osiris's phallus fell into the Nile where it was swallowed by an Oxyrhynchus fish. According to Plutarch, the goddess Isis recovered all the other parts of his body but was unable to retrieve the phallus, so she had to reconstruct it with the aid of magic in order to conceive their son Horus. Plutarch records that the inhabitants of the city of Oxyrhynchus (once a large settlement and now an important archeological site) revered the fish to such an extent that they abstained from eating any fish caught by a hook, their reasoning being that because the Oxyrhynchus was caught by a hook elsewhere in Egypt, the same hook might then be re-used to catch other fish.

The symbolism of this hieroglyph is of the darkness and obscurity of the mud at the bottom of the Nile, and of a creature that has a remarkably well-developed brain and a highly evolved method of perceiving its environment which does not rely on physical abilities such as sight or sound. We can see a parallel between this lowly organism and the story of humankind which has evolved from its obscure origins in the primeval slime to the eventual fulfilment of its ability to use the infinite capacity of its mind rather than rely on its physical body or instincts.

The second hieroglyph in this word has not been conclusively identified but it is often used as a determinative in words that describe bodily growths or diseased conditions. The shape is not well defined but it could illustrate the 'edge' of the bandages placed about an organ or soft tissue. The sign is used in words meaning 'to be painful,' 'to suffer or endure' and 'to be patient with.' It is also found in words that refer to binding, bandaging and embalming, to the soft tissue of the human body and to the process of embalmment. The hieroglyph certainly refers to the human body in some way and implies that the physical body is little more than a shapeless piece of flesh subject to the natural processes of decay. As Blavatsky insisted, "the body is not a principle," merely a temporary vehicle. In contrast to our current obsession with our physical appearance, the lack of definition in the hieroglyph offers a harsh but realistic image of the impermanence of our physical bodies.

The juxtaposition of these two hieroglyphs offers an uncompromisingly realistic view of the essential 'deadness' of the human body, which nonetheless houses a mind that has infinite potential to overcome the limits of physicality. Through their link with the story of Isis and Osiris, these hieroglyphs also refer to the concepts of regeneration and renewal.

Next, the *swyt* or 'shade.' [239]

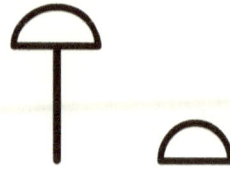

swyt = shade

The hieroglyph illustrates the sunshade that gave necessary protection from the fierce Egyptian sun. Sunshades were often made from ostrich feathers, and while some were small enough to double as a fan or be carried as a parasol, others were larger, more permanent affairs like a canopy or awning. The meaning of this hieroglyph is often likened to the Jungian concept of the 'shadow,' a term which refers to the challenging or unwelcome parts of ourselves which we deny, disown or conveniently ascribe to others. The link between 'shade' and 'shadow' was probably first made by Gardiner in his *Egyptian Grammar* and although it is now widely repeated it does seem to be an inappropriate application of modern psychology to the ancient mind.[240] There is no evidence to suggest that this part of the psyche was recognised by the Egyptians; on the contrary, their belief seems to have been that the shadow cast by the human body was revered as an indication of the sun's light shining through the body rather than of human darkness, or that it was a visible representation of the brightness of the spiritual body which was capable of casting its own shadow. Illustrations of the hieroglyph often depict the sunshade held by a personified ankh, the sign of life, and the connection between the ostrich feather and the balanced, harmonious, light-filled qualities of the goddess *Maat* who wore it as her headdress are an important part of the hieroglyph's symbolism.

The same idea is incorporated in the word below, *swyt neter.*[241]

ntr   swyt
= swyt neter, a sacred figure, the image of a god

This is another example of 'honorific transposition' where the hieroglyph for 'god' is placed first. The combination of these two signs affirms the very positive notion that what we are able to see –

the shadow – is tangible evidence of the existence of a source of light. Far from being an image of negativity the visible shadow is proof of the existence of the sacred, light-filled beings we know as the gods. This positive, affirmative way of looking at a shadow is quite different to our own, but interestingly the habit of 'looking on the bright side' has now been recognised as a positive and creative habit that may add years to our life!

The next two hieroglyphs were both used to illustrate the *bA*, a word which is usually translated as 'soul.' The first sign represents a stork, and the second is a human-headed bird. [242]

bA = the soul

The stork in question is the saddle-billed stork or *Ephippiorhynchus senegalensis*. It was a huge bird, nearly 5 feet in height and having a wing-span of up to 9 feet, making it probably the largest flying bird in ancient Egypt. It is no longer found in Egypt but the earliest representations give such a detailed impression of its appearance that we can assume it was once present in the Nile Valley, probably disappearing during the period of the Old Kingdom.[243] Its feathers are a striking combination of black and white, while its impressively long beak is bright red with a black band around it and a small yellow 'shield' at the base.

Over time, the design of this hieroglyph became less realistic and it tended to take on the appearance of a goose, distinguished only by the long pendulous 'wattle' which protrudes from the bird's chest. Eventually it was often replaced by the slightly comical, short-legged, human-headed bird of the second hieroglyph. The later hieroglyphs give little idea of the size and strength of this extraordinary bird but if one landed in your back garden you would certainly know about it, and its magnificent appearance is worth holding in mind when considering the symbolic meaning of the hieroglyph as a representation of the qualities of the *bA*: immense, powerful, magnificent.

The hieroglyph of the human-headed *bA* bird is usually combined with the incense bowl or burner issuing smoke, a hieroglyph pronounced *sntr* or *seneter* which means 'to cense' or 'to consecrate.' The combination of these two signs poses the questions of what is being consecrated and who or what is responsible for this action? [244] The hieroglyph suggests that it is the *bA* itself which has the power to make sacred, or in other words to reveal the spiritual significance behind everyday objects and actions, and this certainly accords with our present concept of the soul as the wise, immortal part of our being which is an active or causal energy in spiritual work.

The *bA* is also used in words such as *bAkw* which means 'work' or 'task,' as show below.[245] (The hieroglyph of the chick is frequently used to indicate the plural.) The same word, surprisingly, can also mean 'revenues, wages or taxes' but the hieroglyphs are qualified by the determinative of the sealed roll of papyrus which indicates an abstract idea, so we might consider its meaning as a reference to spiritual work and the 'just dues' that are traditionally offered to those engaged in such work.

bA   k   w
= *bAkw*, work, task, wages, taxes

Keeping this in mind, we can add the following word to our understanding of the *bA*. It begins with a hieroglyph of three saddle-billed storks to indicate 'many', and means 'power.' [246]

bA   w

= *bAw*, power

The relationship between the *bA* and the physical body is revealed in the many illustrations that show the *bA* bird returning to, or hovering over, the body of the deceased when it is recumbent in the tomb. The image of the body in the 'tomb' is not solely an illustration of the deceased within the grave but also of the priest or magical worker who, in deep meditation, uses the mind and imagination to enter the realities of the Inner worlds. An important point in Egyptian iconography is that the *bA* appears to have no independent existence of its own but to exist only when its human counterpart is present, which is not quite the same as our current understanding of the nature and function of the human soul, which is that it endures throughout and between each incarnation and is not dependent on the physical body for existence. In fact our current understanding of the soul is perhaps better indicated by the word *bAkw* which suggests the accrual of 'spiritual wealth' or wisdom through hard work.

We can suggest therefore that the *bA* does not indicate the soul as a presence in itself but symbolises the *quality* or *power* of the soul, an energy that might be described as intense aspiration which drives us to seek new experiences and achieve greater spiritual awareness. It enables us to rise into the spiritual worlds after death or in an altered state of consciousness, to benefit from that experience and to bring back what we have learnt in order to enrich our daily lives. According to the symbolism of these hieroglyphs, the power of the *bA* can be experienced as a fiery, driving force which enables us to consecrate or make sacred each moment of our lives by fully realising the potential of the present.

The presence of the *bA* was not confined to humans but was also a part of the gods who, we must assume, also desired to achieve greater spiritual awareness. The sacred texts held in the House of Life were known as the *bA* of the god Re, as if in recognition that all those who read these texts would be inspired by the soul of the sun god and, in turn, would contribute to that Being's greater awareness. The implication is that we are all, in this universe, an aspect of the over-soul of the Sun or Solar Logos.

The hieroglyph shown below depicts the *kA,* and was an ideogram for what is usually now identified as the 'spirit.' [247]

kA = spirit or life-energy

There is some disagreement as to whether this hieroglyph represents the arms held upwards as if in a sign of praise, or extended horizontally to the ground. The gesture is reproduced in statues and illustrations in both orientations, and while it is likely that the Egyptians appreciated the ambiguity, it can be helpful to try the gesture for yourself. If you stand with your arms held level with your shoulders, bent at the elbows and palms facing the floor, the posture lacks meaning and soon becomes tiring. If you raise your forearms so that they are vertical, with your palms facing outwards and ahead, the gesture becomes meaningful and powerful; it enables an exchange of energy between you and the world about you on both an immediate and a subtle level. If you hold the posture for twenty seconds or so you may also find that it becomes revitalising; it encourages you to stand upright and to breathe more deeply.

Although *kA* is generally translated as 'spirit,' the hieroglyph suggests that this isn't quite right. It is difficult to contrive an unambiguous symbol for 'spirit' but outstretched arms don't quite fit the bill, not least because they are so obviously human, and parts of the human body do not make convincing symbols of 'spirit.' The hieroglyph illustrates how we can *use* our bodies to connect with heavenly or spiritual energy and seems to suggest that it is our connection with this energy, rather than spirit as such, which is indicated by the term *kA*. The alternative translation of 'Life-energy' may be a more accurate interpretation.

The use of the hieroglyph in other words is interesting. For example, three *kA* signs means 'food.' [248]

kAw = food

The word below represents a vineyard: [249]

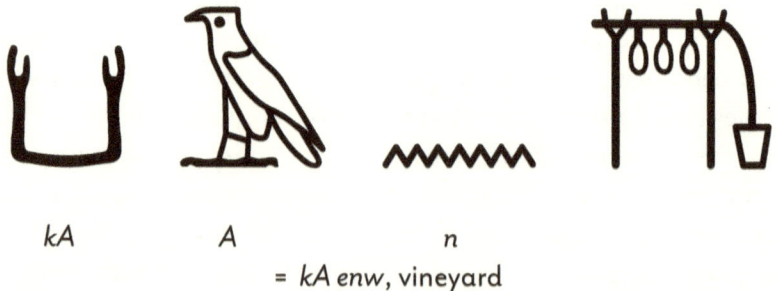

kA   A   n

= *kA enw*, vineyard

In *kA enw*, the *kA* is followed by the White vulture, which symbolises the white light of the spirit manifest in the stars. The third hieroglyph represents moving energy and the pervading connection between all things. So far, the word appears to be concerned with spiritual energy, but the determinative, a lively depiction of grapes supported on wooden props and releasing their juice into a vessel, suggests that the energy described by the previous three hieroglyphs is not 'spiritual' in the sense that we might understand it as rarified or transcendent, but is closely linked to the sustenance of our physical bodies. The sequence of symbolism describes the process by which spiritual or 'life-energy' is transformed into the dense matter of the physical world; it refers to our connection with 'spiritual' energy but emphasises how this can be enjoyed in the physical world!

The word *kA* is also sometimes translated as 'double.' The term indicates something similar to what we now identify as the 'incorporeal double' or 'etheric double.' The latter term was probably only first used in the West in the late nineteenth century but it is an established principle in Eastern thought, for example in Vedantic philosophy, where it is known as the *Linga Sarira* or 'impermanent characteristic pattern.' The etheric body is a combination of the two primary universal principles of energy and substance: the spiritual energy which is constant on all planes of creation combined with the substance or material required for form-building, which is present on each plane and in an increasingly dense form. The etheric body is essential to the survival of the physical body because it attracts, holds and conveys vital energy to the physical body which, as we are reminded by the hieroglyph of the *khat,* is in itself no more than a lifeless piece of flesh. The physical body is sustained by food and drink, but it cannot directly absorb life-energy from the sun. We feel better when the sun comes out because our etheric body has been revitalised, which in its turn revitalises our physical body. The hieroglyph of the *kA* illustrates this exchange of energy between spiritual and physical through the medium of the human etheric body. The Egyptians described dying as 'going to one's *kA*' which suggests the enduring nature of the body of light, in contrast to the brief life of the physical body.

We can perceive or visualise the etheric body as a fine web or network of threads of animated golden light which forms a 'template' upon which elemental substance can be moulded, just as the potter makes a template or inner form for a sculpture. The concept is seen in illustrations of Khnum, the ram-headed god who moulds what appear to be twin figures on his potter's wheel. In fact the second figure is not a sibling but the etheric body. In the earlier dynasties the Pharaoh was believed to possess the combined *kA* of his people, so that the vitality of his etheric body was responsible for transmitting vitalising life-energy to the entire population.

The ram-headed god Khnum moulding the physical body and etheric 'double' on his potter's wheel.

Later, the priesthood, and eventually each individual, recognised their own *kA* and accepted personal responsibility for keeping it pure and vigorous so that it would maintain the physical body in good health.

The modern name 'Egypt' derives from Greek and Latin translations of the phrase *het kA Ptah* or 'House of the *kA* of Ptah,' suggesting a direct link between the *kA* or light-body of the creator god Ptah and the land of Egypt. [250]

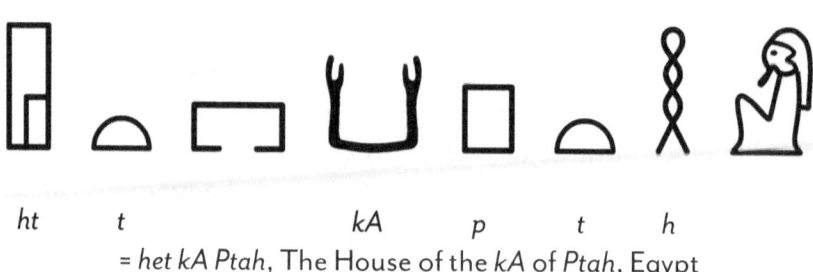

ht   t   kA   p   t   h
= *het kA Ptah*, The House of the *kA* of *Ptah*, Egypt

Above and beyond the *kA* is the *Akh*, whose hieroglyph is shown below.[251]

Akh = spirit

This hieroglyph is usually translated as 'spirit,' 'radiance,' or 'to shine,' but our current understanding of the word 'spirit' is imprecise and it is difficult to be certain what the concept signified to the ancient Egyptians. It can be said that all beings not in physical incarnation are in 'spirit' or, conversely, that nothing exists in the universe *except* spirit, which manifests in varying degrees from a pure energy that is beyond mortal perception to the dense matter of the physical world. Again the question arises as to how any symbol might usefully depict something so nebulous, but a closer study of the hieroglyph reveals some useful ideas.

The hieroglyph that depicts the *Akh* is the Northern Bald ibis, also known as the Hermit ibis or *Geronticus eremita,* although it is often referred to as the Crested ibis. The bird is now considered to be critically endangered and only a few hundred remain in the wild. At least two other types of ibis existed in ancient Egypt: the Glossy ibis and the better-known Sacred ibis that was the especial emblem of Tehuti. Thousands of mummified remains of the Sacred ibis have been found across Egypt in sites connected with Tehuti, although as yet no remains of the Hermit ibis have been discovered. There are however a number of surviving illustrations from the predynastic period which demonstrate the significance of the bird in the earliest years of the Egyptian civilisation.

The usual translation of *Akh* as 'shining spirit, radiance, splendour' can lead to the natural assumption that the bird chosen to symbolise these properties will also be of radiant appearance and possessed of gleaming white feathers, but the *Geronticus eremita* confounds our expectations, because it is a comically ugly bird with black feathers, bright red legs, a bald face and a curved, red bill. Its 'crest' is a punk-like ruff on the back of its neck. However, the bird does shine. In the sunlight its plumage reveals an iridescent sheen of bronze-green, copper and violet, which is particularly noticeable in flight when a blue-green patch on its wing is revealed.[252] Its radiance is therefore not immediately apparent but, like the ugly duckling which transforms into a swan, when its magnificent colours are unexpectedly displayed it symbolises the light of the spirit shining out from the darkness of the physical plane.

Unlike the Sacred ibis, the Hermit ibis is not a river or wading bird, and its natural habitat is the caves and rocky cliffs such as those that form the border between the Nile valley and the desert. It forages for food in this rocky, semi-arid territory by poking its long beak into gaps and fissures in the earth. This is another significant element in the hieroglyph's symbolism because it pertains to the principal distinction in Egyptian magic between the fertile, life-giving properties of the river and the raw power of the desert. The Hermit ibis lives within sight of the Nile yet it 'taps into' the hidden life of the desert. [253]

While the principle meaning of the *Akh* is 'shining radiance' and 'god-like power', it can also signify 'that which is beneficial, useful and good,' and 'profitable'. We can suggest therefore that the meaning of *Akh* is not 'spirit' as such but refers to the condition or quality of the individual who has integrated the light of the spirit into their personality and is able to demonstrate this light shining through their everyday lives. This interpretation accords with the earlier definition of the *bA* as the activity or aspirational force of the soul rather than the soul as an entity in itself, although arguably we are only aware of the soul and spirit by experiencing their effect.

The *Akh* is frequently combined with the hieroglyph of the sieve which is used as a sound complement to emphasise the essential refinement of the coarser elements of our nature and the purity that distinguishes the spirit from other parts of the psyche. [254]

Akh   kh
= spirit

With the addition of the feminine '*t*' and a variety of determinatives, a number of different words are produced, each adding another facet to our understanding of the *Akh*. For example, the determinative of the eye in the word below defines the meaning of the previous three hieroglyphs as 'the eye of a god.' [255]

Akh   kh   t
= the eye of a god

The hieroglyph of the eye is discussed in detail in Chapter Nine: The Eye of Horus. It means 'to do, create, or construct,' indicating actual achievement and accomplishment rather than the expected meaning of 'to see.' It implies a special connection between the gods and those who have achieved the spiritual state of '*Akh*-ness' that enables them to function in a mediatory role as 'the eye of the god' within the world. It suggests that individuals who have achieved this spiritual condition are able to use their ability to bring about creative changes that would normally be considered the work of the gods.

In Chapter Two we looked at the hieroglyph of the horizon or *Akhet*, a word which derives from the root *Akh*. It could be written simply as the ideogram of a single hieroglyph of the sun rising between two hills, or as shown below. [256]

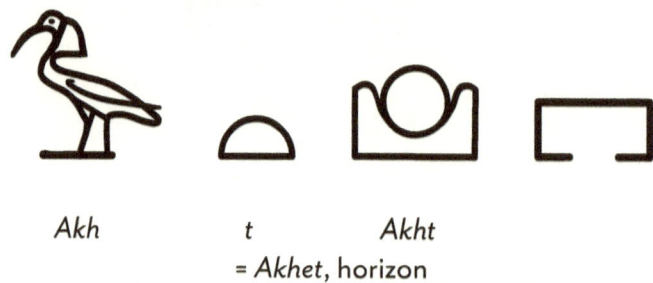

Akh   t   Akht
= *Akhet*, horizon

Here, the symbolic meaning of the *Akh* is expanded by the sound complement of the *Akhet*. The immediate reference is to the place on the horizon where the sun rises or sets, but the symbolism takes us beyond geographical location. The word is determined by the final, unpronounced sign *pr* or *per*. This hieroglyph represents a house or temple and also indicates the concept of 'the house of' in the sense of a group of people which retains its essential identity through successive periods or generations.

The hieroglyph of the *Akhet* illustrates the sun rising or setting between two desert hills, a phenomenon that could be witnessed from almost any location in ancient Egypt. The *Akhet* precisely indicated the place between night and day, because the exact moment of the appearance or disappearance of the sun could precisely be observed, as could the exact moment of the rising or setting of stars. This location in turn symbolised the division between the outer, physical world and the Inner world of the *dwAt*. The symbolic use of the physical horizon as the division between this world and the next is probably unique to Egypt, although the same idea is described in modern esoteric thought as the 'veil between the worlds.' Our perception of the position of the 'veil' varies according to our current level of awareness and our ability to perceive the Inner worlds. The *Akhet* also represents a state of being, the ability to be in this world while maintaining an awareness of the Inner worlds or, conversely, the ability to retain a useful contact with this world even after having passed into the afterlife.

The *Akhu* were the 'dwellers in the horizon,' a group of beings which probably included both the more advanced members of the priesthood and the presence of 'shining spirits' no longer in incarnation. The *Akhu* were not deities but can be likened to those who in other traditions are described as Saints, Inner Plane Adepti or Gurus. They mediate between the outer and the Inner worlds, conveying the truths and guidance of the spiritual worlds to humanity and bearing the invocations of humanity to the gods. As well as guidance of a spiritual and developmental nature they also transmitted a loving kindness and well-being, qualities that are conveyed in the phrase below which means 'do good to' and 'it will be well with you.' [257]

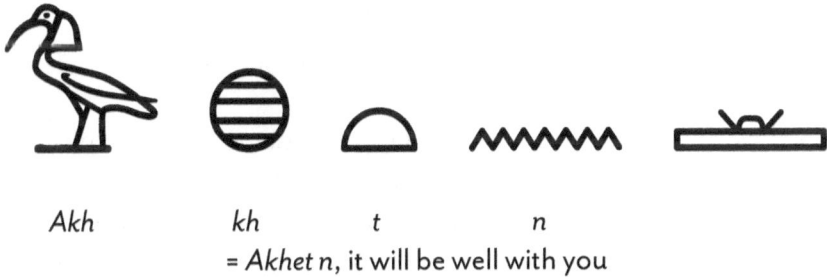

Akh   kh   t   n
= *Akhet n*, it will be well with you

Here, the *Akh* and hieroglyph of the sieve are followed by the hieroglyph '*n*' that indicates the connective energy between all things, while the final sign is the determinative of the sealed roll of papyrus that denotes an abstract idea. The phrase can sound trite but behind the familiar expression is an acknowledgement of the essential goodness and love of creative energy.

The Pyramid Texts describe how, when the Pharaoh achieved the transfigured state of the *Akh* he was said to arise in the East as the 'Morning Star,' the 'Horus Star' or the 'Lone Star.' Although these texts primarily describe an interior, personal or initiatory experience and are not intended to be an accurate depiction of the night sky, the single star is most likely to be Sirius, specifically during the period in which it appeared above the Eastern horizon at the same time as the sun, and heralded the inundation of the Nile. And it may also signify the 'rising' of each individual into their stellar bodies of light. The four-month period of the inundation was called *Akhet,* which was followed by *Peret* the season of planting and then *Shemu,* the period of harvest. The flooding of the land with life-giving waters which coincided with the heliacal rising of Sirius and the sun at its height in the sky is analogous to the flooding of the personality with the light of the spirit.

Finally, the *sAkh,* written in hieroglyphs below. [258]

s   Akh   kh
= sAkh, sah *(s3ḫ)*, to spiritualise or glorify

This word is often translated as *sah,* and identified as a 'spiritual body.' However, the word *sAkh* is a causative verb, not a noun: it doesn't refer to a body of light as such but to the process of causing or enabling a spiritualisation to occur, and in this respect it accords with our earlier suggestions regarding the *bA* and the *kA*. The confusion arises through the transliteration of hieroglyphs for which there is no equivalent letter in the English alphabet, which means that this word is often transliterated as *sah*. The second hieroglyph of *sAkh* is more correctly written as an aleph and pronounced as the 'stop' that occurs for example when you say the word 'rattle' but don't voice the 't.' Usually the letter is transliterated as *A,* a custom which has been adopted throughout this book. The third letter is an 'h' that has a semi-circle underneath it called a breve and is pronounced rather like the 'ch' in 'loch' although is usually transliterated as *kh*. However, rather than use letters not found in the English alphabet, the word is often transliterated as *sAkh* or even *sah*.

The same English letters *sah* are often given as the transliteration of the word for 'mummy' even though this is spelt with an entirely different group of hieroglyphs, as shown below, and is pronounced quite differently. [259]

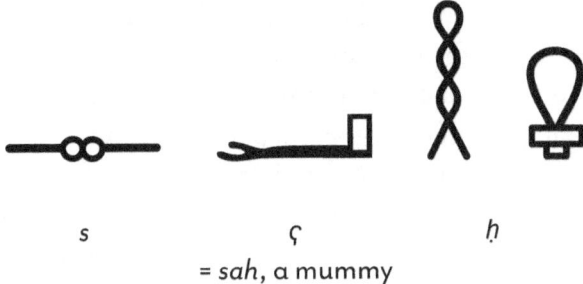

s ꜥ ḥ
= sah, a mummy

The word *Sꜥḥ* meaning 'the mummy' is written with the hieroglyphs of the doorbolt, the lower arm and hand, the lamp wick of twisted linen and the determinative of a cylinder-seal. The second hieroglyph is the ayin which is customarily indicated by a small 'comma' and pronounced with the sort of throaty gurgle that you produce if you try to say 'ah' while swallowing. The final sign of the h with a dot underneath it is pronounced as an emphatic, breathy 'h.'

The problem is compounded through the frequently used transliteration of the word for the constellation of Orion as *sah*, although it should more correctly be transliterated as *s3ḥ* or *sAh*. The hieroglyphs for the constellation of Orion are shown below and are quite different to those for 'the mummy' and 'to spiritualise.'[260]

s3ḥ

= s3ḥ (sAh), Orion

Because the transliteration *sah* is often used for all three words, the impression is created that they are synonymous. The idea is appealing: it seems to make sense that there is a correlation between the mummified body which is transfigured into the body of light, and the body of light which becomes the constellation of Orion, but the hieroglyphs indicate three quite different concepts

The process by which the body of the deceased becomes 're-membered,' just as the body of Osiris was re-membered by Isis and transformed into a body of light within the starry heavens, was an important element of the Egyptian practice of mummification and the elaborate rituals associated with it. The idea of mummification is now difficult for us to comprehend, although as Wallis Budge points out: "The Egyptians were a practical people, and they would never have gone to the expense and trouble of embalming the dead unless they had believed that it was absolutely necessary." [261] The primary purpose of mummification as it is currently understood was to create here on earth a permanent form that could be recognised, ensouled and utilised by the deceased in the afterlife. This was done in the belief that those who had recently passed into the spiritual worlds needed to have access to a recognisable 'light body' in order to retain a sense of self. The notion runs counter to current esoteric belief that our lasting sense of self does not depend on the temporary physical appearance of our most recent incarnation but derives from the immortal reality of our spiritual identity which persists throughout all our lives irrespective of our outer form. It is hard to reconcile two such differing beliefs, particularly in the light of the ancient Egyptians' evident and profound understanding of the spiritual worlds. Were they mistaken? Or have we got it wrong? Time will tell.

Endnotes
235 E.A. Wallis Budge, *A Hieroglyphic Vocabulary to the Book of the Dead* (New York: Dover Publications, Inc. 1991) page 406
236 Alan Gardiner, *Egyptian Grammar* (Oxford, Griffith Institute, 3rd edition 1957) page 172
237 These ideas are developed for example by Gary Lachman, *A Secret History of Consciousness* (Lindisfarne Books 2003)
238 *kha* or *khat*, the physical body: Gardiner K4, Aa2, X1
239 Gardiner S36, X1
240 A.E. Gardiner, *Egyptian Grammar*, page 173
241 *swyt neter*, the image of a god: Gardiner R8, S36

242 *bA*, the soul: Gardiner G29, G53
243 Jiří Janák, *Saddle-billed Stork (Ba-Bird)* UCLA Encylopedia of Egyptology, https://escholarship.org/uc/item/0r77f2f8
244 *seneter*, to cense or consecrate: Gardiner R7
245 *bAkw*, work or task, wages, taxes: Gardiner G29, V31, G43, Y1
246 *bAw*, power: Gardiner G30, G43, Y1
247 *kA*, the life-energy within the etheric body: Gardiner D28
248 *kAw*, food: Gardiner D28, D28, D28
249 *kA-enw*, vineyard: Gardiner D28, G1, N35, M43
250 *het kA ptah*, the house of Ptah, Egypt: Gardiner O6, X1, O1, D28, Q3, X1, V28, A40
251 *Akh*, radiance, spirit: Gardiner G25
252 see Jiří Janák, *Spotting the Akh. The presence of the northern bald ibis in Ancient Egypt and its early decline*, www.academia.edu/894641
253 see Jiří Janák, *Akh*, (2013) UCLA Encyclopedia of Egyptology, 1(1). UCLA: Department of Near Eastern Languages and Cultures. https://escholarship.org/uc/item/7255p86v
254 *Akh*, radiance, spirit: Gardiner G25, Aa1
255 *Akht*, the eye (of a god): Gardiner G25, Aa1, X1, D6
256 *Akhet*, horizon: Gardiner G25, X1, N27, O1
257 *Akhet en*, it will be well with you: Gardiner G25, Aa1, N35, Y1
258 *sAkh*, to glorify or spiritualise: Gardiner S29, G35, Aa1, Y1
259 *sah*, the mummy, Gardiner O34, D36, V28, S20
260 *sAh*, Orion: Gardiner D61,N14,G1,A40.
The symbolism of the hieroglyphs for Orion is discussed in detail in Chapter Five
261 E.A. Wallis Budge, *Osiris and the Egyptian Resurrection* (New York, Dover Publications, 1973) Volume II page 123

The Temple

In contrast to the numinous qualities of the hieroglyphs discussed in the previous two chapters, the following hieroglyphs of the temple and its various functions and ritual artefacts take us back down to earth – although now bringing with us a better understanding of the spiritual worlds. Here is the hieroglyph *pr* or *per*, an ideogram that represents a house, a palace or a temple, and which also stands for 'house of' in the sense of a family, a dynasty or a group of people.' [262]

pr = per, house or temple

The use of the same hieroglyph for house and temple suggests that both were regarded by the ancient Egyptians as sacred, at least in potential, and that the distinction we now make between 'sacred' and 'secular' was less meaningful to them. The hieroglyph *per* could scarcely be more rudimentary in design, but even so it contains features that draw our attention. As with many of the apparently simple hieroglyphs there are no clues as to the size or context of the object illustrated, and while this precludes any precise identification it increases the potential for symbolic meaning. Another significant feature of the hieroglyph is that it illustrates the ground plan of a building rather than the elevation, an apparently odd choice because buildings are best recognised from the appearance of their facade. In fact this ground plan is not typical of an ancient Egyptian house, many of which incorporated an enclosed courtyard to the front or side where much of the cooking was done in a clay oven. A similar design is still often used. The houses were traditionally made from dried mud-and-straw bricks with a flat roof supported by wooden pillars, although their size varied considerably according to the needs and affluence of the family. Larger houses comprised two or more storeys and could contain upwards of twenty rooms. Ventilation was through small windows placed high in the walls which allowed cool air to circulate. The flat roof was used for storage, for keeping chickens and as a sleeping platform in hot weather.

Another significant feature of the hieroglyph is that it is oblong rather than square. By this simple means it conveys a sense of orientation; the building is positioned 'this way' and not 'that way' within the landscape. If you allow your eye to wander over the hieroglyph you will probably find that your attention returns to the doorway. The gap that indicates the doorway is large in proportion to the rest of the building and in some of the earlier illustrations it extends across most of the lower side. We can assume that it is deliberately drawn like this to indicate that the doorway is not just a means of entering the building but comprises an important element in its overall symbolism. If we consider the hieroglyph as a symbol rather than a primitively drawn picture it becomes apparent that the design is not concerned with external appearances but with the inherent qualities that are symbolised by a building and its entrance.

There is nothing in the design of this hieroglyph that provides a clue as to the purpose of the building: its meaning is unrealised until we go through the doorway, and it is our own experience of this transition from the outer world into a sacred space that brings to life the building's inherent qualities. We find the same principle incorporated into in the design of Egyptian temples where the high and comparatively featureless outer walls reveal little of the interior. The entrance symbolises the dividing line between the outer world of physical appearance and the heightened atmosphere of the Inner world that is encountered within, where every carefully chosen image, symbol, perspective and proportion contributes to its power and meaning. Egyptian temples are a symbol in themselves; they present a journey into levels of reality that can be accessed through the power of the mind and creative imagination. What makes a temple a sacred space is not the grandeur of its facade but the ability of its inner structure to resonate with the creative principles of the cosmos and, in turn, to evoke that resonance within the minds of those who step inside.

Other hieroglyphs develop the symbolic content of *per* by combining it with signs which are often symbolically placed across the entrance. For example, here is the hieroglyph for the temple treasury: [263]

per hedj = the treasury

This sign combines *per* with the *hedj*, a type of sceptre or mace whose name means 'white.' A beautiful image of the *hedj* sceptre appears on the Narmer Palette (see the illustration on page 20) where Pharaoh Narmer raises it as a sign of victory over his fallen 'enemy' which may also be an expression of the successful overcoming of the lower self. The quality of 'whiteness' was associated with the god *Hedjwer* or Great White One, a baboon deity who was believed to be an ancestor of the Pharaohs. Although the mace appears to be a symbol of power, its symbolic meaning connects it with the special qualities of the first rays of sunlight at dawn, often noisily greeted by baboons as if in adoration of the light and power of the sun god Re. This quality of dawning light could be seen over the land, *hedj tA*, and was also recognised in the quality of expression on a person's face which revealed their inner state of enlightenment: *hedj her*. The hieroglyph of the sun is used as a determinative in both words.

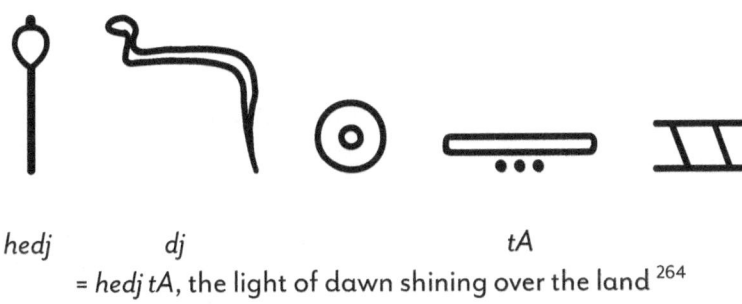

hedj   dj   tA
= *hedj tA*, the light of dawn shining over the land [264]

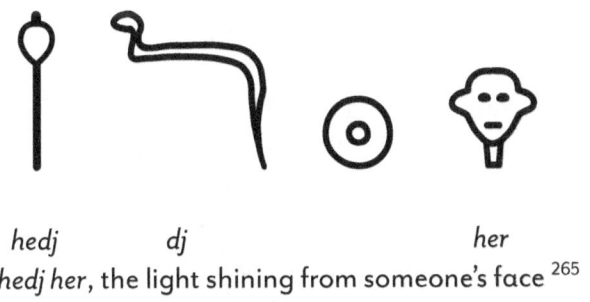

hedj   dj   her
= *hedj her*, the light shining from someone's face [265]

The following two hieroglyphs, *per aA*, originally indicated 'Great House', although the term was later used to refer more specifically to the Pharaoh.[266] Our modern word 'Pharaoh' derives from the Greek pronunciation of these two words – which suggests incidentally that *par* may be a more accurate pronunciation of the hieroglyph than *per*. The second hieroglyph is a wooden column or pillar that was used in buildings and large boats. It indicates 'great' in the sense of both size and quality.

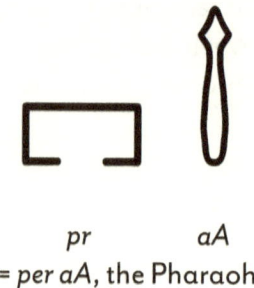

pr   aA
= per aA, the Pharaoh

Per could also be used to represent the tomb, the *per neheh* or House of Eternity.²⁶⁷

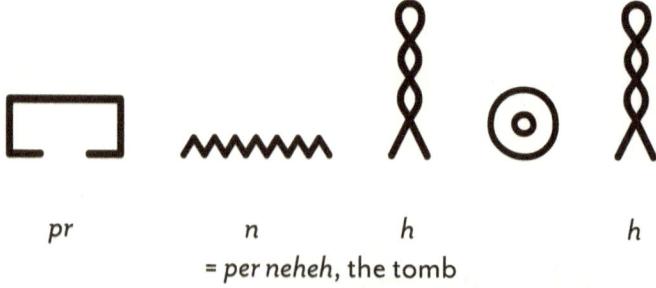

pr   n   h   h
= *per neheh*, the tomb

In the above word, the hieroglyphs of the house, the zig-zag line and the sun have all been discussed previously, but in a striking combination of images the sun is placed between two hieroglyphs of a lamp wick, as if between two pillars. The presence of the sun in a group of signs indicates that they refer in some way to the concept of time or the passing of time, and prompts us to consider a connection between our experience of death, and our experience of time. The word *neheh* refers to the revelation of time through repeated, eternal, cosmic cycles and patterns and suggests that even the sun, although the main indicator of the passage of time here on earth, is itself subject to greater laws and cycles of return.

The lamp wick was made from strands of flax or linen which were rolled and then twisted into a spiral to form a sort of double helix. Our own perception of time is more often helical than linear, and although making an overall progression towards the future it tends to waver between backwards and forwards, depending to a considerable extent on a series of 'markers' such as the amount of daylight, the typical pattern of events during our working day, whether we are hungry or tired, and so on. Eternity, on the other hand, is linked to universal patterns and cycles that are far beyond our normal comprehension. It is said that our perception of time is connected with the mystery of consciousness itself and that those who have reached a state of enlightenment do not experience time as unidirectional but are able to step outside its apparent linear flow. The tomb was literally the place of *neheh,* the fullness of time, and the hieroglyphs make a profound comment on the experience of being in the tomb, whether literally after death or in the altered state of consciousness achieved through spiritual disciplines.

Interestingly, the lamp-wick is also used in the word *pth* or *ptah* meaning 'to create.' The same word with the addition of the determinative of a seated god forms the name of the god Ptah.[268]

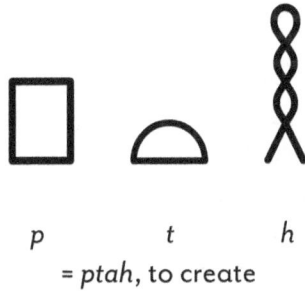

p   t   h
= *ptah*, to create

The room in which the mummification process took place was called *per nefer* and was written as below. [269]

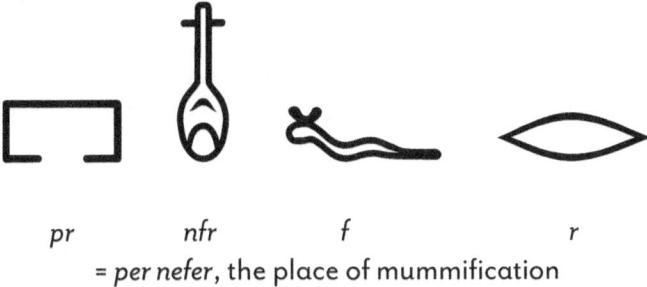

pr   nfr   f   r
= *per nefer*, the place of mummification

The second of these signs, *nefer,* means 'goodness,' 'youth' and 'beauty.' [270] The third and fourth hieroglyphs are sound complements. Again we can only marvel at the originality of Egyptian thought which looked beyond the outer appearances of what now seems to be a somewhat gruesome and unnecessary procedure to the spiritual aims that inspired the rituals of mummification and the hoped-for attainment of the body of light.

The temple's robing room was known as the *per dwAt,* the House of the *dwAt.*[271]

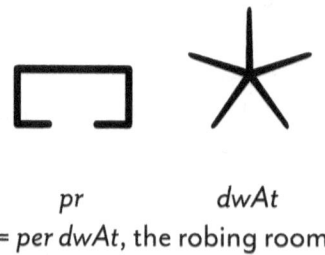

pr   dwAt
= *per dwAt,* the robing room

This simple combination of signs conveys the idea that the act of putting on ceremonial robes plays a significant part in 'taking on' the objective of the ritual. As discussed in Chapter Five, the star hieroglyph can be pronounced as *sabA* or *dwA* and the latter form tends to be used to describe the activities of devotion, and of the praise and worship of the stars. The *dwAt* was a specific area of the Inner worlds which, when successfully navigated, led the questing soul to the place of spiritual dawn. The use of the word in this context indicates that some parts of the temple ritual may have been designed to evoke the conditions of the *dwAt* in order that the participants could experience and overcome its challenges in a sacred environment.

The hieroglyphs of the word below, *djeserw,* illustrate how a building was consecrated or made sacred by using a combination of the spoken word, a magical wand of protection and the appropriate symbolic action.[272]

djsr   r   w
= *djeserw*, sacred place

The first sign is of a forearm bent at the elbow with the hand grasping an object that has been identified as the *nehbet* wand. The earliest illustrations of this wand suggest that it was used defensively, as if to ward off or deflect blows rather than to make an attack, but the idea of repelling the enemy developed into the broader context of establishing a sacred space by creating a defensive boundary, clearing away superfluous material and ridding the space of unwanted influences. The ancient texts refer to the clearing of a path through the sky so that the boat of the sun god Re would be given unimpeded passage, and even speak of the symbolic clearing of an area of the night sky to allow the stars to shine out more clearly in the darkness. We must bear in mind that these are descriptions of an inner process that takes place in the consciousness of the individual. The act of making something sacred also of course provided an element of safety and protection for those within the sacred enclosure.[273]

The procedure described above sounds very like the modern practice of sealing a magical temple or sacred space with ritually drawn pentagrams, and/or with the evocation of god-forms and Archangels, a tradition which is designed to clear the magical space, exclude those whose presence is unwelcome, and consequently heighten the atmosphere within the enclosure which has thus been cleared and secured. The use of the hieroglyph of the mouth in *djeserw*, although functioning as a sound complement, confirms the idea that the power of *djeserw* relied to some extent on invocation and on the deliberate creation of a division or separation – in this instance between the sacred space and the surrounding environment.

The same ideas are developed in the word below, *tA djeser* or 'sacred land,' the Egyptian term for the necropolis.[274] Our modern church graveyards are sacred spaces because they are located within the boundary of the consecrated land of the church but the hieroglyphs suggest that the necropolis was regarded as a type of temple in itself.

tA   djsr   r

= *tA djeser*, the sacred land or necropolis

Moving now to the powers and deities that were invoked within the sacred space, here again is the hieroglyph *neter*, the image of a flag blowing in the wind that is usually translated as 'god.'

ntr = *neter*, god

The word 'god' is imprecise, because of our own uncertainty as to what we mean by 'god' and as an explanation of what the ancient Egyptians meant by the term. Do the gods and goddesses have an objective existence or are they 'the creations of the created?'

An alternative spelling was sometimes used, shown below: [275]

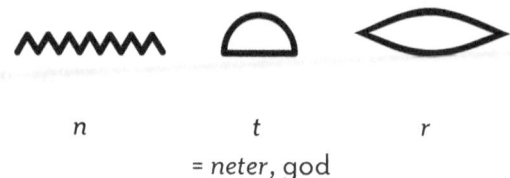

n   t   r

= *neter*, god

Here, although the word is spelled phonetically, it incorporates the symbolism of the 'moving energy' of the first hieroglyph followed by the feminine '*t*,' and the final hieroglyph's suggestion of futurity, of a single entity dividing into two parts, and of the power inherent in the act of giving voice to an idea. Although we tend to reserve the word 'god' for heavenly beings such as Isis, Osiris and Horus, the Egyptians used the word *neter* in connection with any being or entity who possessed power that was beyond ordinary human power. This category did not exclude human beings who had achieved, even if momentarily, god-like qualities, or had '*become neter*,' perhaps in the heightened atmosphere of ritual or through the deliberate evocation of attributes normally associated with the divine. These qualities might be summarised as "... the power to generate life, and to maintain it when generated.' [276]

Although the word *neter* was not gender specific, there was also a word for 'goddess,' *neteret,* shown below. [277] The determinative is the egg, a hieroglyph often used as the final sign in the names of goddesses, particularly of Isis.

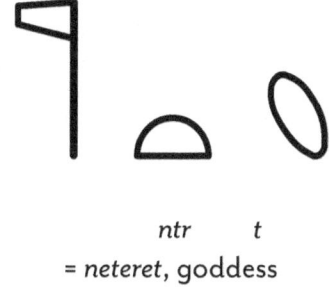

ntr   t
= *neteret*, goddess

An essential quality in the life of the temple was purity. The following sign, *wab,* means 'to bathe, purify or cleanse' and 'to serve as a priest.' [278]

wab = to purify, to serve as a priest

To modern eyes the *wab* hieroglyph is an unlikely assemblage of three entirely separate objects: the line of moving energy more usually seen in its horizontal form as the hieroglyph '*n*,' which here is issuing from an upturned vase or vessel that is improbably balanced at the top of a leg. The leg and foot are a separate hieroglyph in themselves, meaning 'to place' or 'position.' The combined symbolism therefore indicates a place from which pure and purifying energy flows forth.

Bathing in the sacred pool within in the precincts of the temple was an important part of the priest's preparation for temple work, but the significance of this outward action was that it symbolised the required state of inward purity which, then as now, probably took many years to achieve and represented more than outward cleanliness. Purity of motive is the first and constant hurdle in the spiritual life, followed by purity of the emotions in the sense of achieving an objective understanding of the desires for material possession, status, sensual gratification and the uncontrolled feelings they can provoke. Mental purity is attained through regular meditation and the practice of deliberate observation and control of the thoughts, together with the disciplined use of the creative imagination. Eventually, when these have been achieved to a sufficient degree, the state of spiritual purity, which was previously occluded, will inevitably emerge.

In the Book of the Dead the seeker of the spiritual worlds, having made the 'Negative Confession' in which he declares before the gods that he is not guilty of physical, moral or spiritual offences, concludes with the simple affirmation: "I am pure. I am pure. I am pure. I am pure." [279] Those whose vocation was to serve as a priest would aspire to pour out this pure energy in service and benefit to others, whether in daily life or as part of sacred ritual within the temple.

Integral to the magical work of the temple was the knowledge and use of the energy known as *hekA* which written thus: [280]

The Temple

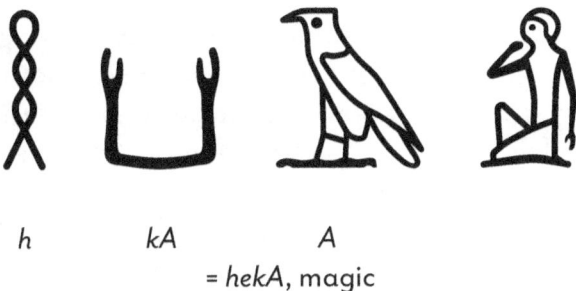

h   kA   A
= hekA, magic

The first three hieroglyphs of *hekA* will be familiar from previous examples and their combination in this word gives a useful indication of what was meant by 'magic' in ancient Egypt. The first sign is the twisted lamp wick which, in addition to its evocation of spiritual fire kindled as the temporal flame within the temple, conveys the idea the idea of time and our perception of time. The second hieroglyph, discussed in detail in the previous chapter, represents the *kA*, which is the vital life-energy focussed within the etheric body, or 'template' for the physical body. The third hieroglyph, used here as a sound complement, is the White vulture frequently found in words connected with the spiritual light of the stars. So these first three hieroglyphs describe three different types or levels of energy and our understanding of them: celestial fire, life-energy and the body of light, all of which are brought together in *hekA*. The 'magician' therefore is one who has knowledge and awareness of all these levels of energy.

In Coffin Text 261, which is headed 'Becoming a Magician', the deceased says: "I am he [i.e. the magician] whom the One God formed before duality existed upon earth." *HeKA* is the creative power of the first utterance of Atum and, paradoxically, 'the son of Her who bore Atum' which suggests that *hekA* was before even Atum. Yet *hekA* is also the power by which Atum's creation is maintained.

The determinative in *hekA* is of a man pointing to his mouth to indicate that the use or invocation of *hekA* is also connected with sound, and may perhaps refer to the idea of sound – such as the OM – as the essence of creation. "In the beginning was the Word, and the Word was with God, and the Word was God." We can understand this in the sense of 'vibration' as well as audible sound. The magician is one who knows the vibration of each living thing and who is able to give voice to this, whether actually or metaphorically. This ability requires a knowledge of universal energies, of the patterns and flow of energy between heaven and earth, of how we relate to that energy and of how it can be controlled and directed. When this energy is invoked and effectively channelled it can be used to universal benefit, to invigorate and regenerate the entire being. Although *hekA* exists irrespective of our ability to contact and use it, its effectiveness also depends on the skills of the magician to work with energy at all levels of manifestation.

> "*My head is like a vulture;*
> *I will ascend, I will rise up into the sky.*
> *My cranium is filled with the starry skies of the god;*
> *I will ascend, I will rise up into the sky.*
> *My eyes are those of the Great God of On, the Place of Pillars.*
> *I will ascend, I will rise up into the sky.*
> *My tongue is the pilot who steers the Ship of Uprightness and Truth;*
> *I will ascend, I will rise up into the sky.*
> *My vertebrae are those of the Two Enneads;*
> *I will ascend, I will rise up into the sky.*
> *It is not I who speaks these words*
> *It is the power of* hekA, *magic, which intuitively knows all things as One*"[281]

The altar or offering table represented another important concept in Egyptian magic: *hotep* or *hetep*, which is written below:[282]

htp = *hetep*, the offering table, peace

The design of this hieroglyph is straightforward – the loaf of offering has been placed on the plinth or mat which serves as an altar – but its meanings of 'peace,' 'contentment' and 'to be pleased or satisfied with' are less obvious. The presence of an altar is familiar in almost every religious context, whether a single candle in the corner of a room, a pile of stones on a hilltop or an elaborately decorated church or temple altar. The altar is a focal point for the symbolic 'sacrifice' or offering up of the lower parts of ourselves to the higher spiritual powers, and the place where the consequent descent of blessing and beneficence is focussed. But the peace, calm and contentment represented by the hieroglyph *hetep* are not always typical sensations as we approach the altar of our religion; aspiration, anxieties and desire for relief from present difficulties are also likely. The emphasis placed by *hetep* on the outcome rather than the process is a confident statement of faith in the future.

The notion that *hetep* represents an ideal state of being rather than a temporary state of ease is suggested by the hieroglyphs which spell *htp m nkh* or *hetep em ankh*: 'to go to rest, to die.' [283]

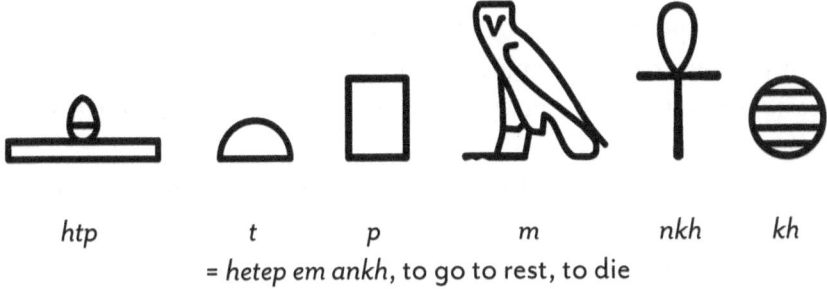

| htp | t | p | m | nkh | kh |

= *hetep em ankh*, to go to rest, to die

The phrase combines hieroglyphs that have been explored in earlier chapters. The altar of peace is followed by the feminine '*t*' and confirmed by the hieroglyph of the small mat that was used as an altar of offering. The owl suggests 'that which is within.' The *ankh* is discussed fully in Chapter Seven but can be summarised as a symbol of the living experience of the entirety of Life. The final hieroglyph is the sieve that represents purification. As a definition of the experience of dying this is not only comprehensive but entirely positive! Esoteric law identifies a number of different stages of 'death' that occur when the various elements that comprise the totality of our self are gradually relinquished during our journey of return to spirit, and *hetep em ankh* suggests that each time we make a symbolic offering at the altar we may experience a taste of the 'death' of one of the lower aspects of human nature.

As part of the symbolism of the temple we must also include some of the hieroglyphs referring to boats, as these often functioned symbolically as a temple. In ancient Egypt the boat was the principle means of transport for both goods and people, and consequently a great deal of symbolic meaning was attached to it. The Nile is the central highway of Egypt and the boat was the natural symbol of travel, whether on the Nile or through the heavens as the sun-boat of the god Re, or as an image of the journey taken by the spiritual seeker through the Inner worlds. The earliest 'everyday' boats – those which were not intended for funeral or ritual purposes but for simple transport across the Nile or for local fishing – were made from papyrus reeds and were quite fragile. These 'reed floats' are frequently mentioned in the Pyramid and Coffin Texts where they become 'the reed floats of the sky.' Later, boats were made from cedar planks and were strong enough to be used in the open sea or for transporting huge blocks of stone to their destination in the construction of the temples, statues and obelisks. Funerary boats, however, were often made in imitation of the early papyrus reed floats.

Models of boats were frequently placed in tombs and a complete, full-size boat about 144 feet long was sealed into a pit at the foot of the Great Pyramid at Giza c 2500 B.C. It was almost certainly made for the Pharaoh Khufu, either as a purely symbolic boat which was not intended for an actual journey, or one that had taken the single voyage to transport the dead Pharaoh from the funerary temple to his tomb. When the boat was discovered it was found to have been dismantled into over 600 separate parts in order to transport it from the Nile, each carefully preserved. Examples even older than this have been discovered at Abydos, the centre of the cult of Osiris, where fourteen ships have been excavated, each with its prow pointing towards the Nile. Traces of pigment clinging to the wooden planks suggest that the boats were painted bright yellow in imitation of the sun. They were all made with unpegged mortice and tenon joints which were easy to dismantle, so the boat could readily be transported to another location and reassembled.

The hieroglyph for 'ship' was written simply as the ideogram of a ship, or as below.[284]

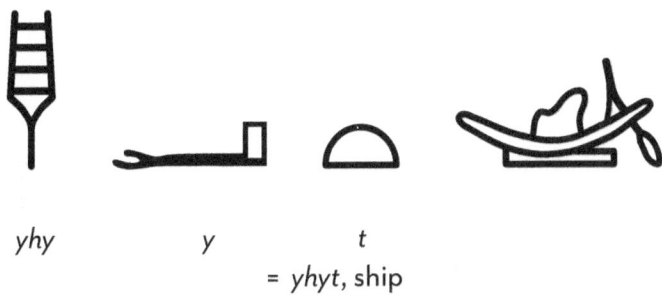

yhy   *y*   *t*
= *yhyt*, ship

The first hieroglyph, *yhy*, is the significant sign in this word, representing the ship's mast. It was combined with other determinatives to produce some quite different meanings. For example, the word below means 'tomb.'[285]

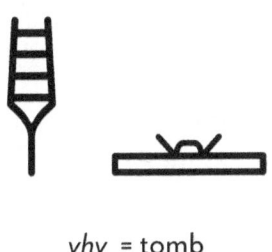

yhy = tomb

Yhy looks like a ladder, although this type of mast was not typical of the appearance of the masts on ancient Egyptian boats, most of which consisted of a single pole. It does however symbolise the concept of 'rising up' which is central to Egyptian sacred and magical thought, as to many other cultures. The determinative of the sealed roll of papyrus indicates that we should regard the 'tomb' as metaphorical; a state of mind or the condition of earthly life rather than a burial chamber.

When followed by the determinative of a slab of stone, *yhy* represents a stele or inscribed stone.[286]

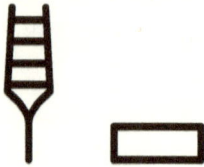

yhy = inscribed stone or stele

These 'stones' – they could also be made of wood – were inscribed with hieroglyphs and were used to mark a tomb and name its owner, or to commemorate an auspicious event such as the victory over a foreign power. They were also used as boundary markers for fields or administrative districts. The best surviving examples of the boundary stelae are those carved into the cliffs on either side of the Nile by Pharaoh Akhenaten to delimit his new city of Akhetaten and to present it as a sacred monument to the visible sun, the Aten. Stelae are a form of public decree or proclamation of identity: 'This is who I am; this is what I stand for.' The combination of the mast and the stele seems surprising but the meaning is clear: the words of the stelae provide a means whereby our consciousness can be raised into the spiritual worlds.

A phrase which is believed to derive from ancient Egypt yet is widely used in esoteric groups today provides an apt conclusion to this study by affirming the link between the spiritual practices of the ancient past and those of the twenty-first century: *khabs em pekht*. When spoken in magical ritual it is usually preceded by the phrase *konx om pax* which is said to be either 'Atlantean' or a sort of pseudo ancient Greek. It is followed by what is assumed to be the translation into English of both phrases: 'Light in Extension.' In modern times these declamations were probably first used in the rituals of the Hermetic Order of the Golden Dawn, where they are intoned as the newly initiated candidate is ceremonially brought from darkness into the light.

The illustration on page 263 is a scan of a hand-copied version of a magical ritual from the 1890s. The signs in the upper row are Egyptian hieroglyphs, the letters of the middle row are Coptic and can be translated as something like '*Kaoubs am Patht*' which sounds very like '*khabs em pekht.*' The four signs in the lower row have no known meaning. [287]

The hieroglyphs are not well drawn but most of them are recognisable, and with some confidence can be reproduced as shown below. The cross at the centre of the group is probably not a hieroglyph, so it has been omitted.

This already begins to look more familiar, and we can apply what we have learnt of these hieroglyphs and their symbolic meaning to make more sense of the phrase. In the first word, the hieroglyph of the star, *sabA,* is probably misplaced. If we move it to the end of the word it functions as the determinative, as in many other words. We could also add the hieroglyph of the White vulture, *A,* as a sound complement to the first hieroglyph, *khA*. As we have seen in many previous examples this sign was frequently used as a sound complement in words referring to the white light of the stars. The first word now reads as *khAbs* which means 'stars.' The hieroglyphs are used phonetically and also contain symbolic meaning. The first sign, the lotus plant, indicates 'a thousand.' The foot and leg mean 'to place or position' and the folded cloth represents 'good health, soundness, lack of disease.' The stars are thus defined as a thousand places of good health.

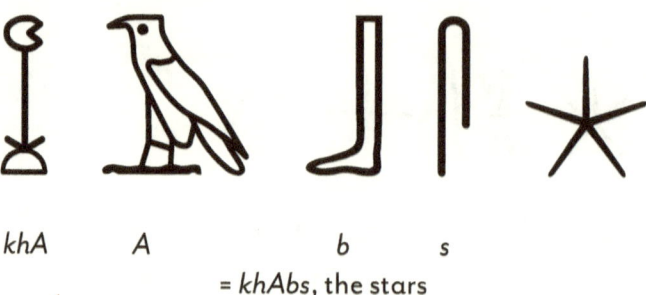

khA   A   b   s
= khAbs, the stars

The next hieroglyph is the owl, '*m*,' which indicates 'by means of,' or 'in.' This leaves us with the final word *pekht*. The hieroglyphs are shown again below, with their transliteration underneath.

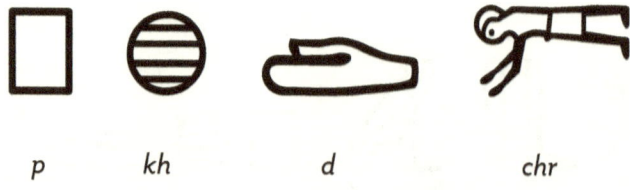

p   kh   d   chr

This word presents more of a challenge and readers will be familiar enough with the general feel of the hieroglyphs to realise that this sequence of signs doesn't look right. The first sign is the mat used in sacred offerings. The sieve indicates refinement and purity. The hieroglyph of the hand means 'to give,' 'put' or 'cause.' The rarely used hieroglyph of the fallen man indicates an enemy who has been overcome or 'thrown down.' It is possible that it should be drawn vertically, in which case it would transform into the more frequently used determinative which indicates an act of praise or adoration, but even if this final sign is an unpronounced determinative, these hieroglyphs don't spell *pekht*.

Peḥt or *Pekht* is, however, an ancient Egyptian word which means 'to arrive at,' 'to attain' and 'to reach the end.' It is written in hieroglyphs as shown below. [288]

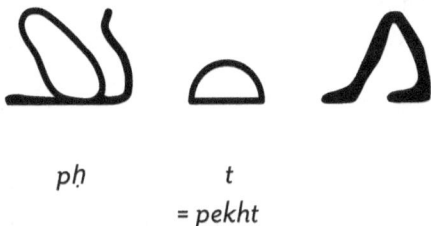

ph   t
= pekht

The 'ḥ' in this word has a dot underneath it, and as we saw in the previous chapter is voiced as a throaty, breathy sound usually transliterated as *kh*. The hieroglyph of the hind quarters of a lion means 'the end' and 'to finish,' with the suggestion that the end of something has been deliberately brought about. Bearing in mind the significance of the direction of north and of the northern circumpolar stars in Egyptian magical thought, it is interesting that *ph* is also used in words that mean 'the far North.' The same hieroglyph is also used as the emblem of *hekA*, the god of magic. Following the feminine '*t*,' the final sign is the determinative of a pair of moving legs which defines the whole word as an action or result which is achieved through your own energy, strength and ability.

There is no way of knowing how, over the millennia, the incorrect hieroglyphs were substituted for these three signs, although one wonders if somewhere along the line a well-meaning scribe decided that the back end of a lion was not a suitable image for such a 'spiritual' phrase. The phrase '*Konx om Pax*' is probably not Greek and certainly not 'Atlantean'; it is either a version of the Coptic *Kaoubs am Patht*, or another way of pronouncing *khAbs em pekht* which may even be closer to the original Egyptian.

This translation of *khAbs em pekht* embodies the aspiration, method and purpose of Egyptian magic:

'By my own efforts I have reached the stars.'

Endnotes

262 *per*, house or temple: Gardiner O1
263 *per hedj*, the temple treasury: Gardiner O2
264 *hedj ta*, the light of dawn over the land: Gardiner T3, I10, N5, N16, N23
265 *hedj her*, the light shining from someone's face: Gardiner T3, I10 N5, D2
266 *per aA*, the Great House, the Pharaoh: Gardiner O1, O29
267 *per neheh*, the tomb, the house of eternity: Gardiner O1, N35, V28, N5, V28
268 *ptah*, to create, the god Ptah: Gardiner Q3, X1, V28
269 *per nefer*, the beautiful house, the mummification room: Gardiner O1, F35, I9, D21
270 *nefer* is discussed in detail in Chapter Eleven
271 *per dwAt*, the House of the Stars or robing room: Gardiner O1, N14
272 *djeserw*, a sacred space: Gardiner D45, D21, G43, O1
273 Review by Carleton T. Hodge of 'Sacred in the Vocabulary of Ancient Egypt: the term DSR, with Special Reference to Dynasties I - XX by James Karl Hoffmeier in *Anthropological Linguistics* volume 27 No 3 (Fall 1985) pp 327-331
274 *tA djeser*, the sacred land or necropolis: Gardiner N16, N21, D45, D21, N25
275 *neter*, god, Gardiner N35, X1, D21
276 E.A. Wallis Budge, 'Neter, the Egyptian word for God', *The Monist*, Volume 13, No. 4 (July 1903) pages 481-92. http://www.jstor.org/stable/27899432.
277 *neteret*, goddess: Gardiner R8, X1, H8
278 *wab*, pure, to cleanse, to serve as a priest: Gardiner D60
279 *The Book of the Dead*: chapter CXXV
280 Gardiner V28, D28, G1, A2
281 A free translation of part of Utterance 539 of the Pyramid Texts
282 *hetep*, the offering table, peace: Gardiner R4
283 *hetep em ankh*, to go to rest, to die: Gardiner R4, X1, Q3, G17, S34, N35, Aa1
284 *yhyt*, ship: Gardiner P6, D36, X1, P1
285 *yhy*, tomb: Gardiner P6, Y1
286 *yhy*, inscribed stone or stele: Gardiner P6, O39
287 http://servitorludi.blogspot.co.uk/2012/04/k-is-for-khabs-am-pekht.html
288 *pekht*, to attain, to arrive at the end: Gardiner F22, X1, D54

Afterword: Becoming a scribe

ss = *sesh*, the scribe

The above hieroglyph, Y3 in Gardiner's sign list, illustrates the Egyptian scribe's materials. It shows a wooden palette with two circular depressions that contained the red and black inks used for written documents, the small bag that held the pigments for mixing the inks, and the cane brush with its softened and frayed end for making curved strokes on the papyrus.

This study of the hieroglyphs has focused on a small selection whose symbolism is particularly evident, but there are many hundreds more. They are easily found in the hieroglyphic dictionaries that are now available as printed books or online. If you would like to continue to explore the hieroglyphs' symbolic potential and to work with them as a system of spiritual and magical development, you might find it rewarding to draw or paint some of them yourself. A ruler and set of French Curves are useful tools, and you can use pen and ink, watercolour, acrylic or poster paint, white or coloured paper – whatever medium suits you best.

Suggestions for further reading are given below.

Maria Carmella Betrò, *Hieroglyphics: The Writings of Ancient Egypt* (New York, Abbeville Press, 1996)

Normandi Ellis, *Awakening Osiris: A New Translation of the Egyptian Book of the Dead* (Grand Rapids, MI, Phanes Press, 1988)

Henry George Fischer, *Ancient Egyptian Calligraphy: A Beginner's Guide to Writing Hieroglyphs* (New York, the Metropolitan Museum of Arts, 1999)

Christian Jacq, trans Catherine Berthier, *Fascinating Hieroglypics: Discovering, Decoding and Understanding the Ancient Art* (New York, Sterling Publishing Co., Inc, 1998)

Jeremy Naydler, *Temple of the Cosmos: The Ancient Egyptian Experience of the Sacred* (Rochester, Vermont, Inner Traditions International, 1996)

Richard H. Wilkinson, *Reading Egyptian Art: A Hieroglyphic Guide to Ancient Egyptian Painting and Sculpture* (London, Thames and Hudson Ltd, 1992)

www.ingramcontent.com/pod-product-compliance
Lightning Source LLC
Chambersburg PA
CBHW022003160426
43197CB00007B/256